USING DISCRETE CHOICE EXPERIMENTS TO VALUE
HEALTH AND HEALTH CARE

THE ECONOMICS OF NON-MARKET GOODS AND RESOURCES

VOLUME 11

Series Editor: Dr. Ian J. Bateman

Dr. Ian J. Bateman is Professor of Environmental Economics at the School of Environmental Sciences, University of East Anglia (UEA) and directs the research theme Innovation in Decision Support (Tools and Methods) within the Programme on Environmental Decision Making (PEDM) at the Centre for Social and Economic Research on the Global Environment (CSERGE), UEA. The PEDM is funded by the UK Economic and Social Research Council. Professor Bateman is also a member of the Centre for the Economic and Behavioural Analysis of Risk and Decision (CEBARD) at UEA and Executive Editor of Environmental and Resource Economics, an international journal published in cooperation with the European Association of Environmental and Resource Economists. (EAERE).

Aims and Scope

The volumes which comprise *The Economics of Non-Market Goods and Resources* series have been specially commissioned to bring a new perspective to the greatest economic challenge facing society in the 21st Century; the successful incorporation of non-market goods within economic decision making. Only by addressing the complexity of the underlying issues raised by such a task can society hope to redirect global economies onto paths of sustainable development. To this end the series combines and contrasts perspectives from environmental, ecological and resource economics and contains a variety of volumes which will appeal to students, researchers, and decision makers at a range of expertise levels. The series will initially address two themes, the first examining the ways in which economists assess the value of non-market goods, the second looking at approaches to the sustainable use and management of such goods. These will be supplemented with further texts examining the fundamental theoretical and applied problems raised by public good decision making.

For further information about the series and how to order, please visit our Website
www.springer.com

Using Discrete Choice Experiments to Value Health and Health Care

Edited by

Mandy Ryan

Health Economics Research Unit, University of Aberdeen, UK

Karen Gerard

Faculty of Medicine, Health and Life Sciences, University of Southampton, UK

Mabel Amaya-Amaya

Health Economics Research Unit, University of Aberdeen, UK

 Springer

A C.I.P. Catalogue record for this book is available from the Library of Congress.

ISBN 978-1-4020-4082-5 (HB)
ISBN 978-1-4020-5753-3 (e-book)

Published by Springer,
P.O. Box 17, 3300 AA Dordrecht, The Netherlands.

www.springer.com

Printed on acid-free paper

TABLE OF CONTENTS

CONTRIBUTING AUTHORS

Mabel Amaya-Amaya, Health Economics Research Unit, University of Aberdeen, UK
Having completed a degree in Economics, M.Sc. in Health Economics and M.Phil. in Applied Economics, Mabel joined the Health Economics Research Unit (HERU) in Aberdeen (Scotland) in 2000 to pursue a Ph.D. in Health Economics funded by the Chief Scientific Office of the Scottish Executive Health Department. Since completing her doctoral studies in 2005, Mabel has been employed as a Research Fellow in HERU. Her main area of research is the valuation of health care benefits using stated preference (SP) survey methods in general and choice experiments in particular. Her Ph.D. thesis constituted one of the first uses in Health Economics of more flexible econometric approaches allowing the enhancement of economic models of choice behaviour with psychological insights about human decision making. One of the main objectives of her current research is the development and application of econometric techniques that allow advance understanding of response variability as a behavioural phenomenon in choice experiments.

Stirling Bryan, Health Economics Facility, School of Public Policy, University of Birmingham, UK
Stirling is a Professor of Health Economics in the Health Economics Facility at the University of Birmingham and in May 2005 was appointed as Director of the Health Economics Facility. For the period August 2005 to July 2006 Stirling was a Harkness Fellow in Health Care Policy, based at the Center for Health Policy at Stanford University, USA. His main qualifications are Ph.D. in Economics, Brunel University, 1999; M.Sc. in Health Economics, University of York, 1988; and BSc (Hons) in Economics, University of Salford, 1987. Stirling is a member of the Standing Scientific Committee for the International Health Economics Association (founding member), the National Institute for Clinical Excellence (NICE) Technology Appraisals Committee, the NHS R&D Health Technology Assessment Programme Pharmaceuticals Advisory Panel, the EuroQol Group, the Medical Research Council's College of Experts and Editorial Board for Chronic Illness. His main research interests lie broadly in the areas of economic evaluation and health technology assessment from applied and methodological perspectives and he has a particular interest in preference elicitation and outcome measurement.

Leonie Burgess, Department of Mathematical Sciences and Centre of Health Economics Research and Evaluation, University of Technology Sydney, Australia
Leonie is a Senior Research Fellow in Mathematical Sciences at UTS. Her research interests include the design and computer-based construction of experiments, and she has published many research papers on the design and construction of optimal choice experiments.

Fiona French, NHS Education for Scotland, Aberdeen, UK
Fiona is the Research and Development Officer for the North-east Deanery. Her interests include the reform of postgraduate medical education, particularly foundation programmes and factors which influence the recruitment and retention of doctors at all levels in Scotland. In the last 5 years, she has co-authored nine papers and ten presentations for a variety of medical education conferences in the UK and abroad.

Karen Gerard, Faculty of Medicine, Health and Life Sciences, University of Southampton, UK
Karen is a Reader in Health Economics at the University of Southampton. In 1982, she graduated from the University of Nottingham with a BA (Hons) in Economics and Econometrics, and a year later, from the University of York with an M.Sc. in Health Economics. Her primary roles are health economics research and education that are of value to the UKNHS, including advice to Southampton and North and West Hampshire Research and Development Support Unit. Her activities support the delivery of efficient and equitable health care services. Her doctorate focused on the role of consumer involvement in health care benefit assessment. This explored policy and methodological issues in the assessment of benefit valuation for out-of-hours health services, using a series of discrete choice experiments.

Dorte Gyrd-Hansen, Institute for Public Health, University of Southern Denmark and Danish Institute for Health Services Research, Denmark
Dorte is a Professor at Institute for Public Health, University of Southern Denmark and is the Director of Research at DSI Danish Institute of Health Services Research. Her main field of interest is methodological issues related to the elicitation of preferences. Research themes include communication of risk, contingent valuation and discrete choice analysis.

Jordan Louviere, School of Marketing, University of Technology Sydney (UTS), Australia
Jordan is Professor of Marketing and Executive Director of the Centre for the Study of Choice (CenSoC) at UTS. Jordan is associated with the Centre for Health Economics Research and Evaluation at UTS. He pioneered the design of stated preference experiments, and currently is focusing on theory and methods for Best-Worst Scaling and modeling the choices of single decision-makers.

Kirsten Major, Director of Strategic Planning and Performance, NHS Ayrshire and Arran Health Board, Scotland, UK
Kirsten is currently Director of Strategic Planning and Performance with NHS Ayrshire and Arran. Through both her current role and professional background as a health economist, she has a long-held interest in methods of resource allocation. Of particular interest to her are the need to ensure that "fair shares" are genuinely based on differences in need for, rather than use of, health services. She is also keen that methods deployed at a national level are used below this level, wherever possible, to ensure equitable distributions of resources at a more local level.

Tami Mark, Associate Director, Thomson Medstat, Washington, DC, US
Tami is an Associate Director in the Outcomes Research department at Thomson Medstat and an Adjunct Assistant Professor at the Johns Hopkins Bloomberg School of Public Health. She has published over 50 peer-reviewed journal articles and book chapters, as well as numerous government reports. Her research interests include mental health and substance abuse services and pharmacoeconomics. She received training in health economics from Johns Hopkins University, MBA from Loyola College and BA from Amherst College.

Gillian Needham, NHS Education for Scotland, Aberdeen, UK
Gillian is the Postgraduate Medical Dean for the North East Region and is a Professional Consultant in Diagnostic Radiology at Aberdeen Royal Hospitals Trust, and Flexible Training Adviser at North East Scotland Postgraduate Medical Centre, Aberdeen. Her interests include appropriate extension of opportunities for Flexible Training and Working in general, and Specialist Training in Radiology in particular. In the last 5 years, she has co-authored 2 books, 13 papers and 14 presentations to learned societies on Radiological Anatomy, Breast Imaging, Image Analysis and Clinical Guidelines.

Tracy Roberts, Health Economics Facility, School of Public Policy, University of Birmingham, UK
Tracy is a Senior Lecturer in Health Economics. She has been involved in health economics since the mid-1990s. Her main qualifications are MPhil in Economics, Wolfson College, University of Oxford, 1992; BSc (Econ) in Economics, University College London, 1990; and Registered General Nurse, St. Bartholomew's School of Nursing, London, 1987. Tracy is currently the coordinator of the Health Technology Assessment applied research theme on diagnostics and screening within HEF. Her research interests span the range of health economics and policy. Special interests include economics of screening, economic evaluation alongside randomised controlled trials, cost-effectiveness systematic reviews, economics of sexual health and economics applied to obstetrics and gynaecology.

Mandy Ryan, Health Economics Research Unit, University of Aberdeen, UK
Mandy joined the Health Economics Research Unit (HERU) in 1987 after graduating from the University of Leicester in 1986 with a BA (Hons) in Economics and from the University of York with an M.Sc. in Health Economics. In 1995, she graduated from the University of Aberdeen with a Ph.D. in Economics, concerned with the application of contingent valuation and discrete choice experiments in health economics. In 1997, Mandy was awarded a 5-year MRC Senior Fellowship to develop and apply discrete choice experiments in health care. In 2002, she was awarded a Personal Chair in Health Economics by the University of Aberdeen, and in 2006, she was elected as a Fellow of the Royal Society of Edinburgh. Mandy has worked with academics, government and the pharmaceutical industry, and has published widely in the field of health economics generally, and monetary valuation more specifically.

Fernando San Miguel Inza, Institución Futuro, Navarra, Spain
Fernando received a Ph.D. in Economics from the University of Aberdeen in 2000, following a Master's degree in Health Economics from the University of York and Bachelor's degree in Economics from the Public University of Navarra. His doctoral thesis empirically investigated some of the crucial axioms of rational choice theory underlying discrete choice experiments. This research led to a number of peer-reviewed publications that have contributed to demonstrate the feasibility of discrete choice experiments within the health and health care field. At present, Fernando coordinates several areas of research within the think tank "Institución Futuro" in Pamplona (Spain). In particular, he acts as a director within the Economics programme. He is also a collaborator in the magazine Tendencias de Futuro.

Anthony Scott, Melbourne Institute of Applied Economic and Social Research, The University of Melbourne, Australia
Anthony is a Professorial Fellow at the Melbourne Institute. He is a health economist and leads the Institute's research into the economics of health care. He has worked at the universities of Aberdeen, Newcastle, Sydney and York. He has a Ph.D. in Economics from the University of Aberdeen. He is also an Honorary Professor in the Health Economics Research Unit at the University of Aberdeen. His research interests have focused on the economics of general practice and primary care, incentives for health care providers and the labour markets of health care professionals. He has also been involved in advising the English and Scottish Health Departments on resources allocation, new contracts for GPs and health care workforce issues. He will build up research at the institute in the area of financing, incentives and organisation of health services.

Marian Shanahan, National Drug and Alcohol Research Centre, University of New South Wales, Australia
Marian is a Health Economist at the National Drug and Alcohol Research Centre, University of New South Wales. She has 15 years experience in applied health economics and health services research and has several publications. Current projects involve evaluating the social and economic impacts associated with the treatment for,

and misuse of, illicit drugs and alcohol, assessing the economic costs of treatment in the Australian Treatment Outcome Study, and the cost-effectiveness of alternate methods of dispensing Suboxone. Additionally, she has experience in the conduct of economic evaluations across a number of contexts, health system reviews and the use of large administrative data sets. She has received an MA in Economics, with a focus on health economics, from McMaster University, Canada.

Diane Skåtun, Health Economics Research Unit, University of Aberdeen, UK
Diane graduated with an MA (Hons) in Political Economy from the University of Glasgow. She then joined the Scottish Doctoral Programme in Economics and gained an M.Sc. in Economics. She continued on the Scottish Doctoral Programme and graduated in 1998 from the University of Aberdeen with a Ph.D. entitled "Econometric Bias and the Estimation of Male–Female Wage Differentials". This reflects her interest in econometric concerns in applied work. Her current work has centred around labour markets within the health care workforce.

Ulla Slothuus Skjoldborg, Institute of Public Health, University of Southern Denmark, Denmark
Ulla is a consultant on health economic issues. Her main area of specialisation is stated preference methods. She has more than 10 years of academic and research experience in health economics, during which she also obtained a Ph.D. At the time of writing her contribution to this book she was an Associate Professor at Institute of Public Health, University of Southern Denmark.

Deborah J. Street, Department of Mathematical Sciences, University of Technology Sydney (UTS), Australia
Deborah is the professor of Statistics in the Department of Mathematical Sciences at UTS. She has worked on the construction of designed experiments for various situations, focusing most recently on the construction of optimal stated choice experiments.

Joffre Swait, Partner, Advanis, Inc., Adjunct Professor, University of Alberta, Alberta, Canada
Joffre conducts research in a number of areas related to consumer behaviour in the marketplace. His particular areas of expertise are choice modelling methods, stated preference (SP) methods, choice data combination methods, and brand equity measurement and management. His research has encompassed a number of different fields: marketing, transportation planning and environmental damage assessment. From 1994 to 1996, he was a faculty member at the Marketing Department, Warrington College of Business Administration, University of Florida; he currently holds a courtesy appointment from the Faculty of Business, University of Alberta. He co-teaches a graduate-level choice modelling course at the University of Alberta, in conjunction with Vic Adamowicz and Ric Johnson. Dr. Swait is also a full-time partner in Advanis Inc., a market research and management consulting firm with offices in Edmonton and Toronto, Canada.

Cristina Ubach, Consorcio para el Desarrollo de Tecnología Avanzada de Imagen Médica, Spain
Cristina joined the Health Economics Research Unit (HERU) in 2000 as part of her M.Sc. in Health Economics at the University of York and worked there as a Research Assistant for the Valuation and Implementation programme until 2002. During this time, her research focused mainly on applications of discrete choice experiments to investigate a variety of issues within health care, including doctors' and pharmacists' preferences for an electronic prescription system, public views on repeated prescription systems and doctors' preferences for their job characteristics. At present, she coordinates a consortium for the development of advanced medical imaging technology in Barcelona (http://www.suinsa.com/cdteam).

Rosalie Viney, Centre of Health Economics Research and Evaluation (CHERE), University of Technology Sydney (UTS), Australia
Rosalie is a Deputy Director at CHERE and Associate Professor of Health Economics at UTS. She holds an honorary Senior Lectureship in the Faculty of Medicine at the University of Sydney and is a Research Associate of the Centre for Applied Economics Research at the University of New South Wales. She has a Ph.D. in Economics from the University of Sydney. Her Ph.D. research focused on the use of discrete choice experiments to value health outcomes and investigate the assumptions underlying quality-adjusted life years (QALYs). She is a member of the Pharmaceutical Benefits Advisory Committee's Economics Subcommittee. Research areas included analysis of health insurance, utilisation of health services, valuation of health outcomes, the use of economic evaluation in resource allocation and measurement of individual's preferences for health care services.

Verity Watson, Health Economics Research Unit, University of Aberdeen, UK
Verity holds a Ph.D. in Economics from University of Aberdeen (2003), an M.Sc. in Economics from Glasgow University (1998) and an MA (Hons) in Economic Science from University of Aberdeen (1997). She has been working for the Health Economics Research Unit (HERU) since 2002. Her area of expertise is non-market valuation using contingent valuation and discrete choice experiments, in particular, considering the validity of the analysis methods and resulting welfare estimates. She applied both methods in her Ph.D. thesis to conduct cost–benefit analyses of decommissioning of offshore installations. For HERU, Verity has applied these methods to inform a range of policy issues. In doing so, she has worked with academics from different fields, the government and the pharmaceutical industry. Recent applied work has focused on the novel application of discrete choice experiments to obtain weights in priority setting frameworks.

PREFACE

USING DISCRETE CHOICE EXPERIMENTS TO VALUE HEALTH AND HEALTH CARE

In recent years, there has been a growing interest in the development and application of discrete choice experiments (DCEs) within health economics. The use of this relatively new instrument to value health and health care has now evolved to the point where a general text for practising professionals seems appropriate. The few existing books in this area are either research monographs or focus almost entirely on more advanced topics. By contrast, this book serves as a general reference for those applying the technique to health care for the first time as well as for more experienced practitioners. Thus, the book is relevant to postgraduate students and applied researchers who have an interest in the use of DCEs for valuing health and health care. Contributions are made by a number of leading experts in the field, enabling the book to contain a uniquely rich mix of research applications and methodological developments.

Part 1 summarises how DCEs can be implemented, from experimental design to data analysis and the interpretation of results. In many ways, this can be regarded as a *crash* course on the conduct of DCEs. Extensive reference is made throughout to other sources of literature where the interested reader can find further details. Part 2 presents a series of case studies, illustrating the breadth of applications in health economics. Part 3 describes some key methodological issues that have been addressed in the application of DCEs in health. Part 4 concludes with an overview of research issues discussed which we believe are at the leading edge of this field.

It is important to acknowledge that any book requires hard work by a large number of people – this one is no exception. We would like to thank all contributing authors for agreeing to participate in this endeavour. We also owe thanks to many individuals who reviewed drafts, suggested resource materials and, in general, gave us necessary support to complete this book. In particular, we acknowledge with special thanks and appreciation the contributions of Barbara Eberth, Verity Watson, Heather Mackintosh and Esther Verdries. We also owe thanks to Ian Bateman for his kind invitation to contribute to the Springer series and for his support throughout the project.

The editors are also grateful for financial support from the Chief Scientist Office of the Scottish Executive Health Department, the University of Aberdeen and the University of Southampton.

Despite the debt owed to our colleagues, the editors and authors are solely responsible for any erroneous interpretation or misuse of data. We accept full responsibility for the final version of the text and sincerely hope that the fruit of these efforts is a book that is both useful and informative. If there are any comments about this book, the editors would be delighted to hear from you. Please email one of us at the addresses below.

Mandy Ryan is Professor of Health Economics at the Health Economics Research Unit, University of Aberdeen, UK. She is also a Fellow of the Royal Society of Edinburgh. m.ryan@abdn.ac.uk.

Karen Gerard is a Reader in Health Economics in the Health Services Research Group, Faculty of Medicine, Health and Life Science, University of Southampton, UK. K.M.Gerard@soton.ac.uk.

Mabel Amaya-Amaya is a Research Fellow at the Health Economics Research Unit, University of Aberdeen, UK. m.amaya@abdn.ac.uk.

The Editors

LIST OF TABLES

xv

LIST OF FIGURES

INTRODUCTION

KAREN GERARD

Faculty of Medicine, Health and Life Sciences, University of Southampton, UK

MANDY RYAN AND MABEL AMAYA-AMAYA

Health Economics Research Unit, University of Aberdeen, UK

1. BENEFIT VALUATION IN HEALTH ECONOMICS

Given the substantial resources devoted to health care in many countries,[1] a fundamental question is: *how does a society determine which health services to provide and the appropriate level at which to provide them?* In many countries, there is a widespread concern that the market mechanism fails to allocate health care resources appropriately. Hence, this task often falls to government.

The dramatic increase in the demand for health care over the last 40 years coupled with the finite nature of those resources (e.g. labour and capital) have led to a growing relative scarcity of health care resources and thus an increasing interest in health care choices and values. Whilst rising costs have spurred numerous cost-containment efforts by governments in the last few decades, the explicit valuation of the benefits of actions improving health care delivery is undoubtedly a crucial aspect of designing effective and efficient policies that accurately reflect the desires of society.

One way health economists can contribute to health policy is by providing explicit measures of benefit valuation for assessing alternative health care interventions. This is no small task since it is accepted that to fully assess the value of benefits in health care, researchers must estimate the value of a wide and at times complex multidimensional array of health care policies, strategies, interventions and treatments. Indeed, the valuation of health care benefits presents one of the greatest challenges facing health economics today. Therefore, it is not surprising to find that different approaches have developed over time reflecting the need to make choices in a diversity of decision contexts. The challenge also justifies the existence of an ongoing programme of research within health economics aiming to better understand the strengths and weaknesses of different methodologies in providing values for use in economic evaluation.

1

M. Ryan, K. Gerard and M. Amaya-Amaya (eds.), Using Discrete Choice
Experiments to Value Health and Health Care, 1–10.
© 2008 *Springer.*

Full economic evaluation techniques include cost-minimisation analysis (CMA), cost-effectiveness analysis (CEA), cost-utility analysis (CUA) and cost–benefit analysis (CBA) (Drummond et al., 2005; Gold et al., 1996). For many years, the method of choice for making policy recommendations has been CEA, which measures benefits as quantity of life using unidimensional clinical measures such as life years saved or deaths averted. The 1980s and the early 1990s saw the development of CUA, which uses a measure of benefit known as "quality-adjusted life years" (QALYs), taking into account both quantity and quality of life generated by health care interventions. Over the years, the QALY measure has gained considerable prominence (Neumann et al., 2005; Stoykova and Fox-Rushby, 2005). It is seen by many health care decision makers as a panacea for priority setting and rationing when used as an input to "cost per QALY" analyses. In addition, CEA/CUA is the method for benefit valuation recommended in guidelines such as those from the National Institute for Health and Clinical Excellence (NICE) in the UK (Department of Health, NHS Executive, 1998) and those in the USA (Gold et al., 1996), Australia (Pharmaceutical Benefits Advisory Committee, 2002), China (China Pharmacoeconomics Center, 2006), the Netherlands (Ziekenfondsraad, 1999), Sweden (Sweden Pharmaceutical Benefits Board, 2003), Poland (Orlewska and Mierzejewski, 2000), Hungary (Szende et al., 2002), Spain (Rovira and Antoñanzas, 1995) and Italy (Garattini et al., 1995) to name a few.[2]

It follows that, unlike in other policy fields such as transportation or the environment, health care policy makers have been reluctant to embrace the valuation of benefits in monetary terms within a CBA framework. CBA presents theoretical advantages such as a firm basis in welfare economics and a common unit of measure for costs and benefits as required to determine whether a policy increases social welfare (*allocative* efficiency). Despite these advantages, most CBA studies in health economics are experimental in nature, attempting to explore measurement feasibility issues rather than being full programme evaluations (Drummond et al., 2005). This historical lack of popularity of CBA in health economics may be partly due to the perceived difficulty associated with placing monetary values on so-called intangible benefits of health care provision and partly to some ongoing conceptual debates concerning what questions should be asked of whom in health care contingent valuation studies (see, e.g. Smith, 2003). However, this view is gradually changing. Significant progress made in monetary valuation methods over the past decade (primarily in the area of environmental economics, but also within the health care arena) holds out the prospect of a move towards decision making based on monetised costs and benefits of alternative policy interventions, as encouraged in the latest HM Treasury's *Green Book* (2003). Indeed, greater use of these methods to facilitate CBA for policy recommendations in health and health care is increasingly advocated.[3] Section 2 outlines the main methods of benefit assessment at the analyst's disposal.

2. MEASURING HEALTH CARE BENEFITS IN MONETARY TERMS

The assessment of health care programmes' benefits in monetary terms is a challenging task because health services are usually not traded in markets and, when they are, prices can be unrealistically low. This means that the standard market-based estimation techniques – which rely on gaining insight from people's preferences for goods and services by reference to patterns of buying and selling – cannot be easily applied.

In their development of monetary benefit valuation techniques, economists have taken two fundamental pathways. The first draws on Samuelson's seminal article (Samuelson, 1948) and involves the exploration of people's preferences as (indirectly) revealed through their actions (choices) in markets specifically related to the value of interest. This group of techniques is known as "revealed preference" (RP) techniques. Examples of such methods include the travel cost method and the hedonic pricing technique. More details on valuation using RP data can be found in Bockstael and McConnell (2006) and Champ et al. (2003). The alternative pathway involves asking the same individuals to state their preferences in hypothetical (or virtual) markets. The methods that follow this strategy are collectively known as "stated preference" (SP) techniques.

A healthy scepticism about relying on what consumers say they will do (SP) compared with observing what they actually do (RP) has typically been displayed in the literature. Yet, there are a number of compelling reasons why health economists should be interested in SP data. Most important in the health sector is that it may not be possible to infer consumer preferences or values from RP data.[4] Many aspects of health care are not traded explicitly in markets, have public good characteristics and are consumed free at the point of service or heavily subsidised via health insurance. Further, an (imperfect) agency relationship exists between the supplier (the doctor or other health care provider) and the consumer (the patient), as the former will generally be better informed than the latter. This problem of *asymmetric* information, linked with the uncertain nature of both health and the outcomes of health care, means that actual decisions may not be solely (if at all) based on consumer preferences. Another reason for favouring SP techniques is that they are based on hypothetical choices that can be precisely specified in advance using a design, which allows straightforward identification of all effects of interest. This is in contrast to RP data, which cannot be controlled a priori so that model identification cannot be guaranteed. Further, SP methods allow large quantities of relevant data to be collected at moderate cost. Furthermore, SP data provides information on current preferences and how these are likely to respond to a proposed change in resource allocation.

As a result, research in the area of health care benefits valuation has seen an increased interest in SP approaches. More recently interest has also been shown in the potential gains from combining RP data, with typically less variability but high validity and reliability, and SP data, with more favourable statistical properties (for more on data enrichment see Chapter 10). The two best-known SP approaches for providing estimates of monetary valuation are the contingent valuation method (CVM) and discrete choice experiments (DCEs). These are outlined below.

2.1. Contingent Valuation Method

The CVM refers to a choice-based approach to value benefits where individuals are asked directly, in a survey, how much they would be willing to pay (WTP) for specific commodities. In some cases, people are asked for the amount they would be willing to accept in compensation (WTAC) to give up a specific good or service. It is called "contingent" valuation, because people are asked to state their WTP, contingent on a particular hypothetical scenario and description of the commodity being valued. The CVM approach can be seen as a holistic approach, with a value being estimated for the good as a whole (for more details see chapter by Boyle in Champ and Welsh, 2006).

CVM is founded in neoclassical welfare economics providing a theoretically correct measure of value. However, its application presents many challenges. Most importantly, it is prone to some known biases.[5] Biased value measures mean that either responses are under-sensitive to manipulations that should affect them (e.g. the "scope" or quantity of the goods or services being valued), or are too sensitive to what should not affect them (e.g. question format or the cost of a good or service). In addition to this, and perhaps not surprisingly within the health care field there are practical problems when asking individuals to express monetary valuations for health care; e.g. individuals may be unfamiliar with the health state under valuation or they may morally object to place a value on health.

All in all, CVM has been applied with varying degrees of success in health care both for benefit valuation and for elicitation of public views. For example, WTP values have been derived for ultrasound in pregnancy (Berwick and Weinstein, 1985) asthma medication (Barner et al., 1999), genetic testing for cancer risk (Bosompra et al., 2001) and cystic fibrosis (Donaldson et al., 1995), community water fluoridation (Dixon and Shackley, 1999) and to set priorities for public sector health care programs (Olsen and Donaldson, 1998) (See Diener et al. (1998); Klose (1999) and Smith (2003) for comprehensive reviews). As monetary benefit valuation is increasingly advocated in health care and many methodological issues become better understood, the use of CVM for valuing the multiple-dimensions of health care benefits can be expected to grow.

2.2. Discrete Choice Experiments

DCEs are an attribute-based approach to collect SP data. They involve presenting respondents with a sequence of hypothetical scenarios (choice sets) composed by two or more competing alternatives that vary along several attributes, one of which may be the price of the alternative or some approximation for it. In a Lancasterian framework (Lancaster, 1966), it is assumed these attribute levels determine the value (utility) of each alternative. For each choice set, respondents are asked to choose their preferred scenario. It is assumed that individuals will consider all information provided and then select the alternative with the highest utility. Responses enable the analyst to model the probability of an alternative being chosen as a function of the attributes and the socio-economic characteristics of the respondents. This allows an estimation of the relative support that respondents show for the various competing alternatives. Other policy outputs include marginal rates of substitution across non-monetary attributes as well as WTP or WTAC for an improvement or deterioration of one of those attribute welfare measures for a proposed change in levels of the attributes and predicted uptake or demand.

The DCE technique was introduced into health economics in the early 1990s to enhance benefit assessment by challenging the presumption that the goal of health services is only to improve health. Benefits can be many sided, e.g. containing elements of the process of care as well as its outcome, and that outcome may extend beyond health benefits such as reassurance or anxiety. The underlying paradigm of the QALY measure was specifically designed to capture heath outcome benefits only. Other concerns, particularly distributional ones, are dealt with by valuing a QALY equally to whoever receives it. If some of the omitted factors are valuable to patients or members of the public, the conclusions reached by policy makers may conflict with those of patients and public (Ryan, 1999). Both CVM and DCE allow for the possibility of measuring benefits beyond health outcome (at least in principle). Advocates of DCEs have argued that DCEs offer several advantages over the CVM (Louviere, 1987; Louviere et al., 1997). First, they enable researchers to collect comparable or higher-quality valuation information at a lower cost. Second, they allow researchers to characterise the incremental benefits that consumers derive from the different individual attributes of health care interventions. Third, they more completely characterise a consumer's underlying utility function, and thus may improve policy makers' ability to perform benefit transfers.[6] Further, it is argued that this method may overcome some of the "biases" encountered in empirical applications using CVM (Hanley et al., 2001). Furthermore, WTP is to be inferred indirectly rather than explicitly pricing the good. This is highly desirable in a health care context where, as mentioned, some individuals may refuse to place a monetary value on human health in the CVM format, increasing the incidence of protest zero bids.

It should be noted that there is now consensus that the choice of SP method depends, in part, on how much detail is required on the characteristics of the health care intervention being valued. Some studies need to answer questions only about the good or service as a whole (e.g. what is the monetary value placed on a screening test). If this is the case, a CVM study is appropriate. In other contexts, what matters is the importance of different characteristics of the programme being valued. In these cases, DCEs are more useful. There are advantages and disadvantages associated with both CVM and DCEs. To the extent that DCEs also allow estimating total values, they provide more information than a single (CVM) experiment. However, this increased information comes at a price: evidence suggests that DCEs are more cognitively demanding for respondents to complete and the study outcomes might be affected (for more on this, see Chapter 9). More generally, some situations can be identified where the two valuation techniques can be used to complement each other; i.e. to increase the robustness of the data or to validate the underlying components of values. The remainder of this book is solely concerned with DCEs and its applications in health economics.

3. PURPOSE AND OUTLINE OF THE BOOK

As interest in the application of DCEs to health care issues continues to grow there is a need for a general reference book which can help to guide those applying the technique to health care for the first time, as well as those more experienced practitioners interested in the current methodological status of DCEs in health economics and debates about future challenges. The book therefore has three aims: (i) to introduce the technique in the health care context; (ii) to demonstrate the broad applicability of the technique, using a range of case studies; and (iii) to provide insight into the methodological status of DCEs in health economics, focusing on current achievements and future challenges. It is thus anticipated that this book will become a key reference for those interested in the application of DCE to the valuation of health care policy, interventions and treatments, as well as useful in better understanding individual behaviour and predicting demand.

The book is presented in four parts. Part 1 has three chapters which together form the building blocks for the reader to understand the theory, methods and application of DCE in health economics. Chapter 1 by Amaya-Amaya et al. provides a comprehensive description of the theoretical underpinnings of DCEs. It also describes the different stages involved in the conduct of an experiment, outlining some important details that the practitioner needs to consider when developing and implementing the survey. Chapter 2 is a technical chapter by Street et al., explaining one way of constructing optimal experimental designs. This will interest the more specialist reader, at the same time giving the general reader an appreciation of what is involved and a sense of the statistical theory that underlies experimental design. Having explained the theoretical underpinnings and methods of a DCE, Chapter 3 by Ryan et al. focuses on application. It is intended for the general reader who is wants to understand some of the practical detail of using an experimental design to collect data and to prepare the data for analysis. This chapter uses a case study in the area of prenatal diagnosis to work through key steps.

Part 2 provides the reader with an appreciation of the breadth of DCE applications in health economics. There are four empirical chapters. Chapters 4–6 illustrate different aspects of using DCE to value health care interventions. Chapter 4 by Ryan et al demonstrates the case of how misleading it can be if benefits are restricted to health outcomes only. It shows how a clinical trial reported no significant difference in clinical benefits of alternative rheumatology appointment systems, but a DCE survey identified reduced waiting times as an important (non-health) benefit to patients. Chapter 4 also considers going beyond the basic model of analysis to allow for different degrees of similarity across alternatives. Chapter 5 by Gerard et al. explores the potential of DCE to predict uptake of a screening programme under different scenarios using a simple binary choice experiment. This chapter also provides an example of alternative coding schemes for the explanatory variables included in the analysis. In Chapter 6, Bryan and Robertson show how the DCE technique can be used in the context of CUA and QALYs to learn more about priority setting rules to inform the debate around the challenge of establishing some "threshold level of cost per QALY (Raftery, 2006). Chapter 7 presents analysis from Scott et al. of an example of using DCE to understand individual behaviour in the form of job satisfaction characteristics for hospital consultants in the UK. This provides a useful exploration of public sector labour market behaviour in a climate of health professional shortages.

It is important to emphasise that these empirical studies were selected to demonstrate the breadth of application possible and not necessarily for their ability to demonstrate good practice over all the stages of undertaking and reporting a DCE. In particular, we are aware that experimental design practices have moved on considerably since these studies were initiated. Given the current state of the art in experimental design of DCE, these examples would be now regarded as *not so good* designs, but they remain appropriate for the purpose they were selected.

The focus in Part 3 is to expose the reader to some examples of methodological issues under debate in the literature. The first that is covered in Chapter 8 by Slothuus and Gryd-Hansen concerns our need to better understand how respondents interpret the price proxy attribute. This chapter considers how method of payment and willingness to engage in compensatory decision making may impact on preferences and what we can do to explore our data sets as thoroughly as possible to avoid misinterpretation of data. Chapter 9 by San Miguel Inza et al. considers the issue of rational choice in the DCE context. The authors demonstrate alternative, more extensive, tests of rationality as well as the benefit of using qualitative methods to enhance the analysts' understanding of how respondents answer DCE questions and thereby better understanding the validity of DCE responses. Chapter 10, the last methodological chapter by Mark and Swait focuses on how combining information on what individuals' say they will do (RP data) with information on what they did do (SP data) – sometimes referred to as data fusion or enrichment – can improve the analyst's understanding of preferences and the implication for future decisions. This is a cutting-edge area of research within health economics. The study described makes use of RP and SP data obtained from doctor's preferences for prescribing in the private US health care system. For health economists operating in publicly funded health care systems one challenge is to find relevant opportunities to use this technique. Whilst it may be harder to find robust RP data in these systems, the future may lie in combining different sources of SP data (e.g. DCE data on indirect WTP with contingent valuation data).

Finally, Part 4 has a single chapter which offers some concluding thoughts from the editors. They first summarise the topics covered in this book, followed by an overview of some directions for research in the future.

ENDNOTES

[1] Health care expenditures are substantial and dramatically rising in most industrialised countries. Over the last 5 years, the increase in health spending, combined with lower economic growth, has driven the share of health expenditure as a percentage of gross domestic product (GDP) up from an average 7.8% in 1997 to 8.5% in 2002 (OECD, 2005).

[2] For more information on some key features of these guidelines in several countries around the world, visit the International Society for Pharmacoeconomics and Outcomes Research (ISPOR) web site: http://www.ispor.org/PEguidelines/index.asp.

[3] See, e.g. Loomes (2002), Hanley et al. (2002) and Ryan (2004). See also Baker et al. (2003) for a recent research proposal on the determination of a monetary value for a QALY to help NICE offering guidance to the National Health Service (NHS) about the uptake (or maintenance) of an intervention.

[4] Where this is possible, i.e. when both RP and SP data are available, the recommendation is to capitalise on the complementary strengths of each source by combining the different data sets (also referred to data fusion) (see, e.g Hensher et al. 1999). See Chapter 10 for more on this and an application in health care.

[5] As noted by Green and Tunstall (1999) the term "bias" is an interesting and potentially dangerous piece of economic labelling that has been used to described both theoretically unexpected and theoretically expected, both undesirable, effects. In either case, the presumption is that the results, the

respondents or the experimental methods are "wrong", so the term has pejorative overtones. Conversely, in psychology "bias" refers to a characteristic of the experimental context that influences respondents in a particular way. Here, unexpected rather than undesirable effects are seen as a way to theoretical development. The term "bias" should therefore be used with extreme caution or indeed avoided altogether by referring to this as an "effect" (e.g. Munro and Hanley, 1999).

[6] Benefit transfers refer to the use of existing estimates of the benefit of a non-marketed good from one or more sites (study sites) to predict the value for the same or for a similar good in a different site (policy site) – see Morrison et al. (2002).

REFERENCES

Baker, R., Chilton, S., Donaldson, C., Jones-Lee, M., Metcalf, H., Shackley, P. and Ryan, M. 2003. Determining the Societal Value of a QALY by Surveying the Public in England and Wales: a Research Protocol. Birmingham: NCCRM Publications, Birmingham, UK.

Barner, J.C., Mason, H.L. and Murray, M.D. 1999. Assessment of asthma patients' willingness to pay for and give time to an asthma self-management program. *Clinical Therapy*, vol 21, 878–894.

Berwick, D.M. and Weinstein, M.C. 1985. What do patients value? Willingness to pay for ultrasound in normal pregnancy. *Medical Care*, vol 23, 881–893

Bockstael, N.E. and McConnell, K.E. (eds) 2006. Environmental and Resource Valuation with Revealed Preferences A Theoretical Guide to Empirical Models Series: The Economics of Non-Market Goods and Resources, vol 7. Dordrecht, The Netherlands: Kluwer Academic.

Bosompra, K., Ashikaga, T., Flynn, B.S., Worden, J.K. and Solomon, L.J. 2001. Psychological factors associated with the public's willingness to pay for genetic testing for cancer risk: a structural equations model. *Health Education Research*, vol 16, 157–172.

Champ, P.A. and Welsh, M.P. 2006. Survey Methodologies for Stated Choice Studies. In: Valuing Environmental Amenities using Choice Experiments: A Common Sense Guide to Theory and Practice. Kanninen, B. (ed.). Boston: Springer Series: The Economics of Non-Market Goods and Resources, vol 8, Series ed.: Bateman, I., 21–42.

Champ, P.A., Boyle, K.J. and Brow, T.C. (eds) 2003. A Primer on Nonmarket Valuation. Series: The Economics of Non-Market Goods and Resources, vol. 3. Dordrecht, The Netherlands: Kluwer Academic.

Chinese Pharmacoeconomic Evaluation Guideline. 2006. China Pharmacoeconomics Center, Chinese Medical Doctor Association. http://www.pe-cn.org/project/guidelines_en.asp

Department of Health, NHS Executive. 1998. A first class service: quality in the new NHS. Leeds: NHS Executive.

Diener, A., O'Brien, B. and Gafni, A. 1998. Health care contingent valuation studies: a review and classification of the literature. *Health Economics*, vol 7, 313–326.

Dixon, S. and Shackley, P. 1999. Estimating the benefits of community water fluoridation using the willingness-to-pay technique: the results of a pilot study. *Community Dental Oral Epidemiology*, vol 27, 124–129.

Donaldson, C., Shackley, P., Abdalla, M. and Miedzybrodzka, Z. 1995. Willingness to pay for antenatal carrier screening for cystic fibrosis. *Health Economics*, vol 4, 439–452.

Drummond, M.F., Sculpher, M.J., Torrance, G.W., et al. 2005. Methods for the Economic Evaluation of Health Care Programme, 3rd edn. Oxford: Oxford University Press.

Garattini, L., Grilli, R., Scopelliti, D. and Mantovani, L. 1995. A proposal for Italian guidelines in pharmacoeconomics. *Pharmacoeconomics*, vol 7, 1–6.

Gold, M.R., Siegel, J.E., Russell, L.B., et al. 1996. Cost-effectiveness analysis in health and medicine. New York: Oxford University Press.

Green, C. and Tunstall, S. 1999. A Psychological Perspective. In: Valuing Environmental Preferences: Theory and Practice of the Contingent Valuation Method in the US, EC and Developing Countries. Bateman, I.J. and Willis, K.G. (eds). Oxford: Oxford University Press, pp 207–257.

Hanley, N., Mourato, S. and Wright, R. 2001. Choice modelling approaches: a superior alternative for environmental evaluation? *Journal of Economic Surveys*, vol 15 (3), 453–557.

Hanley, N., Ryan, M. and Wright, R. 2002. Estimating the monetary value of health care: lessons from environmental economics. *Health Economics*, vol 12, 3–16.

Hensher, D., Louviere, J. and Swait, J. 1999. Combining sources of preference data. *Journal of Econometrics*, vol 89, 197–221.

HM Treasury. 2003. Green Book: Appraisal and Evaluation in Central Government. http://www.hm-treasury.gov.uk/media/05553/Green_Book_03.pdf. Last accessed 28/11/2006.

Klose, T. 1999. The contingent valuation method in health care. *Health Policy*, vol 47, 97–123.

Lancaster, K. 1966. A new approach to consumer theory. *Journal of Political Economy*, vol 74, 132–157.

Loomes, G. 2002. Valuing life years and QALYs: transferability and convertibility of values across the UK public sector. In: Cost Effectiveness Thresholds: Economic and Ethical Issues. Towse, A., Pritchard, C. and Devlin, N. (eds). London: King's Fund and Office of Health Economics.

Louviere, J. 1987. Analyzing Decision Making – Metric Conjoint Analysis. Sage University Paper #67, Newbury Park, CA: Sage Publications.

Louviere, J.J., Oppewal, H., Timmermans, H., et al. 1997. Handling large numbers of attributes in conjoint applications: who says existing techniques can't be applied? But if you want an alternative, how about hierarchical choice experiments? Mimeograph.

Morrison, M., Bennett, J., Blamey, R. and Louviere, J. 2002. Choice modeling and tests of benefit transfer. *American Journal of Agricultural Economics*, vol 84, 161–170.

Munro, A. and Hanley, N. 1999. Information, uncertainty and contingent valuation. In: Valuing Environmental Preferences: Theory and Practice of the Contingent Valuation Method in the US, EC and Developing Countries. Bateman, I. and Willis, K. (eds). Oxford: Oxford University Press, pp 258–297.

Neumann, P.J., Greenberg, D., Olichanski, N.V., Stone, P.W. and Rosen, A.B. 2005. Growth and quality of the cost-utility literature, 1976–2001. *Value in Health*, vol 8, 3–9.

OECD. 2005. Health Data 2005: Statistics and Indicators for 30 Countries. http://www.oecd.org/document/30/0,2340,en_2825_495642_12968734_1_1_1_1,00.html

Olsen, J.A. and Donaldson, C. 1998. Helicopters, hearts and hips: using willingness to pay to set priorities for public sector health care programs. *Social Science and Medicine*, vol 46, 1–12.

Orlewska, E. and Mierzejewski, P. 2000. Polish guidelines for conducting pharmacoeconomic evaluations (project). *Farmakoekonomika*, Suppl 1, 12–20.

Pharmaceutical Benefits Advisory Committee (PBAC). 2002. Guidelines for the pharmaceutical industry on preparation of submissions to the Pharmaceutical Benefits Advisory Committee. http://www.health.gov.au/internet/wcms/publishing.nsf/content/health-pbs-general-pubs-guidelines-index.htm. Last accessed 06/11/06.

Rovira, J. and Antoñanzas, F. 1995. Economic analysis of health technologies and programmes. A Spanish proposal for methodological standardisation. *Pharmacoeconomics*, vol 8 (3), 245–252.

Ryan, M. 1999. A role for conjoint analysis in technology assessment in health care? *International Journal of Technology Assessment in Health Care*, vol 15, 443–457.

Samuelson, P.A. 1948. Foundations of Economic Analysis. Cambridge, MA: McGraw-Hill.

Smith, R.D. 2003. Construction of the contingent valuation market in health care: a critical assessment. *Health Economics*, vol 12 (8), 609–628.

Stoykova, B. and Fox-Rushby, J. 2005. Use of economic evaluation in practice and policy. In: Economic Evaluation. Fox-Rushby, J. and Cairns, J. (eds). Maidenhead: Open University Press.

Sweden Pharmaceutical Benefits Board. 2003. General guidelines for economic evaluation from the Pharmaceutical Benefits Board. http://www.lfn.se/upload/English/ENG_lfnar2003-eng.pdf

Szende, A., Mogyorósy, Z. Muszbek, N., et al. 2002. Methodological guidelines for conducting economic valuation of healthcare interventions in Hungary: a Hungarian proposal for methodology standards. *European Journal of Health Economics*, vol 3, 196–206.

Ziekenfondsraad. 1999. Dutch guidelines for pharmacoeconomic research. Amstelveen, The Netherlands: Health Insurance Council.

PART 1

DCES: WHAT ARE THEY AND THEIR APPLICATION IN HEALTH
A USER'S GUIDE

CHAPTER 1

DISCRETE CHOICE EXPERIMENTS
IN A NUTSHELL

MABEL AMAYA-AMAYA

Health Economics Research Unit, University of Aberdeen, UK

KAREN GERARD AND MANDY RYAN

Faculty of Medicine, Health and Life Sciences, University of Southampton, UK
Health Economics Research Unit, University of Aberdeen, UK

1. INTRODUCTION

Since their introduction in health economics in the early 1990s, research in the area of health care benefits valuation has seen an increased interest in the use of discrete choice experiments (DCEs). This is shown by the explosion of literature applying this technique to direct evaluation of different policy-relevant attributes of health care interventions as well as to look at other issues such as understanding labour supply characteristics, time preferences or uptake or demand forecasting (see Ryan and Gerard, 2003; Fiebig et al., 2005 for recent reviews).

As previously introduced, the DCE is an attribute-based survey method for measuring benefits (utility). DCEs present respondents with samples of hypothetical scenarios (choice sets) drawn a priori from all possible choice sets according to statistical design principles. The choice sets comprise two or more alternatives, which vary along several characteristics or attributes of interest, and individuals are asked to choose one alternative. Most commonly, each respondent faces several choice questions within a single survey. Table 1.1 presents an example of a typical choice presented to individuals. In this case, individuals choose amongst two different prenatal screening tests or having no test. The tests differed in the type and amount of information received; the waiting time (in days) for the test results and cost of the screening test to the respondent (for more details on this study, see Chapter 3 and Ryan et al., 2005).

Drawing upon Lancaster's economic theory of value (Lancaster, 1966), DCEs assume that individuals derive utility from the underlying attributes of the commodity under valuation (rather than the commodity per se) and that individuals'

M. Ryan, K. Gerard and M. Amaya-Amaya (eds.), Using Discrete Choice
Experiments to Value Health and Health Care, 13–46.

TABLE 1.1. *Example of choice task in a DCE*

Choice 1	Test A	Test B	No test
Information	Simple	Comprehensive	No information
Waiting time to receiving results (days)	2	8	No result
Cost of screening test (£)	20	100	0
Please place a tick on the screening test you would choose	☐	☐	☐

preferences (as summarised by their utility function) are revealed through their choices. The results from the experiment are used to model preferences within a random utility maximisation (RUM) framework (McFadden, 1974) as detailed below.

2. THEORETICAL FRAMEWORK OF DISCRETE CHOICE EXPERIMENTS[1]

The theoretical underpinnings of DCEs contain many elements of the standard economic theory of consumer behaviour. As with consumer theory, it is assumed that participants in DCEs are rational decision makers and they seek to maximise innate, stable preferences. That is, when faced with a set of possible consumption bundles of goods, they assign values (preferences) to each of the various bundles and then choose the most preferred bundle from the set of affordable alternatives. Given the traditional properties of the neoclassical consumer,[2] discrete choice behaviour can be formulated as an optimisation problem in which the consumer selects the consumption bundle such that their benefit (utility) is maximised[3] subject to their budget constraint.

However, three extensions to classic consumer theory are important to discrete choice analysis. First, whilst consumer theory assumes homogeneous goods (e.g. a car is a car) and utility a function of quantities, discrete choice theory draws on Lancaster's (1966) idea that it is the attributes of the goods that determine the utility they provide. Changes in those attributes can cause a discrete switch from one bundle of goods to another that will provide the most beneficial combination of attributes. Secondly, as opposed to the continuous (i.e. infinitely divisible) space of products in consumer theory, discrete choice theory deals with a choice among a set of finite and mutually exclusive alternatives (the individual chooses one and only one alternative from this set).[4] This means that, in addition to the budget constraint, further restrictions are added to the optimisation problem (see Hanemann, 1982) for a discussion of problem formulation). Finally, whereas classic consumer theory assumes deterministic behaviour, discrete choice theory introduces the idea that individual choice behaviour is intrinsically probabilistic, hence random. This concept of "random utility" was put forward by Thurstone (1927) in psychology, introduced into economics by Marschak (1960) and further developed by McFadden (1974).

The idea behind random utility in economic theory is that individuals have in their heads some construct of (indirect)[5] "utilities" for choice alternatives and they may have perfect discrimination capability. However, researchers cannot get inside the heads of these individuals and observe all factors affecting preferences. Therefore, as shown in Equation 1.1, the latent utility of an alternative i in a choice set C_n (as perceived by individual n) is considered to be decomposable into two additively separable parts: (1) a systematic (explainable) component specified as a function of (i.e. caused by) the attributes of the alternatives[6] $V(X_{in}, \beta)$; and (2) a random (unexplainable) component ε_{in} representing unmeasured variation in preferences. This random variation may be due to unobserved attributes affecting choice, inter-individual differences in utilities depending upon the heterogeneity in tastes, measurement errors and/or functional specification (Manski, 1977).

$$U_{in} = V(X_{in}, \beta) + \varepsilon_{in} \qquad (1.1)$$

The key assumption is that individual n will choose alternative i if and only if that alternative maximises their utility amongst all J alternatives included in the choice set C_n. That is:

$$y_{in} = f(U_{in}) = \begin{cases} 1 \text{ if } U_{in} = \max_{j} \{U_{ij}\} \\ 0 \quad \text{otherwise} \end{cases} \quad \forall j \neq i \in C_n \qquad (1.2)$$

Where y_{in} is a choice indicator equal to 1 if alternative i is chosen, and 0 otherwise.
From Equation 1.1, alternative i is chosen if and only if:

$$(V_{in} + \varepsilon_{in}) > (V_{jn} + \varepsilon_{jn}) \cdot \forall j \neq i \in C_n \qquad (1.3)$$

Rearranging to place the observable and unobservable components together yields:

$$(V_{in} - V_{jn}) > (\varepsilon_{jn} - \varepsilon_{in}) \qquad (1.4)$$

The analyst does not observe $(\varepsilon_{jn} - \varepsilon_{in})$, hence cannot determine exactly if $(V_{in} - V_{jn}) > (\varepsilon_{jn} - \varepsilon_{in})$. One can only make statements about choice outcomes up to a probability of occurrence.

The probability that a sampled individual n will choose alternative i (described by attributes X_n) equals the probability that the difference between the random utility of any other alternative j and the chosen alternative i is less than the difference between the systematic utility levels of alternatives i and j, for all J alternatives in the choice set C_n (McFadden, 1974). In mathematical terms:

$$\begin{aligned} P_{in} &= \Pr(y_{in} = 1/X_{in}, \beta) \\ &= \Pr(U_{in} > U_{jn}) \forall j \neq i \in C_n \\ &= \Pr(V_{in} + \varepsilon_{in} > V_{jn} + \varepsilon_{jn}) \forall j \neq i \in C_n \\ &= \Pr(\varepsilon_{jn} - \varepsilon_{in} < V_{in} - V_{jn}) \forall j \neq i \in C_n \end{aligned} \qquad (1.5)$$

The analyst does not know the actual distribution of $\varepsilon_{jn} - \varepsilon_{in}$ across the population, but assumes that it relates to the choice probability according to some distribution or density function $f(\varepsilon_{in})$ to be defined. The reader should note that the meaning of this distribution is important and it affects the researcher's interpretation of the choice probabilities. Train (2003) identifies different possibilities. First, the density function can be thought of as the distribution of the unobserved portion of utility within the population of people who have the same observed portion of utility for each alternative as individual n. In this case, the choice probability is the share of people who choose alternative i within that population. Second, the distribution can also be considered to represent the researcher's subjective probability that the unobserved utility of the person will take given values. Then, the choice probability is the probability assigned to each person. Finally, the distribution can represent the effect of unobserved factors that are intrinsic to the person herself (representing, for example, aspects of bounded rationality [March, 1978; Simon, 1955]), such that P_{in} in Equation 1.5 is the probability that these factors induce the individual to choose alternative i given the observed factors.

Different density functions for the unobserved part of the utility ε_{in} lead to families of probabilistic discrete choice models with different statistical and mathematical properties. We review some of these models in Section 3.5.

A critical issue in all discrete choice models is the specification of the "representative" (i.e. estimated) utility function $V(X_{in}, \beta)$, that relates the observed attributes of the alternatives to the utility U_{in} derived from alternative i. It is common to assume linear-in-parameters function as shown in Equation 1.6.

$$V_{in} = \text{ASC}_i + \beta_1 x_{i1} + \ldots + \beta_K x_{iK} \tag{1.6}$$

where there are $k = 1, 2, \ldots, K$ attributes (possibly including price) with generic coefficients (to be estimated) β_k across alternatives.[7] An alternative-specific constant (ASC_i) captures the mean effect of the unobserved factors in the error terms for each of the alternatives.[8]

The assumption of linear-in-parameters utility is made for practical reasons (e.g. simplified welfare analysis (see Section 3.6.2) but is not very restrictive because it allows for any non-linear transformation of the variables x. Indeed, often the researcher might want to test empirically a wide range of non-linear functions (e.g. polynomial, piecewise, logarithmic or exponential) (see Ben-Akiva and Lerman, 1985, p 174).

3. CONDUCTING A DISCRETE CHOICE EXPERIMENT

This section summarises the key steps typically involved in the conduct of a DCE. For the inquisitive minds, further details may be found in Adamowicz et al. (1998) or Ryan and Gerard (2003). These steps should be undertaken with some broad awareness of the downstream implications of the decisions taken at each stage. They should also be seen as an integrated process with feedback: the development of the final design[9] involves repeatedly conducting the steps described here, and incorporating new information as it comes along. Throughout the sections, references to studies in health economics are added to illustrate the state of the practice within the discipline. It is hoped that this will enable the reader to appreciate how the remaining chapters in the book fit into the general debate on the application of DCE in health economics.

3.1. Problem Definition: Characterising the Choice Decision

To best formulate the decision problem, at the outset, the researcher must define and understand the issue under study.[10] In advance of data collection and modelling, analysts must devote sufficient time and resources to understand several important issues such as how individuals become aware of the need to make the decision in question; what are the alternatives; how they think about the evaluative process (i.e. what are the key factors or dimensions driving the choice process); and to identify which of those dimensions (attributes) should be initially[11] included in which of the two components of the utility function (i.e. the systematic and random components).[12] It is also important to identify who are the choosers and possible sources of variability across individuals (e.g. income, education, attitude towards health issues and health experiences) that could lead to important behavioural differences (heterogeneity). These and other items are crucial in formulating the selection problem in terms that the participants understand and that is most akin to the decisions that individuals make in real life.

3.2. Identification of Relevant Attributes, Attributes Levels and "Customisation"

How well we identify, measure and include as many as possible of the factors that influence choice determines our ability to capture the systematic component of the utility function, i.e. the portion of attractiveness that can be related to the attributes of the alternatives. Having identified a potentially long list of factors, the researcher may need to narrow the number of attributes down. The selection of a set of key attributes defining the alternatives and their different values (referred to as "levels") should be guided by the factors that are expected to affect respondents' choices, as well as those attributes that are policy relevant. There are no hard and fast rules used to determine the attributes and levels presented to respondents in a DCE. A good experiment is one that has a sufficiently rich set of attributes and choice contexts, together with enough variation in the attribute levels necessary to produce meaningful behavioural responses in the context of the strategies under study. A starting pointing in the selection process involves secondary research (e.g. policy statements and previous similar studies from both published and grey literature). This can be combined (in a hybrid approach) with primary, qualitative research. For example, focus group studies are becoming increasingly popular to inform about credible attribute levels, possible interaction effects, the best way to present a monetary attribute (if included) and, more generally, to shed some light on the best way to introduce and explain the task to respondents. Having good working relationships with key specialists in the chosen clinical, service or strategy area under study will also prove useful to enhance the realism and plausibility of the study.

The identification and refinement of attribute and attribute levels is not an easy task and the analyst has to make several decisions. For example, for each attribute, a measurement unit must be selected. In most cases, the metric for an attribute is unambiguous. For example, for quantitative attributes such as cost, time and distance, the units can be easily interpreted. However, particular care is needed when using qualitative scales (ordinal or categorical) because depending on how they are expressed, respondents may interpret the levels differently. The researcher needs to try minimising any ambiguity in meaning and connotation in describing qualitative attributes and their levels to avoid confounding real attribute effects with a variety of other interpretations. Further, when comparing marginal utilities of different attributes (i.e. parameter estimates) the researcher must take care to point out the marginal unit of account.

Another decision relates to the number of levels to assign to each attribute, which need not be the same for all the attributes. The number of levels for each attribute will be decided following consideration of the total combinations of attribute levels generated, how attributes and levels are conveyed to the respondent and the need to investigate possible non-linearity in the main effect of an attribute on utility and interaction effects between two or more attributes. Interaction effects refer to situations where the utility brought about by the levels of an attribute (*aka* part-worth or marginal utility) depends on the levels of one or more other attributes. A typical example is price and quality. Individuals might be less sensitive to price for higher than lower quality products, so the marginal utility of price will differ by level of quality. If this is really the case, this interaction needs to be included in the definition of the utility function. Chapter 2 discusses experimental designs allowing for attribute main effects and interactions between pairs of attributes. Non-linear (main) effects refer to a situation where the marginal utility of an attribute differs depending on the level that the attribute takes. When only two levels are defined for an attribute, the marginal utility function can only be linear. The analyst's ability to detect more complex, non-linear utility relationships increases with the number of levels. Three levels would generally suffice to detect non-linear relationships. For continuous attributes, examining whether the effect of the different levels on utility is the same across all levels the analyst can empirically test the linearity of such relationship. Gerard et al. show an example of this in Chapter 5.

More levels might provide a better understanding of the true relationship between an attribute and respondent's utility but there is a trade-off between number of attribute levels and complexity of the experimental design of the study. The practitioner must not forget the size of the experimental design (i.e. the number of possible treatment combinations) increases exponentially with the number of levels. Another dilemma for the analyst arises if she wishes to consider a new attribute or attribute level, which the respondents are unlikely to be familiar with. How far should she go to stretch the respondent's imagination yet at the same time convey information which is treated credibly so not to put the DCE as risk? (An example of this issue is highlighted in Chapter 5.) Finally, at this stage it is important to think about keeping the DCE as realistic as possible. This may involve the need to "customise" the experiment by relating the choice alternatives to actual levels, either by including the current situation as an alternative or by defining some of the attributes with reference to the actual level (e.g. the levels could be set 15% higher or lower than the current level).

3.3. Selection of Experimental Design and Construction of Choice Sets

Once the attributes and corresponding levels have been selected, attribute levels have to be combined into alternatives or treatment combinations (also referred to as scenarios, profiles or options). Respondents could be presented with each of these

looks like DCE assumes non-structural independence in attributes which MAKT

options and asked whether they would choose or not. Chapter 5 presents an example of this dichotomous choice format. More often, the alternatives are placed into binary or multinomial choice sets that individuals are asked to choose from. Experimental design theory is concerned with both selecting the options and placing these into choice sets and doing so in a statistically efficient way (i.e. to estimate reliable parameter estimates). A starting point is a *full factorial* design containing all possible combinations of the attribute levels. By definition this is a statistically efficient design for collecting data. For an experiment with k attributes and each attribute q ($q = 1, 2, \ldots, k$) defined by l_q levels, the total number of possible combinations, L, is given by the product of the number of levels for each attribute, i.e. $\prod_q l_q$.

The advantage of a *full factorial* design is that all effects of attributes on choice can be investigated, i.e. parameter estimates can be obtained not only for the main effect on utility of each attribute singularly but also for all the possible interactions between them. However, for most practical situations, the full factorial design is often very large and not tractable as it would be too cost-prohibitive and tedious to have participants consider all possible combinations. For example, with five attributes ($k = 5$), two at four levels and three at five levels (often denoted $4^2 5^3$), there are 4*4*5*5*5 = 2,000 combinations in the full factorial. Even for a small factorial design (e.g. three attributes at four levels, i.e. 4*4*4 = 64) this can amount to a much larger (and equally unmanageable) number of choice sets depending on the size of the choice set (e.g. for choice sets of size 2 there would be 2,016 unique choice sets to obtain estimates for, i.e. [64*63]/2). For this reason, researchers often select a subset (or fraction) of all possible combinations. The number of combinations chosen should be equal to or greater than the number of parameters the analyst is likely to estimate from data collected using the design (i.e. must be greater than or equal to the *degrees of freedom* of the model). The price of having fewer combinations is that some attributes might be confounded, i.e. they are not distinguishable from each other. The *resolution* of a design identifies which effects, possibly including interactions, are estimable.

For example, in a resolution 3 design, all main effects are estimable free of each other, but some of them are confounded with two-way interactions. To estimate lower-order effects, such as main effects or two-way interactions, we need to assume that higher-order effects are zero or negligible, thus to forfeit some statistical efficiency. This begs the following questions: which effects can be omitted, how much loss in statistical efficiency is acceptable and how should statistical efficiency be assessed? These are big and complex questions to answer and finding "good" (efficient) experimental designs can be quite a challenge for the DCE practitioner and will often require expert advice.

Principles of the statistical theory of design of experiments are often used to select the choice sets to be presented to respondents. Ideally, the design should make the variances of the parameter estimates "small". Unfortunately, we cannot do this unless we know these parameters in advance and, if we knew this we would not need to carry out the experiment in the first place. In such circumstances, the standard approach is to use so-called *orthogonal* designs for linear models (where the variations of the attributes of the alternatives are uncorrelated in all choice sets) and then convert them into choice designs. To that end, several strategies might be used (see, e.g. Street et al., 2005) but the reader should be aware that the *goodness* (statistical efficiency) of the

sounds like Brazzini's orthogonal design for regression models in midyter, where a subset of results is valued. / Combos

final choice design would have to be evaluated in each case. Burgess and Street (2003, 2005) and Street et al. (2005) have derived a "method" that practitioners can use to get designs for generic or unlabelled experiments (see below for an explanation) with known (and good) statistical properties. Chapter 2, by these authors and their colleagues, explains in detail this easy, systematic way of constructing choice sets with any number of options for the estimation of main effects and main effects plus two-factor interactions. Alternative statistical design strategies have also been devised (see, e.g. Zwerina et al., 1996; Kanninen, 2002). Finally, efficient choice designs might be created by making some prior assumptions about the parameter estimates (see, e.g. Sándor and Wedel, 2001, 2002, 2005; Rose and Bliemer, 2005). It is worth noting that these so called D-optimal strategies might result in designs that are non-orthogonal, where some coefficients might be slightly correlated. In particular circumstances, these designs might perform better than orthogonal designs (Rose and Bliemer, 2004) and might require smaller sample sizes for efficient estimation of the model parameters (Bliemer and Rose, 2005). Unfortunately, there is no theory to serve as a guide as to which design method should be employed. Rose and Bliemer (forthcoming) have recently compared the experimental design methods proposed by Street et al. (2001), Sándor and Wedel (2001, 2002, 2005) and Kanninen (2002, 2005). They found that the two latter methods perform better both in terms of statistical efficiency and sample size requirements. All in all, different design strategies embody different assumptions and so are likely to be appealing under different circumstances. Whichever design strategy the analyst selects, testing and assessing the properties of the experimental design before implementation is crucial in order to be confident that the design can match the task at hand.

It is also worth mentioning that, as noted by Louviere (2001, p 29) that "*humans interact with choice experiments in ways not considered by the choice modelling community, such that one must take account not only design efficiency but also 'respondent efficiency' to determine the total efficiency of a choice experiments*". Respondent's efficiency (Severin, 2001) will be determined by her familiarity with the commodity being valued and her motivation to participate in the experiment, the clarity of communication of the exercise, and crucially, the number of choice sets, alternatives, attributes and levels included in the experiment. Extensive evidence from experimental psychology suggest that there is a limit to how much information respondents can meaningfully handle while making a decision (see, e.g. Payne et al., 1993 for a review). Hence, there is the worry that the increased cognitive difficulty associated with certain experimental designs (e.g. including multiple choices between alternatives with many attributes or alternatives very close in utility or "utility balanced" designs (Huber and Zwerina, 1996)) might lower respondent efficiency, offsetting gains from statistical efficiency (Severin et al., 2004). Indeed, there is evidence to suggest that the complexity of the task in a DCE affects, one of the multiple components of the random part of the utility function (Louviere et al., 2002), increasing response variability hence error variances (see, e.g. Swait and Adamowicz, 2001a; Deshazo and Fermo, 2002; Amaya-Amaya and Ryan, forthcoming; Caussade et al., 2005). Ramifications to this research are just beginning to emerge (see, e.g. Hensher, 2006).

As with other applied disciplines, until recently, the majority of studies using DCE within health economics have placed very little emphasis on experimental design issues. For example, 5 (15%) of the 34 studies reviewed by Ryan and Gerard (2003) did not mention the type of experimental design used. Luckily, in a more recent review of a further 25 studies by *Fiebig* et al. (2005) this number had reduced to only one study (4%). In line with this, all empirical chapters in this book provide details of their designs strategies.

Almost all studies in the earlier review have used a fractional factorial design to investigate attribute main effects only (25 studies or 74%). Most empirical chapters in this book are examples of simple designs (yet, as noted in the Introduction, still valid for the purposes they were selected). Again, the practice is changing and the number of applications using more complex design plans is increasing; as shown by six studies (24%) found by Fiebig et al. (2005) including main effects and selected two-way interactions. Chapter 5 shows an example of this. Perhaps, less encouraging is the finding that a considerable proportion of studies (around 15% in both reviews) do not report information concerning the source of the experimental design. For the rest, most applications have relied on software packages (e.g. SPEED or SPSS) and design catalogues for sourcing experimental designs (over 60% of studies in both reviews). All studies have sought to generate orthogonal designs, but we expect applications using D-optimal design strategies in the near future.

As a final note, we wish readers to be aware that understanding how to construct a DCE is becoming increasingly important, particularly as the literature is making clearer the link between the underlying experimental design and the statistical properties of the results obtained. The area of experimental design of DCE has moved on considerably in the last few years and continues to evolve fast. Thus, practitioners are faced with the challenge of keeping pace with these developments.

3.4. Experimental Context and Questionnaire Development

Aside from an optimal design, other important issues must be considered for maximising the amount and quality of information obtained from the respondents. We describe some key issues as follows (there will surely be some more!): whether to include an "opt-out" choice, the use of generic or labelled experiments, how many choice questions each individual will face, the inclusion of further questions for validity or warm up, etc. and sampling.

The first issue is whether to include a base case scenario or an opt-out alternative. This decision should be guided by whether or not the current situation and/or non-participation is a relevant alternative. For example, within the context of health care, individuals may prefer not to take up certain drugs, interventions or screening programmes, regardless of the level of attributes of the service. Alternatively, they may choose to participate only for certain levels of attributes of the alternatives. Failure to include an opt-out or *status quo* alternative, when this is a realistic policy alternative, may overestimate participation distorting welfare measures for non-marginal changes (since at least some individuals might have been *forced* to choose) (Boyle et al., 2001). However, including an opt-out raises issues about how non-participation is accounted for when analysing the data (see, e.g. von Haefen et al., 2005)

A second issue is whether to present the alternatives in the choice sets in a generic (alternatives A, B, C) or alternative-specific form (e.g. GP or hospital consultant) (Blamey et al., 2000). An advantage of using alternative specific labels is familiarity with the context and hence the cognitive burden is reduced. However, the risk is that the respondent may not consider trade-offs between attributes (as the decision may be alternative-based). This approach is preferred when the emphasis is on valuation of the labelled alternatives. When using generic (unlabelled) experiments the respondent will presumably focus more on the attributes. This type of experiment are then preferred when the emphasis is on the marginal rates of substitution between attributes. Whilst in principle, the same design strategies can be applied to both types of experiments, some specification issues arise when using labelled designs. The interested reader is referred to Louviere et al. (2000) and Hensher et al. (2005) for further discussion on this issue.

The analyst must also decide how many choice questions each respondent will be asked to complete. Given that data collection is costly, this number will normally be greater than one. The exact number of questions will depend on the complexity of the particular experiment at hand (see below for further discussion). Each respondent could be given the full set of combinations included the experimental design or only a subset of these, for example, using a blocked design. Louviere et al. (2000) discuss this and other methods to determine the length of each DCE survey.

Another issue is whether further choice questions are added to the experimental design, for example, to check the validity of the results or as a warm-up exercise. Validity refers to the degree to which a study succeeds in measuring the intended values by overcoming potential biases and the hypothetical nature of the valuation exercise. It is customary to include built-in tests in DCEs in order to check if the standard assumptions (axioms) of utility theory hold, for example, rationality (internal consistency) of responses, dominant choice sets, transitivity and monotonicity. Evidence from a large proportion of studies shows that DCEs generally pass these tests of validity, with no strong indications of any axiom violation (Ben-Akiva et al., 1992; Leigh et al., 1984; Hanley et al., 2001; Ryan and Gerard, 2003). Moreover, concerns have been raised as to extent to which failures to satisfy these tests should be interpreted as *irrationalities* (see, e.g. Lancsar and Louviere, 2006). Warm-up questions might help to mitigate violations of further assumptions in DCEs that respondents do not find any problems in completing a choice experiment, and that there are no systematic errors, such as respondents getting tired or changing their preferences as they acquire experience with the experiment, i.e. learning effects. Adding some extra choices to the experimental design (that are discarded from the analysis) or a clearly explained example can help in minimising choice inconsistencies (San Miguel et al., 2004).

Lastly, the analyst must make a decision about sampling issues (framing, size and method) and the administration of the survey. As noted by Viney et al. (2002), the general principles that should drive data collection for DCE are broadly similar to those for all primary data collection, avoiding (or at least minimising) biases and allowing for generalisation to the population of interest (see Champ, (2003), this series for an overview and advice on how to collect survey data for non-market valuation). Otherwise, these concerns are likely to be context specific. Obviously, the sample population will depend on the survey objective. Given this, a sampling strategy has to be determined. A simple random sample is generally a reasonable choice. Yet, a more specific sampling method (e.g. stratified random or choice-based) may be appropriate if there exists a relatively small but important subgroup or one wants to increase the precision of the estimates. Given a sampling strategy, a sample size must be determined. This is a very important issue because samples that are "too large" may waste time, resources and money, while samples that are "too small" (less than 30 individuals) may lead to inaccurate results (imprecise estimates). A number of questions need to be asked (and answered) before a suitable sample size can be determined. First question refers to the level of accuracy (precision) required. In general, the higher the level of accuracy required, the larger the sample size. Sometimes the sample size required is so close to the entire population that it makes more sense to simply survey everyone. More often "smart" designs are used to reduce the required sample size without reducing the accuracy. A second issue is whether estimates for subgroups, as well as for the overall population, are required. The overall sample size needs to be large enough to ensure that an adequate level of accuracy for these subgroups can also be achieved. However, it is worth noting that the population size will play a relatively small role in determining the required sample size, particularly if only a small percentage of the population is being surveyed A third question to consider is the data collection method to be used. Self-completion questionnaires are often cheaper compared to other collection methods such as personal interviews, but their response rates tend to be lower and so the sample size should be larger. Another important issue affecting the sample size required is the level of variability between responses. In general, the less variable the responses are, the smaller sample size that is required to achieve the same level of accuracy. Finally, the burden being placed on respondents needs to be evaluated. In today's society, there are many surveys being conducted for many different purposes. If people or businesses get surveyed too frequently, they are less likely to take the survey seriously. This means that the sample size should not be larger than necessary to obtain the accuracy needed. So, determining the "correct sample size" is not a simple task. In fact, a large part of determining the sample size is not simply "how many should we sample", but how cleverly the sample is chosen. A "smarter" sample design can give more accurate estimates with a smaller sample size. Sample size calculations are available in most survey sampling textbooks (e.g. Cochran, 1977). Louviere et al. (2000, p 262) provide a formula to calculate the minimum sample size needed to measure choice probabilities (or proportions) with some desire level of accuracy using a random sample. The book by Ben-Akiva and Lerman (1985) includes a full chapter on sampling theory (Chapter 8, pp 217–252). Hensher et al. (2005, pp 193–196) also provide an overview of the reality (as opposed to the theory) of sampling practices within studies of choice. Ultimately, the selection of sample strategy and sample size is largely dependent on the budget and resources available for the survey. The same is true for survey administration. While this is generally done with paper-and-pencil tasks, the elicitation scenario can become quite elaborate, involving videotapes, computer simulations, virtual reality, etc. (see, e.g. Bateman et al., 2006). For a review of modes of survey administration, see Champ and Welsh (2006) and Kanninen (2007), in this series (pp 28–36).

3.5. Model Estimation

Once the instrument is devised and the data collected, discrete choice modelling within a RUM framework is used to analyse responses obtained from DCEs.

Recall from Section 2 that choice outcomes can only be determined up to a probability of occurrence and that the probability of an individual n choosing one alternative i over another j from the available choice set C_n is determined by the relative systematic attractiveness of i versus j, as well as the difference in random utility between the alternatives (i.e. $(V_{in} - V_{jn})$ and $(\varepsilon_{jn} - \varepsilon_{in})$ in Equation 1.5). Given the distribution functions of the individual error terms, a distribution function of the difference is derived. This latter distribution will determine the specific model form for the choice probability. The design of the DCE should a priori ensure that, given a maintained hypothesis about the form of the choice model, model parameters can be identified. In practice, DCEs typically can be designed to ensure independent estimation of a wide array of model specifications and parameters conditional on those specifications.

By far, the easiest and most widely used discrete choice model is McFadden's conditional logit model (McFadden, 1974), most commonly referred to as multinomial logit (MNL). However, the MNL model has been widely criticised for reliance on rather restrictive assumptions. Much research effort has been (and continues to be) devoted to increasing the behavioural realism of choice models. Thus, a fairly wide variety of modelling approaches can now be called upon to analyse DCE responses. The remainder of this section reviews the basic specifications for binary choice data, provides an explanation and formulation for the basic MNL model and introduces some of the developments of the MNL model that have been proposed in the literature.

3.5.1. Binary choice

When the choice faced by respondents in a DCE is dichotomous (e.g. would you choose alternative A: yes/no) or if the choice set includes only two alternatives (i.e. would you choose alternative A or B), binary choice models are appropriate. Most commonly, a probit specification is assumed where disturbances ε_{in} are distributed according to standard normal distributions with zero mean and constant variance σ_ε^2 (Butler and Moffit, 1982). Alternatively a logistic distribution could be assumed leading to the binary logit model. Both models, binary probit and logit, lead to equivalent parameter estimates up to scale (Ben-Akiva and Lerman, 1985, p 72). A panel specification (i.e. random effects) can be used in order to take account of the multiple observations generally obtained from each respondent.

Most early applications of DCEs in health economics employed a random effects probit model to analyse the data. For example, using this approach, benefits have been estimated for orthodontic services (Ryan and Farrar, 1994); magnetic resonance imaging for knee injuries (Bryan et al., 1998); in vitro fertilisation (IVF) services (Ryan, 1999); cervical screening programmes (Ryan and Wordsworth, 2000); paediatric out of hours care (Scott et al., 2003); etc. (see also Ryan and Gerard, 2003; Fiebig et al., 2005). Other studies have opted for a logit specification. For example, Gerard et al. (See Chapter 5) use this approach to analyse the determinants of participation rates in a breast cancer screening programme. The extensive use of this modelling approach was partly a reflection of the binary nature of the data collected – "yes/no" (see Chapter 5 for an example of dichotomous choice format); or more commonly forced choices – A or B (see, e.g. Chapters 6 and 7). More recently, studies have collected multinomial rather than binary choice data hence alternative models are increasingly used as detailed in Sections 3.5.2–3.5.7 (see, e.g. Chapter 4).

3.5.2. Multinomial logit

An increase in the number of alternatives in a choice set to three or more introduces a number of challenges that do not exist when analysing binary choice data. In particular, for many years, the application of the probit model (multinomial probit [MNP]) remained hindered by computational difficulties (see below). Instead, the workhorse to analyse multinomial choice has been the logit model (MNL). The MNL model is derived under the assumption that the disturbances ε_{in} are independent and identically distributed (IID) extreme value type I (Gumbel) with mode zero and variance $\mu^2 \pi^2 / 6$, where μ is a positive scale parameter. The individual choice probability is given by (see Ben-Akiva and Lerman, 1985, pp 104–107 for the derivation):

$$P_{in} = \frac{\exp(\mu V_{in})}{\sum_{j \in C_n} \exp(\mu V_{jn})} \tag{1.7}$$

It is important to note that, in a single sample,[13] when, as it is normally the case, the systematic utility function is linear-in-parameters ($V_{in} = \beta'X_{in}$) it is not possible to separately identify the impact of the scale factor from that of tastes. In fact, we identify only the product ($\mu\beta$) (e.g. Ben-Akiva and Lerman, 1985; Swait and Louviere, 1993; Louviere et al., 2000). The traditional assumption to allow identification of the taste vector is $\mu \equiv 1$. (But this need not to be the case. This homocedasticity, i.e. constant variance, assumption might be relaxed. See Section 3.5.3). The likelihood function for the MNL model is:

$$L = \prod_{n=1}^{N} \prod_{i \in C_n} P_{ni}^{y_{in}} \tag{1.8}$$

where N is the sample size and y_{in} is a choice indicator equal to 1 if individual n ($n = 1, 2, \ldots, N$) chooses any alternative i in the available choice set C_n, zero otherwise (see Equation 1.2).

Given the usual assumptions that the systematic utility is linear-in-parameters ($V_{in} = \beta'X_{in}$) and error variances are constant ($\mu \equiv 1$), the MNL model is estimated by finding the values of the βs that maximise the following log-likelihood (LL) function

$$LnL = \sum_{n=1}^{N} \sum_{i \in C_n} y_{in}(\ln(P_{in})) = \sum_{n=1}^{N} \sum_{i \in C_n} y_{in}\left[\beta'X_{in} - \ln \sum_{j \in C_n} \exp(\beta'X_{jn})\right] \tag{1.9}$$

Within health economics, an increasing number of applications of DCEs use the MNL or conditional logit model (Ryan and Gerard, 2003; Fiebig et al., 2005; Chapter 10 of this book), as it is recognised that real life decisions within health are likely not binary in nature. Most times three or more alternative choice options are available to the individual. For example, when choosing treatment for minor illnesses, individuals might have a multiple choice. In addition to this, as mentioned earlier, in some circumstances it is important to allow individuals to be non-demanders. For example, men might prefer not to undertake a drug treatment to alleviate symptoms associated with benign prostate hyperplasia (Watson et al., 2004). No choice should also be an option in the non-urgent rheumatology refer-ral services (see Ryan and Skåtun, 2004 and Chapter 4).

The undoubted popularity of the MNL is due to its simplicity and ease of esti-mation. The assumption of independent errors leads to the independence of irrele-vant alternatives (IIA) property. This behavioural assumption states that, for a given individual, the ratio of the choice probabilities of any two alternatives is unaffected by other alternatives, as seen in Equation 1.10.

$$\frac{P_{in}}{P_{kn}} = \frac{e^{V_{in}}/\sum_j e^{V_{jn}}}{e^{V_{kn}}/\sum_j e^{V_{jn}}} = \frac{e^{V_{in}}}{e^{V_{kn}}} = e^{V_{in}-V_{kn}} \tag{1.10}$$

The implication is that choice probabilities would all change in the same proportion with the introduction of a new alternative or the deletion of an existing one. Put differently, substitution patterns across alternatives are assumed proportional.

The IIA property may be useful from a practical perspective when the number of possible alternatives is large, as it allows consistent estimation of model parameters using only a subset of alternatives for each sampled individual (McFadden, 1978). However, the assumption of independence and the implied equal competition between pairs of alternatives is inappropriate in many situations. For example, the IIA property is difficult to justify in situations where some alternatives compete more closely with each other than they do with other alternatives. In such cases, the MNL model will perform poorly and parameters will be biased (Chipman, 1960; Debreu, 1960) (See also Brownstone and Train, 1999). For example, consider the case of a choice amongst two non-urgent rheumatology services or no service (see Ryan et al., 2005 and Chapter 4). The two services are likely to be more similar to each other than the opt-out alternative. Such similarities, if not included in the measured portion of the utility function, lead to correlation between the errors associated with these alter-natives, a violation of the independence assumption underlying the MNL. If the attributes of one of the rheumatology services (service A say) were to be improved and its choice probability increased, the MNL model would predict that the shares of the other two alternatives would decrease proportionately, decreasing the probability for the clinic referral B and the no service alternative by the same factor. However, it is likely is that the two services compete between each other more intensively than they do with opting out and thus most individuals now choosing service A will be diverted from service B and only some from the no-service alternative. Thus, the MNL model will yield incorrect predictions of diversions from existing modes. One possible solution to circumvent this problem would be to reformulate the model as a nested model, with two nests, one including the two clinic referrals and the other including the no-service (see Chapter 4 for further details).

The validity of the IIA property in a particular application depends on the nature of the data at hand as well as on the theoretical model. The standard procedure to test whether the IIA is problematic in a particular application is the test proposed by

Hausman and McFadden (1984). The intuition for the test is that, if IIA holds, there should be no statistically significant difference in the parameter estimates obtained from an MNL on the full set of alternatives (unrestricted model) and an MNL on a specified subset of alternatives (restricted). The procedure involves constructing a likelihood ratio test around different versions of the model excluding different choice alternatives. Obviously, if the arbitrary exclusion of an alternative changes the estimated parameter vector, the odds ratios are also affected, thus not independent as hypothesised under IIA. Other tests (both formal and informal) have also been proposed in the literature (see, e.g. Train, 2003 and Chapter 4).

Other important restrictions of the MNL model relate to random taste variation and panel data with serial correlation. Regarding the first restriction, in general, it is reasonable to think that different individuals will place a different value or importance on the different attributes defining the alternatives in the choice set. Normally, the analyst will be able to link part of this variation in tastes to observed characteristics such as income or education. For example, individuals with low income are probably more concerned about the price of a dental check-up than higher income people. Older people might appreciate their doctor's advice better than younger members of the population. This systematic (observed) heterogeneity can be incorporated into the MNL model by allowing for interaction terms between socio-economic characteristics (e.g. income or education) and attributes of the alternatives or the constant terms. However, some differences in tastes will remain random to the extent that it cannot be related to observed characteristics. The MNL model cannot represent unobserved heterogeneity (or any other form of unobserved variability for that matter). Similarly, the MNL model will be able to capture any dynamics over the series of questions that DCEs respondents are often presented with as long as they are related to observed factors (e.g. past choices). However, this simple model is not appropriate to analyse panel data when the unobserved factors affecting individual choices are dependent over time.

Developments of the MNL model relax some or all these three restrictions. For example, the IIA property can be partially relaxed (allowing for flexible substitution patterns such as in the nested logit [NL]) or it can be fully relaxed (e.g. the MNP). Figure 1.1. depicts some of the variations of discrete choice models that have been proposed in the literature. We outline each these models below.

3.5.3. Relaxing IIA

There are many ways to relax the IIA assumption. Many variations of discrete choice models aim at doing *just* that. For instance, McFadden (1979, 1981) proposed a class of generalised extreme value (GEV) models that generalises the MNL to allow for explicit correlation among sets (nests) of mutually exclusive groups of alternatives. In so doing, richer substitution patterns can be accommodated. The appeal of the GEV family is its ability to reflect differential degrees of interdependence (i.e. similarity) between subsets of alternatives in a choice set.[14] The simplest and most popular member of the GEV family is the NL, first derived by Ben-Akiva (1973) (for other models in the GEV family see Chapter 4 in Train (2003) and references therein).

The NL model represents important deviations from the IIA property, but retains most of the computational advantages of the MNL model (Borsch-Supan, 1987).

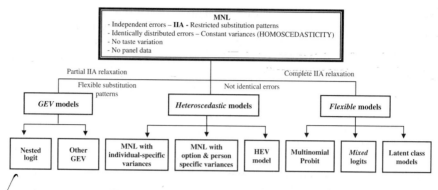

FIGURE 1.1. *State of the art in choice modelling*

The NL model is characterised by grouping (or nesting) subsets of alternatives that are more similar to each other with respect to excluded characteristics than they are to other alternatives. Alternatives in a common nest exhibit a higher degree of similarity and competitiveness than alternatives in different nests. This level of competitiveness, represented by cross elasticities between pairs of alternatives (i.e. the impact of a change in one alternative on the choice probability of another alternative) is identical for all pairs of alternatives in a nest (i.e. IIA holds) but not across nests. For each nest, the joint distribution of the error terms has a specific parameter (λ) that is a measure of the degree of independence in unobserved utilities among all alternatives within that nest. This is often called the dissimilarity parameter and must lie in the range $0 < \lambda \leq 1$ for the NL model to be consistent with utility maximisation (McFadden, 1978). As with MNL, the marginal distribution of each error term is extreme value type I. Chapter 4 presents the formulation of this model.

Very few applications in health economics have used with the NL model to analyse responses. Puig-Junoy et al. (1998) employed this approach to analyse the nature of health care provider choice in the case of patient-initiated contacts. Ryan and Skåtun (2004), within an experiment looking at women's preferences for cervical screening services, used an NL specification to investigate the modelling of responses when an opt-out alternative or a "neither" option is allowed for. Ryan et al. (2005) used a similar approach to estimate the monetary value of reducing waiting time, as well as changes in duration of appointment and the introduction of a pain management service, in the provision of rheumatology services (see also Chapter 4). More recently, Wordsworth et al. (2006) have also used an NL model to allow for no participation when assessing women's preferences for cervical screening.

The NL model avoids some restrictions allowing more flexible substitution patterns than MNL, but does not allow for random taste variation or for multiple observations often obtained from each respondent in a DCE. Models allowing for these factors are often referred to as *flexible* choice models. Recent advances made in the areas of data collection (e.g. information technology, the collection of more refined data, stated preferences and psychometric data), estimation techniques (in particular, the use of the simulation techniques – see, e.g. Stern, 2000), and computational power have made these more complex models more accessible. Next, we briefly review some of these models, specifically the MNP, the random parameter logit (also known as mixed logit) and latent class (LC) models. Before that, another important class of models is presented. These are variants of the MNL relaxing the hypothesis of constant variances (heteroscedastic logit models). For more details on these advanced choice models, the interested reader is referred to the Chapter 10 by Mark and Swait, Kanninen (2007) and Train (2003).

3.5.4. Heteroscedastic models

As explained above, the basic MNL model assumes independent and *identically* Gumbel distributed errors terms. A great deal of research has been concerned with how to circumvent the IIA property of the MNL model by relaxing the independence assumption to allow for correlations across error components (e.g. NL and GEV models). Less attention has been devoted to the assumption of *identical* error distributions (i.e. equal variances) across alternatives and individuals. Yet, as Swait (2006) reminds us, the homocedasticity constraint is also a very important limitation of the MNL model. In logit (and probit) models, ignoring heteroscedasticity results in parameter estimates that are inefficient and, more importantly, biased. This bias will increase when the heteroscedasticity involves the same elements as the independent variables (Yatchew and Griliches, 1984).

Several variants of the MNL allowing for heteroscedasticity can be found in the literature. As in the basic MNL model, heteroscedastic models assume that errors are independent across alternatives and individuals but *not* identically distributed across individuals and/or alternatives. That is, error variances (or equally well inversely related scale factors – remember μ in Equation 1.14) are allowed to vary. The heteroscedasticity may be defined across individuals (e.g. Swait and Adamowicz, 2001a), across alternatives (e.g. the heteroscedastic extreme value model proposed by Bhat (1995) or may be both (Dellaert et al., 1999; Swait, 2006). Either approach offers gains both from an empirical and a behavioural perspective. For example, allowing variances (scales) to differ across individuals implies that for some individuals we are able to explain more of the total utility U than for others (the larger [smaller] the variance [scale μ_n] of the error term ε, the less [more] is captured in the systematic part of the utility V). For example, Swait and Adamowicz (2001a) use this approach to investigate the impact of differential ability to choose across individuals. A similar analysis has been carried out within health care (Amaya-Amaya and Ryan, forthcoming).

In all cases, the scale factor is identified (i.e. separated from taste parameters β) by defining it as a function of individual characteristics (e.g. age, income, education), context-specific variables and/or attributes of the alternatives. It is important to note that depending on the variables used, heteroscedastic models can also capture non-IIA behaviour and so these models are potentially powerful to explain choice behaviour. More applications and further developments of these models could be expected.

3.5.5. Multinomial probit

The MNP model is obtained under the assumption that the joint distribution of the unobserved utility components is normal (Thurstone, 1927; Bock and Jones, 1968; Hausman and Wise, 1978; Daganzo, 1979). This model appears very desirable to the extent that it allows for the most general configuration of substitution across products via arbitrary covariance matrices (see Swait, 2006 for a discussion). It then solves all three restrictions in the MNL logit models allowing for unrestricted substitution patterns, random taste variation (see Hausman and Wise, 1978) and panel data with serial correlation. It can also allow for differences in error variances (heteroscedasticity). This flexibility comes at a price, of course: ease of estimation. The probit probabilities cannot be solved analytically. Simulation techniques have proven to be very useful for approximating probit probabilities numerically (see Hajivassiliou et al., 1996 for a review of simulators). Yet, special restrictions are generally needed to make these models tractable (McFadden, 1981, 1986) and these restricted versions may fall short of being able to represent all behaviours consistent with RUM. This might explain why, despite its current feasibility, the MNP model has never really seen widespread use in the literature. For example, to date we are not aware of any study using this model within health economics. One family of models that is highly flexible and RUM-compatible is the so-called mixed logit as explained next.

3.5.6. Random parameters or mixed logit[15]

The class of RUM-consistent models or *mixed logit* could be located somewhere in between the *logit* (MNL) and the *probit* (MNP) models. Like MNP, the *mixed logit* family has been known for many years but only recently, with the development of convenient numerical simulation methods for estimation, have become fully applicable (Revelt and Train, 1998).

Probably, the more intriguing property of this class of models is that it has been claimed that, with appropriate choice of variables and mixing distribution, the mixed logit can approximate any discrete choice model derived from random utility maximisation (including the MNP) as closely as one pleases (see McFadden and Train, 2000). The mixed logit model structure is also conceptually appealing and easy to understand since it is the familiar MNL model mixed with the multivariate distribution (generally multivariate normal) of the random parameters.

Mixed logits can be derived under a variety of different behavioural specifications that are formally equivalent but provide different interpretation. The most straightforward derivation, and most widely used, is based on random coefficients. In this case the specification is the same as for the standard MNL model except that the vector of parameters of the observed variables (β) are no longer fixed. Rather, it varies over respondents according to some predefined distribution, as a representation of individual tastes. The researcher specifies a distribution for the coefficients and estimates the parameters or *moments* characterising that distribution, e.g. the mean and the standard deviation. In most applications, the density function has been assumed normal or lognormal, but other distributions might be considered (see, e.g. Hensher and Greene, 2003a). The distribution of these individual-specific βs across the population may also be inferred *conditioning on individual tastes* (*COIT*) (Revelt and Train, 2000). Here, the distribution of tastes in the population is estimated first on the pooled data for all sampled individuals. Next, the position of each individual's tastes within the population distribution is inferred by examining the choices of that customer. Mixed logits can also be used simply to represent error components that create correlations among the utilities for different alternatives. This approach is most appropriate when the emphasis is placed on prediction and the primary goal is to represent sufficiently realistic substitution patterns.

The number of empirical applications using variations of mixed logit is increasing quite dramatically in different applied fields such as marketing, transportation and environmental economics. Within health care, several studies have also adopted this modelling approach. For example, Bolduc et al. (1996) to assess the choice of location by general practitioners for establishing their initial practice; Johnson et al. (2000) analysing willingness to pay (WTP) for improved respiratory and cardiovascular health and Hall et al. (2002, 2006) to look at uptake of varicella vaccination and genetic carrier testing. However, it is important to flag up that the application of these models results in a number of challenges that the analyst must face, such as what distribution should be used and what parameters should be specified as random. Identification also becomes an issue (Walker, 2002). Welfare calculations might also become more cumbersome. Hensher and Greene (2003a) present a very intuitive exposition of the model and the state of the practice.

Rather than pre-specifying a continuous distribution of parameter estimates, it can be assumed that there are *groups* of people in the data with similar tastes or utility functions so that latent class [LC] methods could be recalled.

3.5.7. Latent class models

LC models assume that there are two or more classes or groups (segments) of people underlying the data with homogenous (similar) tastes β or utility functions. Segment membership, which is unknown to the analyst, is characterised by unobserved (latent) variables which can be related to a set of discrete observed measures such as general attitudes and perceptions, as well as socio-economic characteristics of the individuals. The probability for the specific choice made by an individual in a particular class is a MNL model.

LC models (LCMs) are semi-parametric models, hence free the analyst from unwarranted distributional assumptions. However, the optimisation may be cumbersome, as discussed by Greene (2001). Another issue to confront is the choice of the *optimal* number of classes. The general strategy is to start with a model with two segments and increase the number gradually. Normally, five classes should suffice. Andrews and Currim (2003) have compared the performance of several segment retention criteria and conclude that a variation of the Akaike's information criterion (AIC) with a per-parameter penalty factor of 3 (Bozdogan, 1993, 1994) is the best. This information criteria is defined as $AIC3 = 2LL - 3K$ where LL is the estimated log-likelihood of the model and K is the number of estimated parameters. So long as we observe decreases on AIC3, adding segments is beneficial. All in all, for a better supported decision regarding the number of segments it is recommended to compare several criteria.

LC *models* have long been applied to count data for the analysis of individual heterogeneity (see Greene, 2001) and they are increasingly used to study discrete choice among multiple alternatives (e.g. Swait, 1994; Swait and Sweeney, 2000; Swait and Adamowicz, 2001b; Boxall and Adamowicz, 2002). Within health economics no published study has yet used an LC specification. Following Swait and Adamowicz (2001b), Amaya-Amaya and Ryan (2003) are exploring the feasibility of this approach to investigate complexity and learning/fatigue effects in a DCE in health care.

Hensher and Greene (2003b) using stated choice data compared LC and mixed logit. They found stronger statistical support overall for the LCM, but results are inconclusive as there is no unambiguous test of the superiority of one approach (mixed logit or LCM) over the other. However, the LCM approach may offer insights into the heterogeneity of consumer preferences that are not readily identifiable through a traditional mixed logit random parameter model, especially when there are reasons to believe that these are clustered around certain values. Similar results have also been found by Scarpa et al. (2004).

3.5.8. Choosing a model

Faced with this wide range of modelling options, the researcher is advised to start her analysis with the *simple* MNL. This will also ensure that there are no problems in the data hindering estimation. Following this, more general models can be estimated to test the restricted assumptions embodied in the MNL model. Which assumption should be relaxed, i.e. which model is most appropriate in each case, depends on the characteristics of the specific choice data at hand. For example, if the alternatives are likely to be clustered into different groups that might share unobserved characteristics an NL specification would be appropriate. When there is the suspicion that tastes might vary considerably across members of the population for some attributes, a random parameters specification should be looked at. LC would be recommendable if two or more groups of people with similar tastes are anticipated. In all cases, the final specification of the model is to be determined empirically. Readily available routines are included in many software packages (e.g. Nlogit/LIMDEP and Stata) that ease the burden of estimating most of these models. Comparing the performance of different model specification is highly recommended.

3.6. Policy Analysis

Once a satisfactory model has been developed and estimated, the results obtained can be used to simulate outcomes that can be used in policy analysis or as components of decision support tools. Applications of DCE to economic policy (e.g. health and health care) are often targeted to predictions of behaviour, generating welfare measures or both. Section 3.6.1 reviews each of these outputs in turn.

3.6.1. Prediction of behaviour

Normally, the starting point of analysis of model results in any study is to consider the overall significance of the model by comparing the value of the LL function (Equation 1.9 for MNL) of the estimated model (at convergence) with that of the base comparison model (normally, a model with constants only or assuming all parameters are zero). This comparison can be accomplished using an LL ratio test as formulated in Equation 1.11

$$-2(LL_{base} - LL_{estimated}) \sim \chi^2_{(number\ of\ new\ parameters\ in\ the\ estimated\ model)} \qquad (1.11)$$

where χ^2_{K-c} is a chi-squared distribution with the difference in the number of parameters estimated in the model (K) and that of the base model (c) as degrees of freedom.

Based on the values of the LL, the model fit is evaluated. Several measures of "goodness of fit" can be used. A common one is McFadden's (1974) pseudo R^2 as shown in Equation (1.12).

$$\text{McFadden } R^2 = 1 - \frac{LL_{\text{estimated}}}{LL_{\text{base}}} \tag{1.12}$$

The pseudo-R^2 can be "adjusted" to impose a penalty for each additional parameter in the model (K), which is subtracted from the numerator of the ratio of LL in Equation 1.12.

The analyst should be aware the pseudo-R^2 of a choice model is *not* exactly the same as the R^2 of a linear regression (although there is a direct relationship between both, see Domencich and McFadden, 1975). The pseudo-R^2 values tend to be much lower. Based on their experience, Hensher et al. (2005, p 339) suggest that a range for pseudo-R^2 between 0.3 and 0.4 can be interpreted as an R^2 between 0.6 and 0.8 for the R^2 in linear regression models (see, e.g. Chapter 3).

An alternative measure for goodness of fit (see, e.g. Chapter 10) defines the pseudo-R^2 in terms of "information". The Akaike R^2 computes the AIC for a constants-only model (AIC_0), then an AIC for the estimated model (AIC_m), and derives

$$R^2_{\text{AIC}} = 1 - \left(\frac{AIC_{\text{base}}}{AIC_{\text{estimated}}} \right) = 1 - \left(\frac{2LL_{\text{base}} - 2K}{2LL_{\text{estimated}} - 2K} \right) \tag{1.13}$$

Another goodness of fit sometimes used in the literature is the percent of correctly predicted observations, i.e the number of times out of the total number of observations when the prediction matches the observed choices (see Chapter 10). However, the researcher should be aware that, as Alberini et al. (2006) note, "in many cases it is easy to predict one particular outcome and much harder to predict others, in which case this measure can be misleading as a goodness-of-fit statistic".

Next, the statistical significance of each of the parameter estimates (or the lack of) is evaluated, generally by looking at the statistical significance of the corresponding Wald test statistic (i.e. the ratio between the estimated coefficient and its standard deviation).

The estimated parameters can then be used to obtain estimates of the indirect utility functions according to the expressions defined in Equation 1.6. Whilst discrete choice models are non-linear, normally the utilities estimates will be linear functions. Substituting back the parameter estimates provides a general formula for the estimated utility, which we can evaluate and compare across alternatives at any actual level of the attributes. The estimated utility expressions can be processed in a spreadsheet to identify how changes in the level of an attribute result in changes of the estimated utility derived from the different alternatives. Chapters 3 and 5 show examples of this calculation.

Based on these estimate utilities, the probability that an individual selects an alternative over all other alternatives contained in the choice set can be predicted (e.g. using Equation 1.7 if an MNL model was used) The applied examples in Chapters 3 and 5 show how to predict choice probabilities. Following this, the analyst should test "what-if" scenarios, i.e. the impact that a variation in the level of one or more attributes has in the selection probabilities. Doing this (at least once) in a spreadsheet, such as Excel (or by hand) will improve the researcher's understanding of how choice models actually work. This justifies the details given for the exercise presented in Chapter 3. In practice, the simulation capability of most software makes this task easier (see, e.g. Chapter 11 in Hensher et al. (2005) for an example of simulation in NLOGIT/LIMDEP).

Before moving onto welfare analysis, we should note that predictions for a specific individual are generally not very useful in helping policy decisions. Instead, most real world decisions are based on the forecast of some *aggregate demand*, i.e. on the predicted share of the population choosing each alternative. Several methods are available for aggregating across individuals. For example, we can create a "representative individual" at the average values of the explanatory variables and approximate the population share by the predicted choice probabilities at those values. More details on other aggregate forecasting techniques can be found in other sources such as Chapter 6 in the book by Ben-Akiva and Lerman (1985).

3.6.2. Welfare analysis

Most commonly, welfare analysis refers to the estimation of WTP for policy changes. When consumers are utility-maximisers and improvements to one attribute can be expressed as an equivalent deterioration in another along an indifference curve (i.e. a compensatory decision process is assumed), a consumer's WTP is measured by the Hicksian consumers' surplus attached to the equivalent price change (Hicks, 1939; Diamond and McFadden, 1974; Varian, 1984; McFadden, 1997). As argued above, generally a linear and additive indirect utility is assumed, so that Hicksian and Marshallian measures of consumer surplus coincide and preferences can be aggregated into representative "community" preferences (Chipman and Moore, 1990; McFadden, 1999). In this case, a general formula to estimate mean aggregate WTP (compensating variation or CV)[16] for a determined change is (Williams, 1977; Small and Rosen, 1981):

$$CV = -\frac{1}{\alpha}\left[\ln \sum_{i \in C} e^{\mu V_{i0}} - \ln \sum_{i \in C} e^{\mu V_{i1}}\right] \tag{1.14}$$

where α is the marginal utility of income, $\ln \sum_{i \in C} e^{\mu V_{i1}}$ (also referred to as the log-sum) is the expected utility that the decision maker obtains from choosing option k ($k = 0, 1$); V_{i0} and V_{i1} represent the indirect observable utility before and after the change under consideration, and C is the choice set. The absolute value of the coefficient of the monetary attribute (if included in the choice model) is taken as an estimate of the marginal utility of income α, which in this simple case is assumed constant.[17]

When the choice set includes a single before and after policy option (referred to in the literature as "state of the world" models (Bennett and Adamowicz, 2001), Equation 1.14 reduces to:

$$CV = -\frac{1}{\alpha}\left[\ln\left(e^{V_{i0}}\right) - \ln\left(e^{V_{i1}}\right)\right] = -\frac{1}{\alpha}[V_{i0} - V_{i1}] \tag{1.15}$$

Moreover, in the case of changes in a single attribute, the implicit price of an attribute further reduces to the ratio between any estimated coefficients (β) over the negative of the estimated coefficient for the monetary price[18]:

$$CV = -\frac{\beta}{\alpha} \tag{1.16}$$

In fact, in most discrete choice models, the ratio of any two estimated coefficients has an economic meaning. It represents people's willingness to give up some amount of one attribute in order to achieve more of another, i.e. it is an estimate of the marginal rate of substitution between the attributes (Hensher and Johnson, 1981). Let x_{ih} be a continuous attribute of alternative i, then $\partial P_{in} / \partial x_{ih}$ is the degree to which changes in those attributes affect the aggregate choice probability P_i. The marginal rate of substitution between two attributes x_{ih} and x_{ik} will be

$$\mathrm{MRS}_{x_{ik}}^{x_{ih}} = \frac{\partial P_i / \partial x_{ih}}{\partial P_i / \partial x_{ik}} = \frac{\hat{\beta}_{ih}}{\hat{\beta}_{ik}} \tag{1.17}$$

This result can be used to assess the relative importance of all attributes by calculating the extent to which each attribute is valued in terms of a numeraire attribute, e.g. time. Such estimates may be very useful from a policy perspective. For example, a DCE looking at the characteristics of alternative screening tests such as the example in Table 1.1 would determine how many days longer people would be willing to wait in exchange for an increase in the amount of information obtained from a particular test. These calculations and other policy outputs for this example will be presented in Chapter 3.

In addition to WTP and MRS, the elasticities of choice probability with respect to each attribute can be evaluated. These express the percentage change in the probability of individual n choosing alternative I (P_{in}) caused by a 1% change in a certain attribute (k) of that alternative. The direct point elasticity[19] is defined as follows:

$$E_{X_{ikn}}^{P_{in}} = \frac{\partial P_{in} / P_{in}}{\partial X_{ikn} / X_{ikn}} = \frac{\partial P_{in}}{\partial X_{ikn}} \cdot \frac{X_{ikn}}{P_{in}} \tag{1.18}$$

For the MNL model the direct elasticity is given by:

$$E_{X_{ikn}}^{P_{in}} = P_{in} \beta_{in} (1 - P_{in}) X_{ikn} / P_{in} = \beta_{ik} X_{ikn} (1 - P_{in}) \tag{1.19}$$

Cross-point elasticities refer to the change in the choice probability of an alternative i, given a change in the kth attribute of another alternative. These can be evaluated as follows:

$$E_{X_{jkn}}^{P_{in}} = \frac{\partial P_{in}}{\partial X_{jkn}} \cdot \frac{X_{jkn}}{P_{in}} = -P_{in} P_{jn} \beta_{jn} X_{jkn} / P_{in} = -\beta_{jk} X_{jkn} P_{jn} \tag{1.20}$$

Recall that, as a consequence of the IIA property, MNL cross elasticities are the same for all $i \neq j$. When the independence assumption is relaxed (e.g. in an NL) the formulation of the elasticities will be different, but the behavioural interpretation is the same.

Most DCEs conducted in health economics have sought to derive welfare estimates. A number of studies have used the coefficients from the estimated models to calculate measures of WTP for individual attributes and for entire goods and services. Most applications have interpreted the marginal rate of substitution in Equations 1.14–1.17 as the marginal WTP for a change in a single attribute. Here, it is considered that the numerator is the marginal utility of the attribute (e.g. continuity of care or waiting time reductions in fertility treatments (Ryan, 1999)) and the denominator is the marginal utility of price or cost. Other studies have calculated the WTP arising from a change in all levels of an alternative by multiplying the marginal WTP for each attribute by the corresponding change in the attribute levels then and adding up. For example, Ryan (1999) used this approach to estimate the welfare gain of providing more expensive fertility treatments with higher chances of success and continuity of contact with same staff (see also Ryan and Hughes, 1997; Johnson et al., 1998; Gyrd-Hansen, 2000; Johnson et al., 2000; Ryan et al., 2000). Very few applications have used the Small and Rosen (1981) formula given in Equation 1.14 for calculating the compensating variation. Lancsar and Savage (2004) is an example of this. Using data from a DCE-investigating preferences for asthma medication, these authors reminded us of the importance of using this formula, which is consistent with random utility theory and welfare theory. The CV method for deriving monetary measures of value provides a more general and possibly accurate measure of welfare than alternative approximations. It considers the changes in both utility and choice probabilities that are likely to follow a variation in the levels of one or more attributes defining the alternatives. Yet, it is important to note that there are some econometric issues arising in the calculation of the compensating variation using this formula (see, e.g. Santos Silva, 2004). These issues become especially challenging as models allow for richer forms of heterogeneity (see Hensher, 2006).

No empirical studies within health economics have reported estimates of direct or cross elasticities. Given the increasing interest in nested structures, we would expect more applications considering these along other figures of merit from DCEs in the near future.

4. CONCLUDING REMARKS

The main purpose of this chapter was to introduce the reader to a comprehensive overview of the theory and methods that underpin the DCE approach to benefit valuation with particular reference to the practice within health economics. This knowledge will be useful throughout the remaining chapters of the book. Chapter 2 builds on the general notions of experimental design provided in this chapter. It explains the theoretical underpinnings and demonstrates the use of one approach to identifying suitable experimental designs for a DCE survey. Following this, Chapter 3 provides an overview of practical issues that arise in carrying out a DCE. Special attention is paid to how to evaluate an experimental design, prepare data for analysis and interpret and use the estimation results for policy analysis.

ENDNOTES

[1] According to Louviere (2000), this is the main feature distinguishing DCEs from traditional conjoint analysis. Conjoint analysis is a theory about the behaviour of sets of numbers in response to factorial manipulations of attributes which eventually may allow studying how holistic preferences for combinations of attribute levels are. DCEs are based on a sound, well-tested, integrated behavioural theory of decision-making and choice behaviour: the random utility theory (RUT). Nonetheless, there remains considerable confusion amongst academics and practitioners about the differences between these two paradigms. Quite too often, one encounters the term "conjoint analysis" referring to any preference elicitation methods that involves manipulation of attributes and levels, including DCEs. This could be taken as if DCEs were one more type of conjoint analysis. In fact, the opposite is true. As a consequence, more attention should be paid to the nomenclature used, as differences between the paradigms turn out crucial for economic valuation exercises (see Louviere, 2000 for further discussion).

[2] See Mas-Collel et al. (1995) for a review.

[3] It is important to note, however, that model derivation consistent with utility maximisation does not preclude decision protocols different from utility maximisation. The process by which a choice is made is not explicitly modelled.

[4] Hanemann (1984) argues that this type of behaviour can solve the utility maximisation problem in two ways. First, there may be some logical or institutional reason why the commodities q_i are mutually exclusive. For example, consider the choice between houses. If a person has only one home, he or she cannot both rent and own. Similarly, in a health context, if somebody needs one (and only one) endoscopic procedure of the digestive tract, they cannot have both a colonoscopy and an ultrasound. Second, even if there is no logical reason why the commodities are mutually exclusive, the consumer's tastes may be such that he or she naturally prefers to select only one of the discrete alternatives at a time. For example, there is no external reason why a person cannot have both electric and gas ovens, but this consumer may prefer to have only one type. Within health care, a person could initially have access to both public and private health care but he or she might prefer to opt out of public services. The discrete model presented here refers to the first of these two cases.

[5] Discrete choice models deal with "indirect" utility that is the maximum utility that is achievable under the given prices and income. As it is customary in the literature the indirect utility function will be refer to simply as "utility" throughout the book.

[6] It should be noted that in empirical applications, the socio-economic characteristics of the individuals are normally also included as an argument as it is necessary to specify how tastes, and therefore utility functions, vary among consumers. As these variables are generally constant for an individual, they are incorporated to the model as interaction terms with the alternative specific constants or the attributes themselves. Chapter 5 presents an example of this. For ease of exposition, here we omit this term and concentrate only on the attributes of the alternatives.

[7] Note this is a common but simplifying assumption. Models that are more general, where the estimated coefficients are specific for each of the alternatives can be estimated. Indeed these might be a good starting point if there are reasons to suspect that the effect of an attribute on utility might differ across alternatives. The equality restriction presented herein should be apparent to test using standard procedures (see, e.g. Greene, 2000)

[8] Note that the meaning of the alternative specific constants (ASC_i) might differ from study to study. For example, in experiments where alternative are labelled (e.g. by brand), the ASC_i might be interpreted as the average utility attached, in general, to a particular alternative or brand, irrespective of its attributes. In studies including an opt-out alternative, the ASC for this option will capture non-participation (Haaijer et al., 2001). It is also important to note that, when using dummy coding for one or more attributes, the value of the ASC_i will also include the reference category for these. This issue is further discussed in Chapter 3.

[9] It is important to distinguish the overall process of designing a DCE from the issue of the statistical design of the experiment. The latter might require specialist support (see under Section 4.4 and Chapter 2); whereas, the overall process can be executed almost mechanically once the options within each stage are known and understood.

[10] It should be noted that the very first is to assess the relevance of the study. Here, it will be assumed the study is sufficiently relevant to be carried out.

[11] The specification of the utility function is likely to (and should) be refined yet further as research progresses (i.e. during the following two stages – firming up attributes and levels and selecting an appropriate experimental design).

[12] It is becoming increasingly popular to view the error component of choice models as an important part of the specification. So it is important to identify which factors are likely to affect mean parameter estimates and those which will affect error variances (see, e.g. Swait and Adamowicz, 2001a, Louviere et al., 2002). We touch on this issue later in this chapter (under Section 3.5). Further discussion is provided in Chapter 11.

[13] Note that if two separate samples are analysed together, the relative scale parameter can be identified, which "accounts for the difference in the variation of the unobserved effects" (Adamowicz et al., 1994; Swait and Louviere, 1993).

[14] Also these models have the advantage that the choice probability usually take a close form such that they can be estimated without resorting to simulation (Train, 2003).

[15] Also termed "multinomial probit with a logit kernel" or hybrid logit (Ben-akiva and Bolduc, 1996).

[16] Note that in reality it is the equivalent variation (before the change) that it is considered. However, under the traditional assumptions of a linear utility function with no income effects the two measures of consumer surplus should coincide and compensating variation is the most common term in the literature.

[17] See Herriges and Kling (1999) and Morey and Rossman (2004) for relaxations of this assumption.

[18] Note that these definitions are true only under certain conditions, more specifically only if disturbances are independent and identically distributed. As discussed in Chapter 11, more flexible models pose a challenge to the calculation of WTP (e.g. see also Louviere (2006)).

[19] This means that the elasticity is valid only at the point at which it is defined. Average (or arc) elasticities over a range of values may be also of interest (see Louviere et al., 2000, pp 279–280).

REFERENCES

Adamowicz, W., Louviere, J. and Williams, M. 1994. Combining revealed and stated preference methods for valuing environmental amenities. *Journal of Environmental Economics and Management*, vol 26 (3) 271–292.

Adamowicz, W., Louviere, J. and Swait, J. 1998. Introduction to attribute-based stated choice methods. Report to NOAA Resource Valuation Branch, Damage Assessment Centre, Advanis.

Alberini, A., Longo, A. and Veronesi, M. 2006. Basic statistical models for conjoint choice experiments. In: Valuing Environmental Amenities using Choice Experiments: A Common Sense Guide to Theory and Practice. Kanninen, B. (ed.). Springer, pp 203–228. Series: The Economics of Non-Market Goods and Resources, vol 8, Series ed.: Bateman, I.

Amaya-Amaya, M. and Ryan, M. 2003. Decision strategy switching in choice experiments: an exploratory analysis in health economics. Paper presented at *Advancing the Methodology of Discrete Choice Experiments in Health Care Workshop*, Oxford, 22–23 September.

Amaya-Amaya, M. and Ryan, M. (forthcoming). Between contribution and confusion: an investigation of the impact of complexity in stated preferences choice experiments. *Journal of Health Economics*.

Andrews, R.L. and Currim, I.S. 2003. A Comparison of segment retention criteria for finite mixture logit models. *Journal of Marketing Research*, vol XL (2).

Bateman, I. et al. 2006. http://www.uea.ac.uk/env/cserge/pub/wp/edm/edm_2006_16.pdf

Ben-Akiva, M.E. and Bolduc, D. 1996. "Multinomial probit with a logit kernel an a general parametric specification of the covariance structure". Working paper, Massachusetts Institute of Technology, Cambridge, MA.

Ben-Akiva, M. and Lerman, S. 1985. Discrete Choice Analysis: Theory and Application to Travel Demand. Cambridge, MA: MIT Press. http://elsa.berkeley.edu/reprints/misc/multinomial.pdf. Last accessed November 2006.

Ben-Akiva, M., Morikawa, T. and Shiroishi, F. 1992. Analysis of the reliability of preference ranking data. *Journal of Business Research*, vol 24, 149–164.

Ben-Akiva, M.E. 1973. Structure of passenger travel demand models. Ph.D. thesis. Department of Civil Engineering, MIT Press, Cambridge, MA.

Bennett, J. and Adamowicz, W. 2001. The Choice modelling approach to environmental valuation. In: Some Fundamentals of Environmental Choice Modelling. Bennett, J. and Blamey, R. (eds). Northampton: Edward Elgar, pp 37–69.

Bhat, C.R. 1995. A heteroscedastic extreme value model of intercity travel mode choice. *Transportation research*, vol 29 (6), 471–486.

Blamey, R.J. Bennett, J., Louviere, M., et al. 2000. A test of policy labels in environmental choice modeling studies. *Ecological Economics*, vol 32, 269–286.

Bliemer, M.C.J. and Rose, J.M. 2005. Efficiency and sample size requirements for stated choice studies. Submitted for publication to *Transportation Research B*. Working paper can be accessed at http://www.its.usyd.edu.au/publications/working_papers/wp2005/itls_wp_05–08.pdf

Bock, R.D. and Jones, L. 1968. The Measurement and Prediction of Judgement and Choice. San Francisco: Holden-Day.

Bolduc, D., Fortin, B. and Fournier, M.A. 1996. The impact of incentive policies to influence practice location of general practitioners: a multinomial probit analysis. *Journal of Labor Economics*, vol 14, 703–732.

Borsch-Supan, A. 1987. Econometric analysis of discrete choice: with applications on the demand for housing in the US and West Germany. Lectures notes in Economics and Mathematical Systems, Heidelberg: Springer-Verlag.

Boxall, P.C. and Adamowicz, V.L. 2002. Understanding heterogeneous preferences in random utility models: the use of latent class analysis. *Environmental and Resource Economics*, vol 23 (4), 421–446.

Boyle, K.J., Holmes, T.P., Teisl, M.F. and Roe, B. 2001. A Comparison of conjoint analysis response formats. *American Journal of Agricultural Economics*, vol 83 (2), 441–454.

Bozdogan, H. 1993. Choosing the number of component clusters in the mixture model using a new informational complexity criterion of the inverse Fisher information matrix. In: Information and Classification. Concepts, Methods and Applications, Proceedings of the 16th annual conference of the "Gesellschaft für Klassifikation e.V.". Opitz, O., Lausen, B. and Klar, R. (eds). Universität Dortmund, 1–3 April 1992, Berlin: Springer-Verlag, pp 40–54.

Bozdogan, H. 1994. Mixture model cluster analysis using model selection criteria and a new informational measure of complexity. In: Multivariate Statistical Modeling. Proceedings of the First US/Japan Conference on the Frontiers of Statistical Modeling. An Informational Approach. Bozdogan, H. (ed.). Dordrecht: Kluwer Academic, pp 69–113.

Brownstone, D. and Train, K. 1999. Forecasting new product penetration with flexible substitution patterns. *Journal of Econometrics*, vol 89, 109–129.

Bryan, S., Buxton, M., Sheldon, R. and Grant, A. 1998. Magnetic resonance imaging for the investigation of knee injuries: an investigation of preferences. *Health Economics*, vol 7, 595–603.

Burgess, L. and Street, D.J. 2003. Optimal designs for 2k choice experiments. *Communications in Statistics – Theory and Methods*, vol 32, 2185–2206.

Burgess, L. and Street, D. 2005. Optimal designs for choice experiments with asymmetric attributes. *Journal of Statistical Planning and Inference*, vol 134, 288–301.

Butler, J. and Moffit, R. 1982. A computationally efficient quadrature procedure for the one-factor multinomial probit model. *Econometrica*, vol 50, 761–764.

Caussade, S., Ortúzar, J., de D Rizzi, L.I. and Hensher, D.A. 2005. Assessing the influence of design dimensions on stated choice experiment estimates. *Transportation Research Part B*, vol 39 (7), 621–640.

Champ, P.A. 2003. Collecting survey data collection for nonmarket valuation. In: A Primer on Nonmarket Valuation. Champ, P.A., Boyle, K. and Brown, T.C. (eds). Boston: Kluwer Academic. Series: The Economics of Non-Market Goods and Resources. vol 3, Series ed.: Bateman, I., Chapter 3.

Champ, P.A. and Welsh, M.P. 2006. Survey Methodologies for stated choice studies. In: Valuing Environmental Amenities using Choice Experiments: A Common Sense Guide to Theory and Practice. Kanninen, B. (ed.). Boston: Springer. Series: The Economics of Non-Market Goods and Resources, vol 8, Series ed.: Bateman, I., pp 21–42.

Chipman, J. 1960. The Foundations of utility. *Econometrica*, vol 28, 193–224.

Chipman, J. and Moore, J. 1990. Acceptable indicators of welfare change. In: Preferences, Uncertainty, and Optimality. Chipman, J., McFadden, D. and Moore, J. (eds). Boulder: Westview Press.

Cochran, W.G. 1977. Sampling Techniques. New York: Wiley.

Daganzo, C. 1979. Multinomial Probit: The Theory and its Applications to Demand Forecasting. New York: Academic Press.

Debreu, G. 1960. Review of R. D. Luce individual choice behavior. *American Economic Review*, vol 50, 186–188.

Dellaert, B., Brazell, J. and Louviere, J. 1999. The effect of attribute variation on consumer choice consistency. *Marketing Letters*, vol 10 (2), 139–147.

Deshazo, J.R. and Fermo, G. 2002. Designing choice sets for stated preference methods: the effects of complexity on choice consistency. *Journal of Environmental Economics and Management*, vol 44 (1), 123–143.

Diamond, P. and McFadden, D. 1974. Some uses of the expenditure function in public finance. *Journal of Public Economics*, vol 3, 3–21.

Domencich, T. and McFadden, D. 1975. Urban Travel Demand: A Behavioral Analysis. Amsterdam: North-Holland.

Fiebig, D., Louviere, J. and Waldman, D. 2005. Contemporary issues in modelling discrete choice experimental data in health economics. Working paper, University of New South Wales. http://wwwdocs.fce.unsw.edu.au/economics/staff/DFIEBIG/ContemporaryissuesHEv120Apr05 .pdf. Last accessed 13 July 2006.

Greene, W. 2001. Fixed and random effects in nonlinear models. Working Paper EC-01-01, Stern School of Business, Department of Economics. http://www.stern.nyu.edu/eco/wkpapers/ workingpapers01/EC-01-01.pdf. Last accessed November 2006.

Greene, W.H. 2000. Econometric Analysis. New Jersey: Prentice Hall.

Gyrd-Hansen, D. 2000. Cost benefit analysis of mammography screening in Denmark based on discrete ranking data. *International Journal of Health Technology Assessment in Health Care*, vol 16 (3), 811–821.

Haaijer, R., Wagner Kamakura, A. and Wedel, M. 2001. The "no choice" alternative in conjoint choice experiments. *International Journal of Market Research*, vol 43, 93–106.

Hajivassiliou, V., McFadden, D. and Ruud, P. 1996. Simulation of multivariate normal rectangle probabilities and their derivatives: theoretical and computational results. *Journal of Econometrics*, vol 72, 85–134.

Hall, J., Kenny, P., King, M., Louviere, J.J., Viney, R. and Yeoh, A. 2002. Using stated preference discrete choice modelling to evaluate the introduction of varicella vaccination. *Health Economics*, vol 11, 457–465.

Hall, J., Fiebig, D., King, M., Hossain, I. and Louviere, J.J. 2006. What influences participation in genetic carrier testing? Results from a discrete choice experiment. *Journal of Health Economics*, vol 25, 520–537.

Hanemann, W.M. 1982. Applied welfare analysis with qualitative response models. Working paper No. 241. Department of Agricultural and Resource Economics, University of California, Berkeley.

Hanemann, W.M. 1984. Discrete/continuous models of consumer demand. *Econometrica*, vol 52 (3), 541–561.

Hanley, N., Mourato, S. and Wright, R. 2001. Choice modelling approaches: a superior alternative for environmental evaluation? *Journal of Economic Surveys*, vol 15 (3), 453–557.

Hausman, J. and McFadden, D. 1984. Specification tests for the multinomial logit model. *Econometrica*, vol 52, 1219–1240.

Hausman, J.A. and Wise, D.A. 1978. A conditional probit model for qualitative choice: discrete decisions recognising interdependence and heterogeneous preferences. *Econometrica*, vol 46, 403–426.

Hensher, D. 2006. Revealing differences in willingness to pay due to the dimensionality of stated choice designs: an initial assessment. *Environmental and Resource Economics*, vol 34 (1), 7–44.

Hensher, D., Rose, J. and Greene, W. 2005. Applied Choice Analysis: A Primer. Cambridge: Cambridge University Press.

Hensher, D.A. and Greene, W. 2003a. The mixed logit model: the state of practice. *Transportation*, vol 30 (2), 133–176.

Hensher, D.A. and Greene, W. 2003b. A latent class model for discrete choice analysis: contrasts with mixed logit. *Transportation Research Part B*, vol 37, 681–698.

Hensher, D.A. and Johnson, L.W. 1981. Behavioural response and form of the representative component of the indirect utility function in travel mode choice. *Regional Science and Urban Economics*, vol 11, 559–572.

Herriges, J. and Kling, C. 1999. Nonlinear income effects in random utility models. *Review of Economics and Statistics*, vol 81, 62–72.

Hicks, J. 1939. Value and Capital. Oxford: Oxford University Press.

Huber, J. and Zwerina, K. 1996. The importance of utility balance in efficient choice designs. *Journal of Marketing Research*, vol 33, 307–317.

Johnson, F.R., Desvousges, W.H., Ruby, M.C, Stieb, D. and De Civita, P. 1998. Eliciting stated preferences: an application to willingness to pay for longevity. *Medical Decision Making*, vol 18 (Suppl), S57–S67.

Johnson, F.R., Banzhaf, M.R. and Desvousges, W.H. 2000. Willingness to pay for improved respiratory and cardiovascular health: a multiple-format stated-preference approach. *Health Economics*, vol 9, 295–317.

Kanninen, B. 2007. Valuing environmental amenities using stated choice studies: A common sense approach to theory and practice. Holland: Springer.

 Kanninen, B.J. 2002. Optimal design for multinomial choice experiments. *Journal of Marketing Research*, vol 39, 214–217.

Kanninen, B.J. 2005. Optimal design for binary choice experiments with quadratic or interactive terms. Paper presented at the 2005 International Health Economics Association conference, Barcelona, July.

Lancaster, K. 1966. A new approach to consumer theory. *Journal of Political Economy*, vol 74, 132–157.

Lancsar, E. and Louviere, J.J. 2006, Deleting "irrational" responses from discrete choice experiments: a case of investigating or imposing preferences? *Health Economics*, vol 15 (8), 797–811.

Lancsar, E. and Savage, E. 2004. Deriving welfare measures from discrete choice experiments: inconsistency between current methods and random utility and welfare theory. *Health Economics*, vol 13 (9), 901–907.

Leigh, T., MacKay, D. and Summers, J. 1984. Reliability and validity of conjoint analysis and self explicated weights: a comparison. *Journal of Marketing Research*, vol 21, 456–462.

Louviere, J.J. 2000. "Why Stated Preference Discrete Choice Modelling is NOT Conjoint Analysis (and what SPDCM IS)", Memetrics white paper.

Louviere, J.J. 2001. Choice experiments: an overview of concepts and issues. In: The Choice Modelling Approach to Environmental Valuation. Bennett, J. and Blamey, R. (eds). Northhampton: Edward Elgar, pp 13–36.

Louviere, J.J. 2006. What you don't know might hurt you: some unresolved issues in the design and analysis of discrete choice experiments. In: Special Issue: Frontiers on Stated Choice Methods. Adamowicz, W. and Deshazo, J.R. (eds). *Environmental and Resource Economics*, vol 34, 173–188.Louviere, J.J., Hensher, D. and Swait, J. 2000. Stated Choice Methods: Analysis and Applications in Marketing, Transportation and Environmental Valuation. Cambridge/England: Cambridge University Press.

Louviere, J.J., Street, D., Carson, R., et al. 2002. Dissecting the random component of utility. *Marketing Letters*, vol 13, 177–193.

Manski, C. 1977. The Structure of random utility models. *Theory and Decision*, vol 8, 29–254.

March, J.G. 1978. Bounded rationality, ambiguity and the engineering of choice. *Bell Journal of Economics*, vol 9, 587–608.

Marschak, J. 1960. Binary choice constraints on random utility indicators. In: Stanford Symposium on Mathematical Methods in the Social Sciences. Arrow, K. (ed.). Stanford: Stanford University Press.

Mas-Collel, A., Whinston, M.D. and Green, J.R. 1995. Microeconomic Theory. Oxford: Oxford University Press.

McFadden, D. 1974. Conditional logit analysis of qualitative choice behavior. In: Frontiers in Econometrics. Zarembka, P. (ed.). New York: Academic Press, pp 105–142.

McFadden, D. 1978. Modeling the choice of residential location. In: Spatial Interaction Theory and Planning Models. Karlqvist, A., Lundqvist, L., Snickars, F. and Weibull, J. (eds). Amsterdam: North-Holland, pp 75–96.

McFadden, D. 1979. Quantitative methods for analyzing travel behavior of individuals: some recent developments. In: Behavioural Travel Modelling. Hensher, D. and Stopher, P. (eds). London: Croom Heml, pp 279–318.

McFadden, D. 1981. Econometric models of probabilistic choice. In: Structural Analysis of Discrete Data with Econometric Applications. Manski, C. and McFadden, D. (eds). Cambridge: MIT Press, pp 198–272.

McFadden, D. 1986. The choice theory approach to market research. *Marketing Science*, vol 5 (4), 275–297.

McFadden, D. 1997. Measuring willingness-to-pay in discrete choice models. In: Essays in Honor of John Chipman. Moore, J. and Hartman, R. (eds). London/New York: Routledge.

McFadden, D. 1999. Computing willingness-to-pay in random utility models. In: Trade Theory and Econometrics. Moore, J., Reizman, R. and Melvin, J. (eds). London: Routledge, pp 253–274.

McFadden, D. and Train, K. 2000. Mixed MNL models for discrete response. *Journal of Applied Econometrics*, vol 15, 447–470.

Morey, E.R. and Rossman, K.R. 2004. Calculating with varying types of income effects, closed-form solutions for the compensating variation associated with a change in the state of the world. July 2004. http://www.colorado.edu/Economics/morey/papers/MoreyStatetoState CV06282006.pdf

Payne, J.W., Bettman, J.R. and Johnson, E.J. 1993. The Adaptive Decision Maker. Cambridge, MA: Cambridge University Press.

Puig-Junoy, J., Saez, M., Martinez-Garcia, E. (1998). "Why do patients prefer hospital emergency visits? A nested multinomial logit analysis for patient-initiated contacts". *Health Care Management Science*, vol 1 (1), 39–52.

Revelt, D. and Train, K. 2000. Specific taste parameters and mixed logit. Working paper No. E00-274, Department of Economics, University of California, Berkeley.

Revelt, D. and Train, T. 1998. Mixed logit with repeated choices: households' choice of appliance efficiency level. *Review of Economics and Statistics*, vol LXXX (4), 647–657.

Rose, J. and Bliemer, M. 2004. The design of stated choice experiments: the state of the practice and future challenges Institute Transport and Logistics Studies. Working paper 04-09 http://www.its.usyd.edu.au/publications/working_papers/wp2004/its_wp_04-09.pdf

Rose, J. and Bliemer, M. 2005. Constructing efficient choice experiments. ITLS Working Paper ITLS-WP-05-07. Download/http://www.its.usyd.edu.au/publications/working-papers/wp2005/itls-wp-05-7.pdf

Rose, J. and Bliemer, M. (forthcoming). Stated preference experimental design strategies. In: Handbook in Transport Modelling. Hensher, D.A. and Button, K. (Series and volume eds). Oxford: Pergamon Press.

Ryan, M. 1999. Using conjoint analysis to take account of patient preferences and go beyond health outcomes: an application to in vitro fertilization. *Social Science and Medicine*, vol 48 (4), 535–546.

Ryan, M. and Farrar, S. 1994. A pilot study using conjoint analysis to establish the views of users in the provision of orthodontic services in Grampian. Health Economics Research Unit Discussion Paper No 07/94, University of Aberdeen, Aberdeen.

Ryan, M. and Gerard, K. 2003. Using discrete choice experiments to value health care programmes: current practice and future research reflections. *Applied Health Economics and Health Policy*, vol 2 (1), 55–64.

Ryan, M. and Hughes, J. 1997. Using conjoint analysis to assess women's preferences for miscarriage management. *Health Economics*, vol 6, 261–273.

Ryan, M. and Skåtun, D. 2004. Modelling non-demanders in discrete choice experiments. *Health Economic Letters*, vol 13, 397–402.

Ryan, M. and Wordsworth, S. 2000. Sensitivity of willingness to pay estimates to the level of attributes in discrete choice experiments. *Scottish Journal of Political Economy*, vol 47, 504–524.

Ryan, M., McIntosh, E., Dean, T. and Old, P. 2000. Trade-offs between location and waiting times in the provision of health care: the case of elective surgery on the Isle of Wight. *Journal of Public Health Medicine*, vol 22, 202–210.

Ryan, M., Major, K. and Skåtun, D. 2005. Using discrete patient choices to go beyond clinical outcomes when evaluating clinical practice. *Journal of Evaluation in Clinical Practice*, vol 11, 328–339.

San Miguel, F., Ryan, M. and Amaya-Amaya, M. 2004. Irrational stated preferences: a quantitative and qualitative investigation. *Health Economics*, vol 14 (13), 307–322.

 Sándor, Z. and Wedel, M. 2001. Designing conjoint choice experiments using managers' prior beliefs. *Journal of Marketing Research*, vol 38, 430–444.

Sándor, Z. and Wedel, M. 2002. Profile construction in experimental choice designs for mixed logit models. *Marketing Science*, vol 21 (4), 455–475.

Sándor, Z. and Wedel, M. 2005. Heterogeneous conjoint choice designs. *Journal of Marketing Research*, vol 42, 210–218.

Santos Silva, J.M.C. 2004. Deriving welfare measures in discrete choice experiments: a comment to Lancsar and Savage. *Health Economics*, vol 13 (9), 913–918.

Scarpa, R., Willins, K.G. and Acutt, M. 2004. Comparing individual-specific benefit estimates for public goods: finite versus continuous mixing in logit models. Foundation Eni Enrico Mattei Nota Di Lavoro 132.2004.

Scott, A., Watson, M.S. and Ross, S. 2003. Eliciting preferences of the community for out of hours care provided by general practitioners: a stated preference discrete choice experiment. *Social Science and Medicine*, vol 56, 803–814.

Severin, V. 2001. Comparing statistical and respondent efficiency in choice experiments. Unpublished Ph.D. dissertation. Department of Marketing, University of Sydney, Sydney, Australia.

Severin, V.C., Burgess, L., Louviere, J. and Street, D.J. 2004. Comparing statistical efficiency and respondent efficiency in choice experiments. Research report to the Department of Mathematical Sciences, University of Technology, Sydney, Australia.

Simon, H.A. 1955. A behavioural model of rational choice. *Quarterly Journal of Economics*, vol 69, 99–118.

Small, K.A. and Rosen, H.S. 1981. Applied welfare economics with discrete choice models. *Econometrica*, vol 49 (3), 105–130.

Stern, S. 2000. Simulation based inference in econometrics: motivation and methods. In: Simulations-based inference in econometrics: methods and applications. Mariano, R., Schuermann, T. and Weeks, M.J. (eds). Cambridge: Cambridge University Press.

 Street, D.J., Bunch, D.S. and Moore, B.J. 2001. Optimal designs for 2^k paired comparison experiments. *Communications in Statistics, Theory, and Methods*, vol 30 (10), 2149–2171.

 Street, D.J., Burgess, L. and Louviere, J.J. 2005. Quick and easy choice sets: Contructing optimal and nearly optimal stated choice experiments. *International Journal of Research in Marketing*, vol 22, 459–470.

Swait, J. 1994. A structural equation model of latent segmentation and product choice for cross-sectional revealed preference choice data. *Journal of Retail and Consumer Services*, vol 1 (2), 77–89.

Swait, J. 2006. Advanced choice models. In: Valuing Environmental Amenities Using Stated Choice Studies: A Common Sense Approach to Theory and Practice. Kanninen, B. (ed.). Dordrecht: Springer. Series: The Economics of Non-Market Goods and Resources, vol 8, Series ed.: Bateman, I., Chapter 9.

Swait, J. and Adamowicz, W. 2001a. Choice environment, market complexity, and consumer behaviour: a theoretical and empirical approach for incorporating decision complexity into models of consumer choice. *Organizational Behaviour and Human Decision Processes*, vol 86 (2), 141–167.

Swait, J. and Adamowicz, W. 2001b. The influence of task complexity on consumer choice: a latent class model of decision strategy switching. *Journal of Consumer Research*, vol 28, 135–148.

Swait, J. and Louviere, J.J. 1993. The role of the scale parameter in the estimation and comparison of multinational logit models. *Journal of Marketing Research*, vol 30, 305–314.

Swait, J. and Sweeney, J. 2000. Perceived value and its impact on choice behaviour in a retail setting. *Journal of Retailing and Consumer Services*, vol 7 (2), 77–88.

Thurstone, L.L. 1927. A law of comparative judgment. *Psychological Review*, vol 34, 273–286.

Train, K. 2003. Discrete Choice Methods with Simulation. Cambridge: Cambridge University Press.

Varian, H. 1984. Microeconomic Analysis, 2nd edn. New York: Norton.

Viney, R., Lanscar, E. and Louviere, J. 2002. Discrete choice experiments to measure consumer preferences for health and healthcare. *Expert Review of Pharmacoeconomics Outcomes Research*, vol 2 (4), 319–326.

von Haefen, R.H., Massey, D.M. and Adamowicz, W. 2005. Serial non-participation in repeated discrete choice models. *American Journal of Agricultural Economics*, vol 87 (4), 1061–1076.

Walker, J. 2002. The mixed logit (or logit kernel) model: dispelling misconceptions of identification. *Transportation Research Record*, vol 1805, 86–98.

Watson, V., Ryan, M., Barnett, G., Ellis, B., Emberton, M. and Brown, C. 2004. Eliciting preferences for drug treatment of lower urinary tract symptoms associated with benign prostatic hyperplasia. *Journal of Urology*, vol 172, 2321–2325.

Williams, H.W.C.L. 1977. On the formation of travel demand models and economic evaluation measures of user benefit. *Environment and Planning*, vol A9, 285–344.

Wordsworth, S., Ryan, M., Skåtun, D. and Waugh, N. 2006. Women's preferences for cervical cancer screening: a study using a discrete choice experiment. *International Journal of Technology Assessment in Health Care*, vol 22 (3), 344–350.

Yatchew, A. and Griliches, Z. 1984. Specification error in probit models. *Review of Economics and Statistics*, vol 66, 134–139.

Zwerina, K., Huber, J. and Kuhfeld, W. 1996. A general method for constructing efficient choice designs. SAS working paper. Download/http:qSqqSqftp.sas.comqSqtechsupqSqdownloadqSq technoteqSqts629.pdf

CHAPTER 2

DESIGNING DISCRETE CHOICE EXPERIMENTS FOR HEALTH CARE

DEBORAH J. STREET

Department of Mathematical Sciences, University of Technology Sydney (UTS), Australia

LEONIE BURGESS

Department of Mathematical Sciences and Centre of Health Economics Research and Evaluation, University of Technology Sydney, Australia

ROSALIE VINEY

Centre of Health Economics Research and Evaluation (CHERE), University of Technology Sydney (UTS), Australia

JORDAN LOUVIERE

School of Marketing, University of Technology Sydney (UTS), Australia

1. INTRODUCTION

As noted in Chapter 1, the application of discrete choice experiments (DCEs) in health economics has seen an increase over the last few years. While the number of studies using DCEs is growing, there has been relatively limited consideration of experimental design theory and methods. Details of the development of the designed experiment are rarely discussed. Many studies have used small fractional factorial designs (FFDs), generated with commercial design software packages, e.g. orthogonal main effects plans (OMEPs), sometimes manipulated in ad hoc ways (e.g. randomly pairing up scenarios or taking one scenario from the design and combining it with every other scenario). Such approaches can result in designs with unknown statistical design properties, in particular with unknown correlations between parameter estimates.

Consideration of the design of the experiment is important for a number of reasons. Because SP data are collected in controlled experiments, the researcher decides in advance what data to collect, and this determines the models that can be estimated. It is not possible to analyse the impact of attributes or combinations of attributes that have not been anticipated in the design of the experiment. The design should take

M. Ryan, K. Gerard and M. Amaya-Amaya (eds.), Using Discrete Choice
Experiments to Value Health and Health Care, 47–72.
© 2008 *Springer.*

account of the form of the utility function to be estimated, including non-linearities. A limitation of OMEPs is that only strictly linear additive utility functions can be estimated, with no interaction effects. The main effects that can be estimated will be correlated with unobserved and unobservable interaction effects. Unless these interaction effects are non-significant, the main effects estimated will be biased (El-Helbawy and Bradley, 1978). Larger designs may be desirable because they allow greater coverage of response surfaces.

Balanced against this is the fact that collection of survey data is costly. An objective in the design of any DCE should be maximising the information that can be obtained from the data collection (e.g. ensuring that different functional forms can be tested, and that all relevant attributes and levels have been incorporated in the experiment), or minimising the cost of collecting the data required to test particular hypotheses. While larger designs allow more effects to be estimated, they also often entail larger sample sizes, more choice sets per respondent and larger choice sets. The principles of designing optimal experiments can be used to reduce the cost of data collection by reducing the number of respondents required for the same level of accuracy (Atkinson and Donev, 1992).

Choice experiments are complex cognitive tasks for respondents, and it is important to consider the impact of the design of the experiment on choice behaviour of respondents. When relevant attributes are not included in an experiment, respondents may infer levels for these attributes, introducing unobservable biases in parameter estimates (Louviere et al., 2000). However, as task complexity increases, cognitive burden for respondents increases, increasing random variability in responses, and reducing the efficiency of estimation (Louviere et al., 2000).

Louviere et al. (2000) identify four design objectives for choice experiments: (1) *identification*, ensuring that the desired forms of utility function can be estimated from the experiment; (2) *precision*, ensuring that the statistical efficiency of the experiment allows the parameters to be estimated precisely; (3) *cognitive complexity*, concerned with ensuring that the experiment does not impose an excessive cognitive burden on respondents; and (4) *market realism*, addressing whether the way the choices in the experiment represent the choice process and the actual choices presented are realistic. As noted above, an additional objective that is relevant in most data collection contexts is cost minimisation. While achieving market realism is context specific, the use of the principles of designing optimal experiments can ensure that the other objectives are met for most choice experiments.

This chapter describes an easy, systematic way of constructing choice sets with any number of options for estimating main effects and main effects plus two-factor interactions. The designs for the estimation of main effects have known optimality properties and have desirable structural properties such as minimum attribute-level overlap and balance. The designs are no larger than ones currently employed and are no more difficult for respondents to complete than currently used designs, but generally give more information from the same number of respondents.

In Section 2, we give a definition and example of a DCE, focusing on moving from design coding to actual choice sets. Section 3 discusses the current methods of constructing DCEs within health economics. In Section 4, we discuss the model that we use, and the effects that can be estimated. Section 5 discusses how designs can be compared using the variance–covariance matrix of the estimated effects. In Section 6, we discuss how to construct optimal and near-optimal designs for a number of situations that arise in the health area. We look at the estimation of main effects in a forced choice setting. We then consider the construction of (near-)optimal designs when main effects plus two-factor interaction effects are to be estimated. We briefly consider the construction of (near-)optimal designs when a "none-of-these" option is to be included, and when a common base alternative appears in every choice set. In the penultimate section we look at a number of areas where further work is required.

2. DEFINITION AND EXAMPLE

Recall from Chapter 1 that a DCE consists of several choice sets, each of which includes two or more options, sometimes called treatment combinations. In experiments with a small number of choice sets, each respondent may be asked to choose from each of the choice sets included in the experiment. In larger experiments, the full set of choice sets may be blocked into smaller subsets, often using random assignment, and each respondent is randomly assigned to respond to a particular subset.

Throughout this chapter, we assume that all options in a choice set (except the "none-of-these" option, if it is present) are described by several (k) attributes and that each attribute q has two or more levels (l_q). The levels are coded and represented numerically by $0, 1, \ldots, l_q-1$. Assume that all the choice sets in a particular experiment have the same number of options. Let m be the size of each of the choice sets. If all the choice sets have two options ($m = 2$), then we often speak of a paired comparison design.

It is further assumed that these options are generic or unlabelled; see Louviere et al. (2000) for specification issues for labelled experiments where the label of the alternatives in the choice set conveys information to individuals that may not be ignored.

The next example describes a DCE used to elicit preferences for asthma medications.

Example 1

Here are some symptoms, which are the attributes, and the corresponding levels, from a study of asthma medications (McKenzie et al., 2001). The five attributes in the experiment are given in the first column of Table 2.1. Each attribute has three levels, which are shown in the other columns of the table. The design codes (0,1,2), which are the same for all of the attributes, are given in the final row of the table. The combinations of levels and attributes are arranged into choice sets, describing pairs of symptoms for a person suffering asthma. So, in this example, $k = 5, l_q = 3, q = 1, \ldots, 5$ and $m = 2$.

A possible choice set and the wording of the question are shown in Table 2.2. This choice set can be represented in design code by the pair (20212, 00100).[1]

Section 3 discusses the current methods used to construct DCEs.

3. CURRENT METHODS OF CONSTRUCTION

As reviewed in Chapter 1, most methods of construction for DCEs use only a subset of size f of all possible combinations of attribute levels. These subsets are called FFDs. Most commonly within the applied literature, OMEPs, equivalently FFDs of

TABLE 2.1. *Attributes, levels and coded levels from a study of asthma medications*

Attributes	Levels		
Cough	None	Some but no restricted activities	Lots and restricted activities
Breathlessness	None	Some but no restricted activities	Lots and restricted activities
Wheeze	None	Some but no restricted activities	Lots and restricted activities
Chest tightness	None	Some but no restricted activities	Lots and restricted activities
Sleep disturbance	None	Woken once	Woken 2 or 3 times
Coded levels	0	1	2

TABLE 2.2. *One choice set from a study of asthma medications*

Suppose that your asthma can be controlled to some extent by medication and that as a result the next week you would have one of the following two sets of symptoms. Which of these two would you prefer or is there no difference?		
	Week A	Week B
Cough	A lot of coughing with restricted activities	No cough
Breathlessness	No breathlessness	No breathlessness
Wheeze	Very wheezy with restricted activities	Some wheezing but with no restricted activities
Chest tightness	A little tightness	Chest not tight
Sleep disturbance	Awoken 2–3 times with cough/breathlessness	No sleep disturbance

resolution 3, are employed. To say an FFD is of *resolution 3* is to say that for any two attributes all combinations of pairs of levels appear with proportional frequencies. By this we mean that if we let r_{xq} be the number of times that level x appears in column q of the array, then for any pair of columns q and p, the number of times that the ordered pair (x,y) appears in the columns is $r_{xq}r_{yp}/f$. These are the smallest designs available for the estimation of main effects only in the ordinary least squares situation (linear models). However, these designs do have limitations: a resolution 3 design does not permit the estimation of any interaction effects between any subsets of attributes, and main effects will be confounded with the interaction effects. To allow for the estimation of interaction effects between pairs of attributes (two-factor interactions), a resolution 5 design is required. The pairwise interactions are estimated under the assumption that all interaction effects involving three or more attributes are zero. We can easily check if a design is of resolution 5 by checking that any combination of levels from any four attributes appear in the same number of treatment combinations. More details may be found in Dey and Mukerjee (1999).

Whilst most applications of DCEs have employed FFDs, a number of different approaches have been adopted to generate the choice sets included in the DCEs. The most common early approach was to obtain an OMEP from computer software (often SPEED) and then to pair the resulting profiles randomly into a number of choices (Ryan et al., 2001; Ryan and Gerard, 2003). Another approach is to take several FFDs and randomly choose the first option from the first FFD, the second option from the second FFD, and so on, until there are m options. Another method is to construct an OMEP with $m \times k$ attributes in total and use the first k attributes for the first option, the second k for the second option and so on. This final construction method has been called the L^{MA} approach by some authors (see Louviere et al., 2000). It should be noted that L^{MA} designs are not designed to be used to estimate main effects but instead are intended to allow one to test violations of the identically distributed (IID) errors assumptions and hence to estimate mother logit models, if appropriate.

The above approaches gave very little consideration to the properties of a good design. More recently, consideration has been given to the properties of a good design, initially drawing on the work of Huber and Zwerina (1996). They describe a set of features they believe are characteristic of optimal choice designs:

1. *Level balance* – all the levels of each attribute occur with equal frequency (often called equi-replicate in the statistical literature).
2. *Orthogonality – the levels of each attribute vary independently of each other*. This means that for any two attributes all combinations of pairs of levels appear with proportional frequencies.
3. *Minimal overlap – the probability that an attribute level repeats itself in each choice set should be as small as possible*. We can achieve this if the difference between the number of times that any two levels of an attribute are replicated is at most one.
4. *Utility balance* – options within a choice set should be equally attractive to respondents.

Orthogonality is a term that has been used by various people to mean various things and it is important to understand what someone means when they use the term. One common usage is to say that two effects that are uncorrelated are orthogonal. In the context of an OMEP this is the usage that is being referred to – the main effects estimated from an OMEP in a linear models setting are uncorrelated (see Dey and Mukerjee, 1999).

In a choice experiment, it is not the attributes or the options that need to be uncorrelated but the estimates obtained from the choice experiment. The way that we judge this is to consider the information matrix, represented by C later, and see if that matrix is diagonal, in which case all components of all effects are independent. This matrix can be block diagonal (i.e. has non-zero block matrices of order $(l_q - 1)$ on the diagonal and all other entries 0), in which case main effects from different attributes are independent but components of the main effect from one attribute may not be.

It is convenient to start with an OMEP when constructing a choice experiment because it is then often easy to construct choice sets, and hence a choice experiment, in which the information matrix has the right (block diagonal) form.

Minimal overlap is a desirable feature for main effects only, of course, as Huber and Zwerina point out also, since it precludes the estimation of interaction effects.

In one of the applications of the Huber and Zwerina approach within the discipline, Phillips et al. (2002), use it to construct 11 choice sets of size 2 for a situation with six attributes with 3, 4, 4, 3, 5 and 2 levels, respectively. It should be noted that a design which satisfies the four Huber and Zwerina criteria above is not necessarily optimal, and an optimal design does not necessarily satisfy their criteria (see Street and Burgess, 2007). For any design constructed by any of the available methods the optimality properties of the design need to be evaluated on a case-by-case basis.

We now discuss some variations of generic choice experiments described above. Sometimes one of the alternatives has been selected from the profiles generated and then paired up with the rest. This common base alternative may be chosen to represent the current situation (Ryan and Hughes, 1997; Ryan and Farrar, 2000; Longworth et al., 2001) or may be randomly chosen from the OMEP (Ryan, 1999; Ryan et al., 2000; Scott, 2002). van der Pol and Cairns (2001) chose the choice sets pragmatically, "using three criteria: (1) inclusion of all possible scenarios; (2) a wide range of implied discount rates; (3) one discrete choice set representing a negative discount rate".

Good techniques for constructing designs for generic choice experiments now exist. Burgess and Street (2003a, 2005) and Street and Burgess (2004a, b) give constructions that give optimal designs for the estimation of main effects and of main effects plus two-factor interactions. These constructions are easy to implement and give designs that turn out to have the good properties identified by Huber and Zwerina (1996). These constructions are described in Sections 6 and 7. But first we consider an appropriate model for a choice experiment and how to compare two, or more, choice experiments.

4. THE MODEL AND PARAMETER ESTIMATION

Within a random utility maximisation framework as described in Chapter 1, the objective of any DCE is to identify which attributes are important in determining utility and how these attributes interact. In terms of the design, we want to be able to compare any pair of designs and say which is better in achieving this objective. To do this we need to consider the form of the utility function in advance in order to know the effects to be estimated in a particular experiment and the model that is to be used.

The model estimated depends on assumptions made about the distribution of the random component of the utility ε_{ij}, and the nature of the choice being modelled. Often it is assumed that the ε_{ij} are independently and identically distributed, with a Gumbel (often called extreme value type 1) distribution, resulting in a multinomial logit (MNL) model. Following on from Equation 1.7, we will use the notation in Burgess and Street (2003a) for the model and likelihood function. We let the T_{ij} be the m different options in the choice set and $\pi_{ij} = \exp(\mu\beta' X_{ij})$. Then the probability that option T_{i_1} is preferred to the other $m-1$ options is given by:

$$P(T_{i_1} > T_{i_2}, \ldots, T_{i_m}) = \frac{\exp(\mu V_{i_1})}{\sum_j \exp(\mu V_{i_j})} = \frac{\exp(\mu\beta' X_{i_1})}{\sum_j \exp(\mu\beta' X_{i_j})} = \frac{\pi_{i_1}}{\sum_{j=1}^{m} \pi_{i_j}}$$

for $i_j = 1, 2, \ldots, f$ treatment combinations, where no two options are the same. We let $\pi = (\pi_1, \pi_2, \ldots, \pi_f)$ and let $\gamma = \ln(\pi)$. Using the likelihood function given in Equation 1.8, we can find the information matrix of γ, which we denote by Λ (see Street and Burgess, 2006 for details).

To define Λ we first define $\lambda_{j, i_2, \ldots, i_m} = n_{i_1, i_2, \ldots, i_m}/N$, where $n_{i_1, i_2, \ldots, i_m} = 1$ if $(T_{i_1}, T_{i_2}, \ldots, T_{i_m})$ is a choice set and is 0 otherwise. Then the entries of Λ, which is a square matrix with rows and columns labelled by treatment combinations, are given by

$$\Lambda_{i_1, i_1} = \pi_{i_1} \sum_{i_2 < i_3 < \ldots < i_m} \frac{\lambda_{i_1, i_2, \ldots, i_m} \sum_{j=2}^{m} \pi_{i_j}}{\left(\sum_{j=1}^{m} \pi_{i_j}\right)^2} = \sum_{i_2 < i_3 < \ldots < i_m} \frac{\lambda_{i_1, i_2, \ldots, i_m}(m-1)}{m^2}$$

if all $\pi_{ij} = 1$, where the summations are over all choice sets that contain item T_{i_1}, and

$$\Lambda_{i_1, i_2} = -\pi_{i_1} \pi_{i_2} \sum_{i_3 < i_4 < \ldots < i_m} \frac{\lambda_{i_1, i_2, \ldots, i_m}}{\left(\sum_{j=1}^{m} \pi_{i_j}\right)^2} = -\sum_{i_3 < i_4 < \ldots < i_m} \frac{\lambda_{i_1, i_2, \ldots, i_m}(m-1)}{m^2}$$

if all $\pi_{ij} = 1$, where the summations are over all choice sets that contain items T_{i_1} and T_{i_2} (see Burgess and Street, 2003a for more details).

As we choose different forms for V_i, such as main effects or main effects plus two-factor interactions, the corresponding entries in β can be written as $\beta = B\gamma$ with information matrix $C = B\Lambda B'$.

If we are interested in estimating the main effects of each of the attributes, then we are interested in estimating $B_M\gamma$ where B_M is the contrast matrix for main effects and has one column for each treatment combination in the complete factorial. Recall that the *main effect* of an attribute with l_q levels has $l_q - 1$ degrees of freedom. These degrees of freedom can be represented by $l_q - 1$ polynomial contrasts and we use these polynomial contrasts as the rows of the matrix B_M. Hence, an attribute with two levels has one row in the B_M matrix, with entries equal to -1, when the level of the corresponding attribute is at the low level, and 1, when the level of the corresponding attribute is at the high level. If an attribute has three levels, then there are two rows in the B_M matrix. There are entries of -1, 0 and 1 in one row, corresponding to the linear polynomial, and $1, -2$ and 1 in the other row, corresponding to the quadratic polynomial, for the three levels of the attribute. If an attribute has four levels, then there are three rows in the B_M matrix. There are entries of $-3, -1, 1$ and 3 in one row, corresponding to the linear polynomial, $1, -1, -1$ and 1 in the second row, corresponding to the quadratic polynomial, and $-1, 3, -3$ and 1 for the third row, corresponding to the cubic polynomial for the four levels of the attribute. In all cases, we normalise the entries so that $B_M B'_M = I$. The information matrix for the estimation of $B_{M\gamma}$ is given by $C_M = B_M \Lambda B'_M$. Healy (2000) provides a useful summary of matrix theory for non-mathematicians and Kuehl (1999) has polynomial contrasts of higher orders.[2]

Properties of the information matrix C_M, and of its inverse, the variance–covariance matrix, determine the properties of the corresponding design. In particular, if the information matrix is diagonal (i.e. has all off-diagonal elements equal to zero), so is the variance–covariance matrix, and all the effects are independently estimated. If the information matrix is block diagonal, so is the variance–covariance matrix and, while components of a particular effect may be correlated, the different effects are independently estimated.

Next we present an example illustrating all the concepts above.

Example 2

Suppose $k = 2$ (there are two attributes), $m = 3$ (there are three options in each choice set), $l_1 = 2$ (the first attribute has two levels, coded 0 and 1) and $l_2 = 3$ (the second attribute has three levels, coded 0, 1 and 2). In this case there are six possible treatment combinations, 00, 01, 02, 10, 11 and 12, and they can be combined into choice sets of any size from $m = 1$ (choose yes or no) to $m = 6$.

Let $P_1 = \{(00, 01, 10), (00, 01, 11), (00, 02, 10), (00, 02, 12), (00, 10, 11), (00, 10, 12), (01, 02, 11), (01, 02, 12), (01, 10, 11), (01, 11, 12), (02, 10, 12), (02, 11,12)\}$, and consider using these 12 choice sets of size $m = 3$ as a choice experiment.

We can write the six possible treatment combinations in the order 00, 01, 02, 10, 11 and 12 (called *lexicographic order*), and use these to label the rows and columns of Λ. To get the entries in the first row of the Λ matrix observe that options 00 and 01 both appear together in two choice sets so $\Lambda_{1,2} = -2/(m^2 \times N) = -2/(3^2 \times 12)$. Similarly $\Lambda_{1,3} = \Lambda_{1,5} = \Lambda_{1,6} = -2/(3^2 \times 12)$ and $\Lambda_{1,4} = -4/(3^2 \times 12)$ since option 00 appears with 10 in four choice sets. The diagonal entry in the first row is the negative of the sum of these entries and so $\Lambda_{1,1} = 12/(3^2 \times 12)$. Continuing in this way, under the null hypothesis $\pi_i = 1$, $i = 1, \ldots, 6$, we get the Λ matrix below.

The contrast matrix B_M has three rows; one row for the two level attribute, with entries -1 and 1 corresponding to the coded levels 0 and 1, respectively, and two rows for the three-level attribute, with entries $-1, 0$ and 1 in the first row, for the linear contrast and $1, -2$ and 1 in the second row, for the quadratic contrast. We then normalise the rows to get the B_M matrix given below (e.g. for the first row we divide each element

by $\sqrt{(-1)^2 + (-1)^2 + (-1)^2 + (1)^2 + (1)^2 + (1)^2} = \sqrt{6}$).
Finally calculate $C_M = B_M \Lambda B'_M$.

① sum of two entries of ←

$$\Lambda = \frac{1}{108}\begin{bmatrix} 12 & -2 & -2 & -4 & -2 & -2 \\ -2 & 12 & -2 & -2 & -4 & -2 \\ -2 & -2 & 12 & -2 & -2 & -4 \\ -4 & -2 & -2 & 12 & -2 & -2 \\ -2 & -4 & -2 & -2 & 12 & -2 \\ -2 & -2 & -4 & -2 & -2 & 12 \end{bmatrix}, \quad B_M = \begin{bmatrix} \frac{-1}{\sqrt{6}} & \frac{-1}{\sqrt{6}} & \frac{-1}{\sqrt{6}} & \frac{1}{\sqrt{6}} & \frac{1}{\sqrt{6}} & \frac{1}{\sqrt{6}} \\ \frac{-1}{2} & 0 & \frac{1}{2} & \frac{1}{2} & 0 & \frac{1}{2} \\ \frac{1}{\sqrt{12}} & \frac{-2}{\sqrt{12}} & \frac{1}{\sqrt{12}} & \frac{1}{\sqrt{12}} & \frac{-2}{\sqrt{12}} & \frac{1}{\sqrt{12}} \end{bmatrix}$$

and $C_M = \begin{bmatrix} \frac{4}{27} & 0 & 0 \\ 0 & \frac{1}{9} & 0 \\ 0 & 0 & \frac{1}{9} \end{bmatrix}$.

Suppose we use the choice sets in $P_2 = \{(00, 01, 12), (00, 02, 11), (00, 11, 12), (01, 02, 10), (01, 10, 12)$ and $(02, 10, 11)\}$ as a choice experiment.
Then B is the same but now

$$\Lambda = \frac{1}{54}\begin{bmatrix} 6 & -1 & -1 & 0 & -2 & -2 \\ -1 & 6 & -1 & -2 & 0 & -2 \\ -1 & -1 & 6 & -2 & -2 & 0 \\ 0 & -2 & -2 & 6 & -1 & -1 \\ -2 & 0 & -2 & -1 & 6 & -1 \\ -2 & -2 & 0 & -1 & -1 & 6 \end{bmatrix}, \quad \text{and so } C_M = \begin{bmatrix} \frac{4}{27} & 0 & 0 \\ 0 & \frac{1}{6} & 0 \\ 0 & 0 & \frac{1}{6} \end{bmatrix}.$$

Recall that the inverse of C_M is the variance–covariance matrix for the estimates of the main effects. As C_M is diagonal, so is the variance–covariance matrix. Hence, we see that in either of these choice experiments, estimates of the main effects are independent of each other.

5. COMPARING DESIGNS

5.1. D-Optimality

We can compare estimates by considering the form of the information matrix (e.g. C_M if we are estimating main effects) or the variance–covariance matrix. More often the generalised variance, which is the determinant of the variance–covariance matrix (i.e. $\det(C^{-1})$), is used to compare different designs. We want $\det(C^{-1})$ to be as small as possible and, since $\det(C^{-1}) = \det(C)^{-1}$, we want $\det(C)$ to be as large as possible (see Atkinson and Donev, 1992 for more details).

The design with the largest value of $\det(C)$ is defined to be the D-optimal design and we write this largest value of $\det(C)$ as $\det(C_{opt})$.

For any design d with information matrix C_d the D-efficiency of d is given by

$$\text{D-eff} = \left[\frac{\det(C_d)}{\det(C_{\text{opt}})} \right]^{\frac{1}{p}}$$

if there are p parameters to be estimated. For main effects $p = \sum_{q=1}^{k} (l_q - 1)$, for example, and for estimating main effects plus two-factor interactions

$$p = \sum_{q=1}^{k} (l_q - 1) + \sum_{q=1}^{k} \sum_{r=q+1}^{k} (l_q - 1)(l_r - 1)$$

Clearly the D-efficiency of the optimal design is 100%.

5.2. Estimating Main Effects Only

Suppose that we want to compare designs for the estimation of main effects only. Consider again the designs in Example 2. We have for P_1, $\det(C_M) = (1/27)(1/9)^2 = 0.00182899$ and for P_2, $\det(C_M) = (4/27)(1/6)^2 = 0.00411523$.

Thus, for estimating main effects only, we choose P_2 rather than P_1 since both designs have a diagonal C matrix and P_2 is more efficient than P_1.

Example 3 extends the comparison to seven different designs.

Example 3

We consider seven designs for $k = 2$, $l_1 = 2$ and $l_2 = 3$. Each design is made up of choice sets of size 3, i.e. $m = 3$ (often called triples) or unions of these sets. P_1 and P_2 are as before and we let $P_3 = \{(00, 01, 02), (10, 11, 12)\}$.

TABLE 2.3. *Seven choice experiments with choice sets of size 3 for a design with $k = 2$, $l_1 = 2$ and $l_2 = 3$*

Design	Number of sets (N)	det (C_M)	Diagonal entries of C	Efficiency (%)
P_1	12	0.00182899	$\frac{4}{27}, \frac{1}{9}, \frac{1}{9}$	76.3
P_2	6	0.00411523	$\frac{4}{27}, \frac{1}{6}, \frac{1}{6}$	100
P_3	2	0	$0, \frac{1}{6}, \frac{1}{6}$	0
P_1 and P_3	14	0.00179966	$\frac{8}{63}, \frac{5}{42}, \frac{5}{42}$	75.9
P_1 and P_2	18	0.00248946	$\frac{4}{27}, \frac{7}{54}, \frac{7}{54}$	84.6
P_2 and P_3	8	0.00308642	$\frac{1}{9}, \frac{1}{6}, \frac{1}{6}$	90.9
P_1, P_2 and P_3	20	0.00237037	$\frac{2}{15}, \frac{2}{15}, \frac{2}{15}$	83.2

In Table 2.3 we give the triples that make up the design, the number of triples, the determinant of the C_M matrix (all the C_M matrices in this example are diagonal) and the efficiency of each design.

In the previous example, we saw that the best design was the one in which all the options were as different as possible. This turns out to be the case always when one only wants to estimate main effects. The next definition measures this difference for each attribute.

We let S_q be the largest number of pairs of options that can have different levels for attribute q in a choice set. For a choice set of size m there are $m(m-1)/2$ distinct pairs of options and clearly we can have this many differences only if an attribute has more levels than there are options in a choice set. When there are fewer levels than there are options in a choice set then we want each of the levels to appear "about the same number of times" which gives rise to the values of S_q given below.

For a given choice set size, m, the least upper bound for S_q is

$$S_q = \begin{cases} (m^2-1)/4 & l_q=2, m \text{ odd}, \\ m^2/4 & l_q=2, m \text{ even}, \\ (m^2-(l_q x^2+2xy+y))/2 & 2<l_q<m, \\ m(m-1)/2 & l_q \geq m. \end{cases}$$

where positive integers x and y satisfy the equation $m = l_q x + y$ for $0 \leq y < l_q$.

Example 4

Consider again the designs P_1, P_2 and P_3 from Example 3. For each of these sets we can calculate the corresponding values of S_1 and S_2 since the sets were chosen to contain all triples with the same values for the pair (S_1, S_2).

In $P_1 = \{(00, 01, 02), (10, 11, 12)\}$ we see that the levels for the first attribute are always the same so $S_1 = 0+0+0 = 0$ and the attribute levels for the second attribute for any pair of options are always different so $S_2 = 1+1+1 = 3$.

Similarly for P_2 we have that $S_1 = 0+1+1 = 2$ and $S_2 = 1+0+1 = 2$; and for P_3 we have $S_1 = 0+1+1 = 2$ and $S_2 = 1+1+1 = 3$.

The largest possible value for S_1 is $(m^2-1)/4 = 2$ and the largest possible value for S_2 is $m(m-1)/2 = 3$.

So how do we go about finding choice sets that are optimal for the estimation of main effects only? We make systematic level changes so that there are as many pairs of options as possible with different levels for each attribute. This is discussed further in Section 6.

We then compare the determinant of the resulting design to the upper bound on $\det(C_M)$ which is given by

$$\det (C_{M, opt}) = \prod_{q=1}^{k} \left[\frac{2S_q l_q}{m^2(l_q-1)L} \right]^{l_q-1} \tag{2.1}$$

5.3. Estimating Main Effects plus Two-Factor Interactions

If we also want to estimate some, or all, of the interaction effects, then we adjoin rows to B_M for the contrasts corresponding to the interactions effects to get B_{MI} and evaluate $C_{MI} = B_{MI} \Lambda B'_{MI}$.

Burgess and Street (2003a) show that if all k attributes have two levels, the maximum possible value of $\det(C_{MI})$ is given by

$$\det(C_{MI,\,opt}) = \begin{cases} \left(\dfrac{(m-1)(k+2)}{m(k+1)2^k} \right)^{k+k(k-1)/2} & k \text{ even,} \\[4mm] \left(\dfrac{(m-1)(k+1)}{mk2^k} \right)^{k+k(k-1)/2} & k \text{ odd.} \end{cases}$$

In other cases we do not have an upper bound on $\det(C_{MI})$. For some small values of k, m and l_q optimal designs are known (see Burgess and Street, 2003b). We can always compare any set of proposed designs and decide which is the best.

Example 5

Let $k = 2$, $m = 3$, $l_1 = 2$ and $l_2 = 3$ and suppose that we want to estimate the interaction effect as well as the main effect. That means that we need to adjoin two further rows to the B matrix and these rows are, before normalisation $(1, 0, -1, -1, 0, 1)$ (the component-wise product of the first row of the matrix B_M and the second row of the matrix B_M) and $(-1, 2, -1, 1, -2, 1)$ (the component-wise product of the first row of the matrix B_M and the third row of the matrix B_M). Then, we get the results shown in Table 2.4.

TABLE 2.4. *Seven choice experiments with choice sets of size 3 for a design with $k = 2$, $l_1 = 2$ and $l_2 = 3$*

Design	Number of sets	$\det(C_M)$	Diagonal entries of C	Efficiency (%)
P_1	12	0.0000401424	$\dfrac{4}{27}, \dfrac{1}{9}, \dfrac{1}{9}, \dfrac{4}{27}, \dfrac{4}{27}$	99.0
P_2	6	0.0000352814	$\dfrac{4}{27}, \dfrac{1}{6}, \dfrac{1}{6}, \dfrac{5}{54}, \dfrac{5}{54}$	96.5
P_3	2	0	$0, \dfrac{1}{6}, \dfrac{1}{6}, \dfrac{1}{6}, \dfrac{1}{6}$	0
P_1 and P_2	18	0.0000418325	$\dfrac{4}{27}, \dfrac{7}{54}, \dfrac{7}{54}, \dfrac{7}{54}, \dfrac{7}{54}$	99.9
P_1 and P_3	14	0.000040922	$\dfrac{8}{63}, \dfrac{5}{42}, \dfrac{5}{42}, \dfrac{19}{126}, \dfrac{19}{126}$	99.4
P_2 and P_3	8	0.0000381039	$\dfrac{1}{9}, \dfrac{1}{6}, \dfrac{1}{6}, \dfrac{1}{9}, \dfrac{1}{9}$	98
P_1, P_2 and P_3	20	0.00237037	$\dfrac{2}{15}, \dfrac{2}{15}, \dfrac{2}{15}, \dfrac{2}{15}, \dfrac{2}{15}$	100

Similarly, it is possible to decide to estimate only some of the interaction effects, say just the linear × linear component for instance. The effects that are to be estimated (linear, quadratic, interactions) determine the entries in the B matrix. The options that occur together in a choice set determine the entries in the Λ matrix and $C = B \Lambda B'$ is then the information matrix for the DCE.

For main effects we always know what $\det(C_{M, \text{ opt}})$ is (see above) but for other B matrices $\det(C_{\text{opt}})$ may not be known and it may be sufficient to know that all effects of interest can be estimated from the proposed design.

In Sections 6 and 7, we discuss how to construct (near-)optimal designs for estimating main effects, in a forced choice setting, when a "none-of-these" option appears in each choice set, and when there is a common base alternative in all choice sets. We go on to give some ideas for constructing designs that can estimate interaction effects in all of these situations. We use typical examples from the health services literature to illustrate our constructions.

6. OPTIMAL DESIGNS FOR MAIN EFFECTS ONLY

The aim of this section is to show how to use the results in Burgess and Street (2003a, 2005) and Street and Burgess (2004a, b) to construct optimal forced choice DCEs. These designs are all for generic alternatives although all the first options (and all the second options and so on) constitute a main effects plan.

As seen above, to make an optimal choice experiment to estimate main effects we must make systematic level changes, preferably starting from an OMEP in which all attributes have equal replication of all levels, so that there are as many pairs of options as possible with different levels for each attribute within each choice set, i.e. the upper bound S_q is attained for each attribute.

This suggests that for binary attributes (attributes with two levels) about half the options in each choice set should have one level and the other half should have the other level. For attributes with three levels about one third should have each of the levels and so on. We discuss some examples below.

Example 6
Suppose that there are $k = 5$ attributes, each with two levels and that the aim is to estimate main effects. Each respondent is presented with several sets of pairs of options (so $m = 2$) and for each pair they are to say which option they prefer.

Find a resolution 3 FFD (OMEP). Although commercially available software packages could be used, the easiest way to do this is to use Sloane (2005). The web site uses *oa.N.k.s.t.name* to denote an orthogonal array (a particular class of OMEPs) with N runs, k factors (or attributes), s levels (for each of the attributes), and strength t (equivalently resolution $t + 1$). We see that there is an oa.8.5.2.2 so we can use this as the starting design for our construction. Click on the link and you will obtain the design in Table 2.5. Each run represents a treatment combination. These are the first options in each choice set.

To generate the choice sets from this OMEP we need to change systematically the treatment combinations in the OMEP to create the second option in each choice set. More precisely, since the maximum possible S_q is $m^2/4 = 2^2/4 = 1$ we will need to change the level of each attribute for each option to get the second option in each

TABLE 2.5. *The oa.8.5.2.2*
from Sloane's web site

00000
10011
01010
00101
11001
10110
01111
11100

TABLE 2.6. *An optimal set of pairs for estimating main effects*

0	0	0	0	0	1	1	1	1	1
1	0	0	1	1	0	1	1	0	0
0	1	0	1	0	1	0	1	0	1
0	0	1	0	1	1	1	0	1	0
1	1	0	0	1	0	0	1	1	0
1	0	1	1	0	0	1	0	0	1
0	1	1	1	1	1	0	0	0	0
1	1	1	0	0	0	0	0	1	1

choice set. Thus, interchanging all 0s and 1s gives the second option in each choice set and the resulting design appears in Table 2.6. (This is often called "folding over" the first option to get the second.) Each row is a choice set in the choice experiment. By calculating B_M, Λ and hence C_M, and comparing $\det(C_M)$ to the bound given earlier, we know that this design is optimal (and so is 100% efficient, of course).

Suppose that you are interested in five attributes, each with two levels, but now suppose that you want to estimate main effects by presenting respondents with choice sets of size 3 ($m = 3$). Then, you need to change levels so that you have two options with the attribute at one level and one option with the attribute at the other level and this is true for each attribute. There are many ways that this can be done. If we change the levels of attributes 1, 2 and 3 to get the second option in each choice set, and attributes 4 and 5 to get the third option in each choice set, we get the choice sets shown in

TABLE 2.7. *Optimal choice sets of size 3 for estimating main effects*

0	0	0	0	0		1	1	1	0	0		0	0	0	1	1
1	0	0	1	1		0	1	1	1	1		1	0	0	0	0
0	1	0	1	0		1	0	1	1	0		0	1	0	0	1
0	0	1	0	1		1	1	0	0	1		0	0	1	1	0
1	1	0	0	1		0	0	1	0	1		1	1	0	1	0
1	0	1	1	0		0	1	0	1	0		1	0	1	0	1
0	1	1	1	1		1	0	0	1	1		0	1	1	0	0
1	1	1	0	0		0	0	0	0	0		1	1	1	1	1

Table 2.7. To check the design is optimal, calculate B_M, Λ and hence $\det(C_M)$ and see that it equals the value given in Equation 2.1.

This design is not unique because we can swap the levels in any sets of attributes as long as $S_q = 2$ for each attribute. So we could swap the levels in attributes 1, 4 and 5 for the first option and in attributes 2, 3 and 4 for the second option, and the resulting design would also be optimal.

To talk of "swapping levels" becomes more difficult as the number of levels that an attribute has increases. Instead, we use the mathematical idea of modular arithmetic to describe how options are to be created from the entries in the FFD. We describe this below for 2, 3 and 4 levels, although the same idea will work for any number of levels (see Insall and Weisstein, 2006).

If we interchange 0s and 1s for a binary attribute, then we are adding 1 modulo 2. We write $0 + 0 = 1 + 1 = 0 \pmod 2$ and $0 + 1 = 1 + 0 = 1 \pmod 2$. We can represent this in an addition table such as the one below.

+	0	1
0	0	1
1	1	0

For three-level attributes we work modulo 3 and for four-level attributes we do the addition modulo 4. The corresponding addition tables appear below.

+	0	1	2
0	0	1	2
1	1	2	0
2	2	0	1

+	0	1	2	3
0	0	1	2	3
1	1	2	3	0
2	2	3	0	1
3	3	0	1	2

We usually write the elements to be added as a k-tuple since there are k attributes. For the position corresponding to attribute q, addition is modulo l_q since attribute q has l_q levels. So we get the second options in Table 2.7 by adding (11100) (to each of the rows or runs in the OMEP) and we get the third options by adding (00011). These are called the *generators* of the choice experiment.

We illustrate this for non-binary attributes in the next example.

Example 7

Suppose that each option is described by four attributes; the first two attributes have two levels, the third attribute has three levels and the fourth attribute has four levels. Suppose that you want to estimate the main effects of each of the attributes using a DCE with choice sets of size 2. No initial design with this arrangement of attribute levels is given in Sloane (2005). However, there is a resolution 3 FFD with 16 rows with five attributes each with four levels. It appears in Table 2.8.

To get the design that we need we delete one of the attributes (we have chosen to delete the fifth attribute) and in three of the remaining attributes we *collapse levels*. We make the first two four-level attributes into two two-level attributes by changing all 2s to 0s and all 3s to 1s. Any two levels of the four-level attribute can be equated to give

TABLE 2.8. *An oa.16.5.4.2 from Sloane's web site*

0	0	0	0	0
0	1	1	1	1
0	2	2	2	2
0	3	3	3	3
1	0	1	2	3
1	1	0	3	2
1	2	3	0	1
1	3	2	1	0
2	0	2	3	1
2	1	3	2	0
2	2	0	1	3
2	3	1	0	2
3	0	3	1	2
3	1	2	0	3
3	2	1	3	0
3	3	0	2	1

the two-level attribute; hence, the way that we have chosen to do this is one of several possible ways. For the third attribute we change all the 3s to 2s. Again we can equate any two levels to change the four-level to a three-level attribute. The resulting design appears in Table 2.9. Note, however, that there can be problems when collapsing more than one attribute; this is discussed at some length in Street and Burgess (2006).

If we want to use choice sets of size 2 ($m = 2$), the maximum number of attribute differences for each pair is $S_1 = S_2 = S_3 = S_4 = 1$. Using the upper bound for the determinant of the information matrix, given in Equation 2.1, and remembering that $L = 2 \times 2 \times 3 \times 4 = 48$, we get

$$\det(C_{M,\,opt}) = \left[\frac{2 \times 1 \times 2}{2^2(2-1)48}\right]^{2-1} \left[\frac{2 \times 1 \times 2}{2^2(2-1)48}\right]^{2-1} \left[\frac{2 \times 1 \times 3}{2^2(3-1)48}\right]^{3-1} \left[\frac{2 \times 1 \times 4}{2^2(4-1)48}\right]^{4-1}$$

$$= \frac{1}{48} \times \frac{1}{48} \times \left(\frac{1}{64}\right)^2 \times \left(\frac{1}{72}\right)^3$$

$$= 2.83897 \times 10^{-13}$$

TABLE 2.9. *An OMEP with 16 rows, two attributes with two levels, one attribute with three levels and one attribute with four levels*

0	0	0	0
0	1	1	1
0	0	2	2
0	1	2	3
1	0	1	2
1	1	0	3
1	0	2	0
1	1	2	1
0	0	2	3
0	1	2	2
0	0	0	1
0	1	1	0
1	0	2	1
1	1	2	0
1	0	1	3
1	1	0	2

If we use the generator (1111) (a shorthand way of saying that we will add 1 mod 2 to the first two attributes, 1 mod 3 to the third and 1 mod 4 to the fourth), we get 16 pairs which are 96.8% efficient since $\det(C) = 2.25718 \times 10^{-13}$ and so we get

$$\text{D-eff} = \left[\frac{\det(C_d)}{\det(C_{M,opt})} \right]^{\frac{1}{p}} = \left[\frac{2.25718 \times 10^{-13}}{2.83897 \times 10^{-13}} \right]^{\frac{1}{7}} = 96.8\%.$$

By considering the C_M matrix we can see that all effects are independently estimated except for the linear and cubic components of the attribute with four levels (since all the other off-diagonal elements of C_M are 0).

$$C_M = \begin{bmatrix} \frac{1}{48} & 0 & 0 & 0 & 0 & 0 & 0 \\ 0 & \frac{1}{48} & 0 & 0 & 0 & 0 & 0 \\ 0 & 0 & \frac{7}{384} & 0 & 0 & 0 & 0 \\ 0 & 0 & 0 & \frac{21}{1664} & 0 & 0 & 0 \\ 0 & 0 & 0 & 0 & \frac{1}{80} & 0 & \frac{1}{240} \\ 0 & 0 & 0 & 0 & 0 & \frac{1}{96} & 0 \\ 0 & 0 & 0 & 0 & \frac{1}{240} & 0 & \frac{3}{160} \end{bmatrix}$$

If we use the generators (1111) and (1112), we get 32 pairs which are 98.4% efficient and again the linear and cubic components are not independently estimated. If we use the generators (1111), (1112) and (1113), we get 48 pairs that are 99.1% efficient and all effects are independently estimated (so the C_M matrix is diagonal).

If we use choice sets of size 3, then $S_1 = S_2 = 2$ and $S_3 = S_4 = 3$ and the generators (1111) for the second options and (1122) for the third options we get 16 choice sets of size $m = 3$ that are optimal (have the largest possible value of $\det(C_M)$).

If we use choice sets of size 4, the generators (1111) for the first options, (1022) for the second options and (0123) for the third options, we get 16 choice sets of size 4 that are 99.96% efficient and have a diagonal C_M matrix. If instead we use the generators (1111), (1012) and (0123), the linear and quadratic components of the three-level attribute are not independent. This shows the importance of the particular generators used when the initial array does not have all levels of all attributes appearing equally often. If instead we use the OMEP in Table 2.10 (available in Sloane, 2005), all attributes have all levels appearing equally often.

7. NEAR-OPTIMAL DESIGNS FOR MAIN EFFECTS PLUS INTERACTION EFFECTS

To construct an optimal or near-optimal choice experiment to estimate main effects plus two-factor interactions, we need to start with a complete factorial or a fractional factorial of resolution 4 or 5, preferably with equal replication of levels for

TABLE 2.10. *An OMEP with 24 rows, two attributes with two levels, one attribute with three levels and one attribute with four levels*

0	0	0	0
1	1	0	0
0	0	1	0
1	1	1	0
0	0	2	0
1	1	2	0
1	0	0	1
0	1	0	1
1	0	1	1
0	1	1	1
1	0	2	1
0	1	2	1
0	0	0	2
1	1	0	2
0	0	1	2
1	1	1	2
0	0	2	2
1	1	2	2
1	0	0	3
0	1	0	3
1	0	1	3
0	1	1	3
1	0	2	3
0	1	2	3

each attribute, depending on how many two-factor interactions are to be estimated. We can evaluate $C_{MI} = B_{MI} \Lambda B'_{MI}$ and if the attributes all have two levels, then the efficiency can be calculated, otherwise we can compare values of $\det(C_{MI})$ for various designs.

In the next example we consider a design for six attributes, three with two levels and three with four levels, where we are interested in the main effects of the binary attributes and the linear and quadratic components of the four-level attributes and the linear × linear interaction of each pair of the four-level attributes. The choice sets are of size $m = 2$. The theory behind these ideas is developed in Burgess and Street (2005).

Example 8

Once again we need to find a suitable design and collapse levels. In this case, we find a design of resolution 4 with 6 attributes each with four levels (oa.64.6.4.3 in Sloane (2005)) and we collapse the first three attributes so that they each have only two levels with equal replication. This design is given in Table 2.11.

TABLE 2.11. *A resolution 4 fractional factorial with six attributes, three with two levels and three with four levels*

0	0	0	0	0	0	0	0	0	1	3	2	1	0	0	2	1	3	1	0	0	3	2	1
0	0	0	1	1	1	0	0	0	0	2	3	1	0	0	3	0	2	1	0	0	2	3	0
0	0	1	2	2	2	0	0	1	3	1	0	1	0	1	0	3	1	1	0	1	1	0	3
0	0	1	3	3	3	0	0	1	2	0	1	1	0	1	1	2	0	1	0	1	0	1	2
0	0	0	1	2	3	0	0	0	0	1	1	1	0	0	3	3	0	1	0	0	2	0	2
0	0	0	0	3	2	0	0	0	1	0	0	1	0	0	2	2	1	1	0	0	3	1	3
0	0	1	3	0	1	0	0	1	2	3	3	1	0	1	1	1	2	1	0	1	0	2	0
0	0	1	2	1	0	0	0	1	3	2	2	1	0	1	0	0	3	1	0	1	1	3	1
0	1	0	2	3	1	0	1	0	3	0	3	1	1	0	0	2	2	1	1	0	1	1	0
0	1	0	3	2	0	0	1	0	2	1	2	1	1	0	1	3	3	1	1	0	0	0	1
0	1	1	0	1	3	0	1	1	1	2	1	1	1	1	2	0	0	1	1	1	3	3	2
0	1	1	1	0	2	0	1	1	0	3	0	1	1	1	3	1	1	1	1	1	2	2	3
0	1	0	3	1	2	0	1	0	2	2	0	1	1	0	1	0	1	1	1	0	0	3	3
0	1	0	2	0	3	0	1	0	3	3	1	1	1	0	0	1	0	1	1	0	1	2	2
0	1	1	1	3	0	0	1	1	0	0	2	1	1	1	3	2	3	1	1	1	2	1	1
0	1	1	0	2	1	0	1	1	1	1	3	1	1	1	2	3	2	1	1	1	3	0	0

Now we need to construct the appropriate B matrix. In this case, we will have one row for the main effect for each of the two-level attributes, two rows for each of the three four-level attributes, one for the linear component and one for the quadratic component, and finally we will have three linear × linear contrasts for the three pairs of four-level attributes. Thus, we see that B has $3 + (2 \times 3) + 3 = 12$ rows. To get the rows for main effects we need only substitute "−1" for "0" for the two-level attributes and we create two rows for each of the four-level attributes. In the first "0, 1, 2, 3" are replaced by "−3, −1, 1, 3", respectively, and in the second "0, 1, 2, 3" are replaced by "1, −1, −1, 1", respectively. For the linear × linear interaction the levels of both attributes involved in the interaction need to be considered. So 00 is replaced by $-3 \times 1 = -3$, 01 by $-3 \times -1 = 3$, 02 by $-3 \times -1 = 3$ and so on.

Remember that the treatment combinations in the complete factorial label the columns of B. Thus, the first 6 columns of B are labelled by treatment combinations (000000), (000001), (000002), (000003), (000010) and (000011) and the last six columns by treatment combinations (111322), (111323), (111330), (111331), (111332) and (111333). These columns of the B matrix are given in Table 2.12.

Adding the generator (111111) to the design given in Table 2.11 results in 64 choice sets with $\det(C_{MI}) = 9.201 \times 10^{-36}$. Using three generators (111131), (111312) and (111223), results in 192 choice sets with $\det(C_{MI}) = 2.372 \times 10^{-35}$. In both cases the C_{MI} matrix is diagonal so all effects are uncorrelated. More discussion about the choice of generators may be found in Street et al. (2005) and Street and Burgess (2006).

TABLE 2.12. *B matrix for the first six and last six treatment combinations of example 8*

Effect	Contrasts												
A	−1	−1	−1	−1	−1	−1	...	1	1	1	1	1	1
B	−1	−1	−1	−1	−1	−1		1	1	1	1	1	1
C	−1	−1	−1	−1	−1	−1		1	1	1	1	1	1
D (lin)	−3	−3	−3	−3	−3	−3	...	3	3	3	3	3	3
D (quad)	1	1	1	1	1	1		1	1	1	1	1	1
E (lin)	−3	−3	−3	−3	−1	−1	...	1	1	3	3	3	3
E (quad)	1	1	1	1	−1	−1		−1	−1	1	1	1	1
F (lin)	−3	−1	1	3	−3	−1	...	1	3	−3	−1	1	3
F (quad)	1	−1	−1	1	1	−1		−1	1	1	−1	−1	1
DE (lin × lin)	9	9	9	9	3	3	...	3	3	9	9	9	9
DF (lin × lin)	9	3	−3	−9	9	3		3	9	−9	−3	3	9
EF (lin × lin)	9	3	−3	−9	3	1		1	3	−9	−3	3	9

8. DESIGNS WITH "NONE OF THESE"

Although many health settings require that the patient choose some form of inter-vention, there are situations when it makes sense to give the respondent the opportunity not to choose any of the options from a choice set, i.e. to include a "none-of-these" option in every choice set. One such situation is described in Chapter 3.

The Λ matrix now has an additional row and column, corresponding to the none option but is defined as before. The contrast matrix B_n is given by

$$B_n = \begin{bmatrix} B & \mathbf{0} \\ \frac{1}{d}\mathbf{j} & \frac{-L}{d} \end{bmatrix}$$

where $\mathbf{j}$ is a row vector with all entries equal to 1 and $\mathbf{0}$ is a column vector of 0s and $d^2 = L(L+1)$.

Street and Burgess (2007) show that the same designs that are optimal for the esti-mation of main effects or main effects plus two-factor interactions are also optimal when a "none-of-these" option is to be included in each choice set. The determinant of $C_{M,n}$ matrix of the optimal is given by

$$\det (C_{M,n,\text{opt}}) = \frac{m(L+1)}{L(m+1)^2} \prod_{q=1}^{k} \left[\frac{2S_q l_q + m(l_q - 1)}{(m+1)^2 (l_q - 1)L} \right]^{l_q - 1}$$

Example 9

Once again we consider the seven designs described in example 3. In Table 2.13 we give the efficiency of each of these designs when used to estimate main effects or main

TABLE 2.13. *Seven choice experiments, three options per choice set, for a design with $k = 2$, $l_1 = 2$ and $l_2 = 3$*

Effects	Main effects		ME and 2fi	
Type	Forced (%)	With "none" (%)	Forced (%)	With "none" (%)
Design				
P_3	0	80.9	0	95.5
P_1	76.3	89.4	99.0	99.8
P_2	100	100	96.5	99.2
P_1 and P_3	75.9	89.1	99.4	99.8
P_2 and P_3	90.9	96.2	98.0	99.5
P_1 and P_2	84.6	93.1	99.8	99.9
P_1, P_2 and P_3	83.2	92.4	100	100

effects plus two-factor interactions and when presented as experiments where one of the options must be chosen ("forced choice") or when a "neither-of-these" option is included in each choice set ("none"). We have that $L = 6$, $m = 2$, $S_1 = S_2 = 1$, so

$$\det(C_{M, n, \text{opt}}) = \frac{2(6+1)}{6(2+1)^2}\left[\frac{2\times1\times2+2(2-1)}{(2+1)^2(2-1)6}\right]^{2-1}\left[\frac{2\times1\times3+2(3-1)}{(2+1)^2(3-1)6}\right]^{3-1}$$

Observe that all of the designs (including P_3) can now be used to estimate all of the effects. However, although all of the designs are highly efficient within the class of designs in which a none option is included in each choice set, the designs are much less efficient than the best forced choice experiment. On the other hand, the inclusion of a "none" option may make the task much more realistic and so mean that the respondents perform it more thoughtfully. Also remember that usually the C_{MI} matrix for the estimation of main effects and two-factor interactions from a small choice experiment results in estimates for the effects that are correlated.

9. DESIGNS WITH A COMMON BASE ALTERNATIVE

In this setting, one option, often the current situation, appears in each choice set. We call this the *common base alternative*. We assume that the choice sets are of size $m = 2$ throughout this section. To get an optimal design for this situation the common base alternative needs to be one of the treatment combinations in the OMEP; this can always be the case by choosing a suitable labelling of the levels. Any level changes that give the right option in the fraction can be used. Thus, if 00. . .0 is in the OMEP, assign level 0 of attribute 1 to the level of attribute 1 for the common base, and so on for the other attributes.

If all the levels of all the attributes are equally replicated, we can give an explicit expression for $\det(C_{M,c})$. We will let $p = \Sigma^k_{q=1}(l_q - 1)$, the total degrees of freedom for main effects, and $L = \prod^k_{q=1}l_q$ (the total number of treatment combinations) and we will let F be a resolution 3 FFD with equal replication of levels and with f treatment combinations. Choose any treatment combination (i.e. row) in F to be the common base and create $(f-1)$ pairs by pairing the common base with each of the other treatment combinations in turn. This is commonly known in the health economics literature as choosing a constant comparator.

Then

$$\det(C_{M, c, \text{opt}}) = \frac{1+p}{(4(f-1))^p}\left(\frac{f}{L}\right)^p$$

Hence, we can evaluate the efficiency of the choice experiment with the common base. See Street and Burgess (2007) for more details.

Example 10

Consider an experiment where there are four attributes describing each option. Three of the attributes have two levels and one has four levels. So $p = 1+1+1+3 = 6$ and $L = 2\times2\times2\times4 = 32$. Using an OMEP with eight runs and using any treatment combination as a common base gives a design with $f = 8$ and so $\det(C_{M,c}) = 3.55\times10^{-12}$

while using the complete factorial (so $f = 32$) and letting any treatment combination be the common base gives a design with $\det(C_{M,c}) = 1.93 \times 10^{-12}$.

In Scott (2002) a similar experiment was carried out with four attributes, two with two levels, one with three levels and one with four levels, and using 16 choice sets. In this case the efficiency depends on the treatment combination chosen to be the common base. If the common base has the three-level attribute which appears eight times, then $\det(C_{M,c})$ is less than if the common base has either of the other levels of the three-level attribute which appear four times each (see Street and Burgess, 2007).

10. FURTHER COMMENTS

Throughout this chapter we have assumed that we want to have as few choice sets as possible to estimate the effects of interest. It is possible to include more choice sets than the construction gives by repeating the construction using a different OMEP, different generators or both, and combining the choice sets obtained from the two constructions.

All efficiencies are quoted assuming no prior knowledge about the values of the coefficients in the utility function. If indicative values of the coefficients are known, it may be possible to improve on the designs given here but these designs will still be optimal unless there are one or two options which are extremely popular (or unpopular). In such cases, the designs developed here easily identify the extreme options (Street and Burgess, 2006). Some authors use prior information to specify a prior distribution for the unknown parameter values and use that when designing the choice sets (see, e.g. Sandor and Wedel, 2001).

The techniques that we have described in the paper do not seem to lend themselves to avoiding dominated alternatives automatically. The use of an initial OMEP that does not contain 00. . .0 and the use of a generator with different levels for some pairs of attributes are both techniques that will help avoid having many choice sets with dominating alternatives. Street and Burgess (2006) give some specific constructions and advice.

The number of choice sets that respondents can reliably complete has been the subject of some debate (Louviere et al., 2000; Louviere, 2001) but if the number of choice sets that result from the constructions given here are larger than one respondent can complete, we recommend randomly dividing the choice sets into smaller sets as long as there are a minimum of 3–4 responses for each choice set.

11. CONCLUSION

This chapter describes a technique for the construction of optimal designs for the estimation of main effects for choice experiments of any size, be they forced choice experiments or choice experiments in which a "none-of-these" option is included in each choice set. The same technique can be used to give near-optimal designs for the estimation of (subsets of) two-factor interaction terms, as well as main effects. The techniques require less effort than variants on thoughtful pairing and give designs with a more reliable performance than random pairing.

ENDNOTES

[1] A feature of the experiment given in this example is the fact that all the attributes are ordered in utility terms, such that the first level for each attribute will always be preferred to the second level, and so on. This feature can give rise to concerns about dominance, whereby for particular choice sets, all the attributes in one option are preferred to all the attributes in the other options, as in the choice set in the table. Where dominance occurs, the choice set cannot provide any information about how respondents trade-off between alternatives. This feature can arise in any choice experiment where the attributes have a clear preference ordering, particularly if some or all of the attributes are expressed in quantitative rather than qualitative terms. Dominance is discussed briefly in Section 10.

[2] It should be noted that this decomposition assumes that we are using design codes, which are equally spaced. If we use the actual attribute levels and there were non-equidistant these "standard" orthogonal polynomial coefficients cannot be used so different polynomial need to be defined (see e.g. Narula (1978))

REFERENCES

Atkinson, A.C. and Donev, A.N. 1992. Optimum Experimental Designs. Oxford: Clarendon Press.

Burgess, L. and Street, D. 2003a. Optimal designs for 2^k choice experiments. *Communications in Statistics – Theory and Methods*, vol 32, 2185–2206.

Burgess, L. and Street, D. 2003b. Optimal Designs for Asymmetric Choice Experiments. Sydney: Department of Mathematical Sciences, University of Technology.

Burgess, L. and Street, D. 2005. Optimal designs for choice experiments with asymmetric attributes. *Journal of Statistical Planning and Inference*, vol 134, 288–301.

Dey, A. and Mukerjee, R. 1999. Fractional Factorial Designs. New York: Wiley.

El-Helbawy, A.T. and Bradley, R.A. 1978. Treatment contrasts in paired comparisons: large-sample results, applications and some optimal designs. *Journal of the American Statistical Association*, vol 73, 831–839.

Healy, M.J.R. 2000. Matrices for Statistics. Oxford: Oxford University Press.

Huber, J. and Zwerina, K. 1996. The importance of utility balance in efficient choice designs. *Journal of Marketing Research*, vol 33, 307–317.

Insall, M. and Weisstein, E.W. 2006. Modular Arithmetic. From *MathWorld* – A Wolfram Web Resource. http://mathworld.wolfram.com/ModularArithmetic.html

Kuehl, R. 1999. Design of Experiments: Statistical Principles of Research Design and Analysis. Pacific Grove, CA: Duxbury Press.

Longworth, L., Ratcliffe, J. and Boulton, M. 2001. Investigating women's preferences for intrapartum care: home versus hospital births. *Health and Social Care in the Community*, vol 9, 404–413.

Louviere, J. 2001. Choice experiments: an overview of concepts and issues. The choice modelling approach to environmental valuation. Bennett, J. and Blamey, R. (eds). Northhampton: Edward Elgar, pp 13–36.

Louviere, J.J., Hensher, D.A. and Swait, J.D. 2000. Stated choice methods: analysis and applications. Cambridge: Cambridge University Press.

McKenzie, L., Cairns, J. and Osman, L. 2001. Symptom-based outcome measures for asthma: the use of discrete choice methods to assess patient preferences. *Health Policy*, vol 57, 193–204.

Narula, S. 1978. Orthogonal polynomial regression for unequal spacing and frequencies. *Journal of Quality Technology*, vol 10, 170–179.

Phillips, K.A., Maddala, T. and Johnson, F.R. 2002. Measuring preferences for health care interventions using conjoint analysis: an application to HIV testing. *Health Services Research*, vol 37, 1681–1705.

Ryan, M. 1999. Using conjoint analysis to take account of patient preferences and go beyond health outcomes: an application to in vitro fertilisation. *Social Science and Medicine*, vol 48, 535–546.

Ryan, M. and Farrar, S. 2000. Using conjoint analysis to elicit preferences for health care. *British Medical Journal*, vol 320, 1530–1533.

Ryan, M. and Gerard, K. 2003. Using discrete choice experiments to value health care programmes: current practice and future research reflections. *Applied Health Economics and Health Policy*, vol 2, 55–64.

Ryan, M. and Hughes, J. 1997. Using conjoint analysis to assess women's preferences for miscarriage management. *Health Economics*, vol 6, 261–273.

Ryan, M., McIntosh, E., Dean, T. and Old, P. 2000. Trade-offs between location and waiting times in the provision of health care: the case of elective surgery on the Isle of Wight. *Journal of Public Health Medicine*, vol 22, 202–210.

Ryan, M., Bates, A., Eastmond, C.J. and Ludbrook, A. 2001. Use of discrete choice experiments to elicit preferences. *Quality in Health Care*, vol 10 (Suppl 1), i55–i60.

Sandor, Z. and Wedel, M. 2001. Designing conjoint discrete choice experiments using managers' prior beliefs. *Journal of Marketing Research*, vol 38, 430–444.

Scott, A. 2002. Identifying and analysing dominant preferences in discrete choice experiments: an application in health care. *Journal of Economic Psychology*, vol 23, 383–398.

Sloane, N.J.A. 2005. Tables of Orthogonal Arrays. http://www.research.att.com/~njas/oadir/

Street, D. and Burgess, L. 2004a. Optimal and near-optimal pairs for the estimation of effects in 2-level choice experiments. *Journal of Statistical Planning and Inference*, vol 118, 185–199.

Street, D. and Burgess, L. 2004b. Optimal stated preference choice experiments when all choice sets contain a specific option. *Statistical Methodology*, vol 1, 37–45.

Street, D. and Burgess, L. 2007. The Construction of Optimal Stated Choice Experiments: Theory and Methods. New York: Wiley.

Street, D.J. and Burgess, L. and Louviere, J. 2005. Quick and easy choice sets: constructing optimal and nearly optimal stated choice experiments. *International Journal of Research Marketing*, vol 22, 459–470.

van der Pol, M. and Cairns, J. 2001. Estimating time preferences for health using discrete choice experiments. *Social Science and Medicine*, vol 52, 1459–1470.

CHAPTER 3

PRACTICAL ISSUES IN CONDUCTING A DISCRETE CHOICE EXPERIMENT

MANDY RYAN AND VERITY WATSON

Health Economics Research Unit, University of Aberdeen, UK

KAREN GERARD

Faculty of Medicine, Health and Life Sciences, University of Southampton, UK

1. INTRODUCTION

This chapter walks the reader through the stages of a discrete choice experiment (DCE) application drawing on concepts introduced in Chapters 1 and 2. A case study eliciting women's preferences for prenatal screening is used to illustrate the points (Ryan et al., 2005). It should be noted that this data was collected several years ago, and therefore adopted old methods of experimental design. The sample size is also small. We have chosen it because it demonstrates nicely the many potential uses of a DCE, it addressed a policy-relevant question at the time, and it represents one of the few studies in health economics where the scientists (geneticists) worked with the evaluators (economists) and implementers (obstetricians) to look at development, evaluation and implementation of prenatal screening programmes. In Section 2 the background to the study is described, and the attributes and levels of the DCE defined. Section 3 describes the experimental design used. Based on criteria of a good design presented in Chapter 2, the properties of this design are assessed. Section 4 discusses issues that arise in data input. Consideration is given to the formation of the data matrix for analysis for two commonly used statistical software packages, LIMDEP and STATA. In Section 5, we present the analysis commands for these software packages and use them to estimate a multinomial logit (MNL) model. Further we interpret the output from this study, showing its relevance for policy. Section 6 provides some concluding comments on key issues for design, data input, analysis and interpretation. In the Appendix, the efficiency of the experimental design used in this chapter is assessed by Leonie Burgess and Deborah Street, using the methods presented in Chapter 2. They also suggest a more efficient method of designing this experiment.

M. Ryan, K. Gerard and M. Amaya-Amaya (eds.), Using Discrete Choice
Experiments to Value Health and Health Care, 73–97.
© 2008 *Springer.*

2. IDENTIFICATION OF ATTRIBUTES AND LEVELS

As noted in Chapter 1, DCEs are an attribute-based measure of value. Thus, the first stage in a DCE is to define the attributes and levels. The application presented in this chapter is concerned with eliciting women's preferences for prenatal diagnosis (Ryan et al., 2005). The attributes were defined from the policy question. In Scotland, prenatal diagnosis by karyotype analysis is offered to pregnant women at increased risk of fetal chromosome abnormality. This is the most informative prenatal diagnostic test, detecting common abnormalities (e.g. Down's syndrome) as well as other rare chromosomal disorders and the gender of the fetus. Results are generally reported within 13–21 days. Recently, a rapid test has been developed to detect common abnormalities (e.g. Down's syndrome). This test can produce results within 2 days of sampling, but does not provide information on other rare chromosomal disorders nor on the gender of the fetus. The Scottish Executive is now funding this rapid test for all at-risk pregnancies in Scotland. With over 30,000 amniocenteses performed in the UK each year, this policy has an obvious cost implication. There is now a debate about whether rapid diagnosis should be used as the sole diagnostic tool for certain referral groups (e.g. those at risk of Down's syndrome on biochemical screening) (UK Department of Health, 2003).

In this study, we used a DCE to help address this question. The DCE was used to estimate the trade-offs individuals were willing to make between waiting time and level of information, as well as to estimate marginal willingness to pay (MWTP) for proposed "simple and quick" (rapid analysis of specific chromosomes) versus "comprehensive and longer" (karyotype analysis) prenatal diagnosis programmes. Using the results of the MNL model we consider the policy implications of introducing a new screening test and calculate the resulting welfare (compensating variation) of changing the available screening tests.

The policy question resulted in three attributes being chosen: information received from the test; the number of days wait from having the test to receiving the result; and cost of the screening test. Including the price proxy allowed us to estimate willingness to pay (WTP), a monetary measure of benefit, for individual attributes as well as different attribute combinations for the prenatal screening test. The "information received from the test" attribute took two levels, "comprehensive" (whether or not the fetus had Down's syndrome, other rare chromosomal conditions and gender) and "simple" (whether or not the fetus had Down's syndrome). The waiting time attribute took four levels: 2, 8, 16 and 30 days, these levels were based on current waiting times. The cost attribute also took four levels: £20, £100, £250 and £500 per test (see Table 3.1). These levels were based on a contingent valuation study conducted during pilot work to estimate WTP for prenatal screening. This is a recommended approach for assessing levels to include for the price proxy in DCEs.

Following on from Chapter 1, we are modelling the probability a respondent will select a specified screening test. The probability of choosing a given alternative is determined by the indirect utility. Here, we assume utility is linear and additive:

$$V = \beta_1 SIMPLE + \beta_2 COMP + \beta_3 WAIT + \beta_4 COST \qquad (3.1)$$

TABLE 3.1. *Attributes and levels*

Attributes	Levels
Level of information	Comprehensive, simple
Number of days' wait for results	2, 8, 16, 30
Cost to you (£)	20, 100, 250, 500

where V is the utility derived from a given prenatal screening programme as opposed to no screening, SIMPLE refers to having simple information rather than no information, COMP refers to having comprehensive information rather than no information, WAIT refers to the number of days waiting for results and COST refers to the cost of the screening test.

3. EXPERIMENTAL DESIGN

The attributes and levels resulted in 32 profiles (two attributes at four levels and one attribute at two levels = $2^1 \times 4^2$), and 496 possible pairwise choices ((32*31)/2). Experimental design techniques were employed to reduce the number of choices to be presented to individuals. As noted in Chapter 2, at the design stage the researcher should consider the specification of the utility function to be estimated, taking account of potential interaction terms, non-linearities and the choice between labelled and generic experiments. Consistent with most applications of DCEs, within health economics and elsewhere, only main effects were estimated, with non-linearities and interactions assumed negligible. Further, a generic design was employed.

The creation of choices in this study followed older design methods rather than those outlined in Chapter 2. The software package SPEED (Bradley, 1991) was used to reduce the full factorial design of 32 profiles to a fractional factorial design (FFD) of 16 profiles. From these 16 profiles choice sets were created by randomly allocating them into eight choice sets with the further restriction that each choice set included both a simple information profile and a comprehensive information profile. These choice sets are shown in Table 3.2.

A relevant question when designing a DCE is whether to include an opt-out choice. For this specific study, an opt out should be included since pregnant women may choose not to have a screening test. When including an opt out it is crucial to define the levels of the attributes. These may be included in the choice sets presented to ensure that respondents understand the implications of choosing the opt out. This study defined the opt-out alternative as receiving no information with zero days wait for results and zero cost. Table 3.3 shows incorporation of the opt-out alternative into the choice set.

3.1. Checking Properties

Chapter 2 outlined the characteristics of a good design, and how to measure D-efficiency. Below we consider level balance, orthogonality and minimum overlap

TABLE 3.2. *DCE design*

		Alternative A			Alternative B	
Choice	INFO	WAIT (days)	Cost (£s)	INFO	WAIT (days)	COST (£s)
1	Comprehensive	16	500	Simple	2	250
2	Comprehensive	8	20	Simple	30	100
3	Comprehensive	30	500	Simple	8	250
4	Comprehensive	16	250	Simple	2	500
5	Comprehensive	8	100	Simple	30	20
6	Comprehensive	30	250	Simple	8	500
7	Comprehensive	16	100	Simple	2	20
8	Comprehensive	2	100	Simple	16	20

TABLE 3.3. *Example of choice with "opt-out" choice*

Choice 1	Test A	Test B	No test
Information	Simple	Comprehensive	No information
Waiting time to receiving results (days)	2	8	No result
Cost of screening test (£)	20	100	0
Please place a tick on the screening test you would choose	☐	☐	☐

for the design in Table 3.2. Given we had no a priori information on parameter estimates utility balance is not considered. It should be noted, as mentioned above, that the methods adopted to design the DCE here (taking FFD and randomly pairing into choice sets) are no longer recommended. What follows does, however, demonstrate how to consider the characteristics of a good design and provides some insight of design efficiency when optimal methods are not employed. The D-efficiency of the above design is considered in the Appendix written by Leonie Burgess and Deborah Street, based on the methods presented in Chapter 2. This Appendix then constructs a design for this case study using the methods in Chapter 2, and compares the efficiency and properties of this design with the one above.

3.1.1. Level balance

Level balance requires all levels of each attribute to appear with equal frequency across profiles. Thus, for a two-level attribute each level should appear in 50% of the profiles, for a four-level attribute each level should appear in 25% of the profiles. This is reported in Table 3.4. Before the opt out was introduced there was level balance in the design, with the four levels of cost and waiting time each appearing 25% of the time, and the two levels of information each appearing 50% of the time. However, introducing the neither option has compromised the level balance of the design.

3.1.2. Orthogonality

This criterion requires that the levels of each attribute vary independently of each other. In Chapter 2, Street et al. note that orthogonality has been interpreted to mean different things by different people. One common interpretation is to look at the correlations between two attributes, and if this is zero or low, then it is defined as orthogonal. When looking at an orthogonal main effects plans this is what is being referred to. The design used in this case study was generated from a main effects plan taken from SPEED. The correlations for this design are shown in Table 3.5, and are seen to be low. Such correlations can be estimated in any statistical analysis package. The appropriate

TABLE 3.4. *Level balance with opt out*

Attribute	Level	No. of appearances in DCE (%)
Information	No information	8
Information	Simple	8
Information	Comprehensive	8
Waiting time to result	0 days	8
Waiting time to result	2 days	4
Waiting time to result	8 days	4
Waiting time to result	16 days	4
Waiting time to result	30 days	4
Cost of screening	£0	8
Cost of screening	£20	4
Cost of screening	£100	4
Cost of screening	£250	4
Cost of screening	£300	4

TABLE 3.5. *Correlation coefficients of the SPEED design*

	Information	Wait	Cost
Information	1	0.0679	−0.0819
Wait	0.0679	1	−0.0489
Cost	−0.0819	−0.0489	1

test depends on the nature of the attributes and an introductory statistics book will tell you what test should be used. Hensher et al. (2005) note the Pearson product moment (PPM) correlation coefficient is a good approximation for all correlations.

Street et al. in Chapter 2 note that within a DCE it is not the attributes or options that need to be uncorrelated, but the estimates obtained from the choice experiment. They note that the way to judge this is to test if the information matrix is diagonal, indicating all components of all effects are independent. This definition of orthogonality is considered in the Appendix.

3.1.3. Minimum overlap

This criterion requires that the probability of a repeated attribute level within a choice set be minimised. This ensures that the experiment provides maximum information regarding respondents' trade-offs; if an attribute takes the same level in each choice, no information is revealed about preferences. From the design in Table 3.2, within each choice set attribute levels are different.

3.1.4. Statistical efficiency

As noted in Chapters 1 and 2, more recently researchers have attempted to maximise some measure of statistical efficiency when designing DCEs. The Appendix presents the statistical efficiency of the design used in this application, using the methods developed in Chapter 2. Our design is calculated to be 88.5% efficient relative to the optimal design. Burgess and Street suggest an alternative simple way to design the same experiment, resulting in 16 choices with a D-efficiency of 98.58% relative to the optimal design or eight choices with a D-efficiency of 99.6% relative to the optimal design. They also note, from the estimation of the C matrix, that whilst the pairs of main effects are correlated in our design, all effects are uncorrelated in their two proposed designs. Another important observation from this Appendix is that the initial design from SPEED does not appear to be of resolution 3 (i.e. for any two attributes, the combinations of pairs of levels do not appear with proportional frequencies).

4. DATA PREPARATION

Following the generation of a design for the DCE this has to be incorporated into a questionnaire that will be used to collect the data. All the generic issues of survey research apply here. We recommend readers unfamiliar with survey research consult reference texts such as Dillman (2000) and Presser et al. (2004). This study was administered as a pencil-and-paper questionnaire to pregnant women attending the maternity hospital in Aberdeen for their booking scan. Fifty women were invited to take part in the study. It is recognised that the sample size for this study is very small, and probably at the minimum level for any reliable statistical estimates.

The practitioner should be aware of the requirements of the statistical software packages they are using to analyse the data. This section presents useful tips to prepare data for analysis in two commonly used packages: STATA and LIMDEP.

As with any data set it is useful to start by ordering the variables in some logical way. One suggestion is to present all the variables in a sequence that first describes how the data are organised (e.g. respondent identifier, choice set identified), then present the independent variables from the experimental design followed by the dependent variable. Data sets also include other variables relating to the individual such as socio-economic characteristics. One feature common to all DCE data sets is that respondents answer more than one discrete choice question, resulting in multiple observations for each individual. Further, choice sets presented to individuals contain two or more alternatives, thus, we have multiple observations for each choice set (the chosen alternative and the not chosen alternative(s)). The number of observations in a data set depends on the number of respondents, the number of choice sets per respondent and the number of alternatives in each choice set. For instance, in the pre-natal study there are three alternatives in each choice set (two screening tests and the "opt out"). Thus, each choice set contributes three observations to the data set (one chosen alternative and two non-chosen alternatives). Further, each respondent is presented with eight choices. As each choice contributes three observations and each respondent faces eight choices, there are 24 observations per respondent (eight choices × three observations per choice). A sample of the data for the case study is shown in Table 3.6. This shows the first, second and eighth choices for respondent 1 and the first and second choices for respondent 2.

The first variable is an identification variable unique to each respondent (id). This is followed by a variable representing the choice number in the DCE questionnaire (*cno*), as there were eight choices *cno* will range from 1 to 8. Within each choice, the alternatives presented to respondents are described by *alt* (where *alts* = 1 represents the first alternative in the choice set (test A in Table 3.2)). Following this *cset* indicates how many alternatives were in a choice set. In this case, there were always three alternatives. Following this there are three variables *alt1*, *alt2*, and *alt3* these identify each of the alternatives, thus *alt1* takes the value 1 for all observations arising from alternative 1 and 0 otherwise, and so on for *alt2*, and *alt3*. The variables *alt*, *cset*, and *alt1*, *alt2* and *alt3* are required by LIMDEP for the statistical analysis. The variable *c_id* is required if analysis is conducted in STATA, where this *c_id* takes a unique value for each choice set, this identifies the observations that when grouped together represent *each* unique choice. For individual 1 this will range from 1 to 8, and for individual 2 this will range from 9 to 16. Thus, for choice 3 presented to respondent 2 *c_id* = 11.

The attributes in this study are a mixture of quantitative and qualitative variables. The two quantitative variables (wait and cost) take values in the data set that

TABLE 3.6. General choice data entry format

Id	Cno	Alt	Cset	Alt1	Alt2	Alt3	C_id	Infos	Infoc	Info0	Wait	Cost	Choice	Age
1	1	1	3	1	0	0	1	0	1	0	16	500	1	35
1	1	2	3	0	1	0	1	1	0	0	2	250	0	35
1	1	3	3	0	0	1	1	0	0	1	0	0	0	35
1	2	1	3	1	0	0	2	0	1	0	8	20	0	35
1	2	2	3	0	1	0	2	1	0	0	30	100	1	35
1	2	3	3	0	0	1	2	0	0	1	0	0	0	35
1	8	1	3	1	0	0	8	0	1	0	8	100	1	35
1	8	2	3	0	1	0	8	1	0	0	16	20	0	35
1	8	3	3	0	0	1	8	0	0	1	0	0	0	35
2	1	1	3	1	0	0	9	0	1	0	16	500	0	40
2	1	2	3	0	1	0	9	1	0	0	2	250	0	40
2	1	3	3	0	0	1	9	0	0	1	0	0	1	40
2	2	1	3	1	0	0	10	0	1	0	8	20	0	40
2	2	2	3	0	1	0	10	1	0	0	30	100	1	40
2	2	3	3	0	0	1	10	0	0	1	0	0	0	40

correspond to the levels presented in the questionnaire. The qualitative information variable was entered in the form of dummy coded variables. When including dummy coded variables the effect of a level of an attribute is estimated relative to a base comparator or reference point. An alternative approach for analysis is effects coding, where coefficients are estimated for all levels of attributes. For an example of effects coding, see Chapter 5. For more on dummy variable and effects coding within a DCE, see Louviere et al. (2000).

The three levels for the information attribute need to be represented: (1) simple information; (2) comprehensive information; and (3) no information. These are represented by three dummy variables *infos*, *infoc* and *info0*. Dummy variables take the value of 1 if the level is present in the alternative and 0 otherwise. For instance, the first alternative in choice set 1 is a test where comprehensive information is received, thus *infoc* = 1, with both *infos* and *info0* = 0. Further, it should be noted that in each choice set alternative 3 was the "opt out" and this was the same for all choice sets.

The dependent variable (*choice*) is the respondent's choice of test; test A, test B or "opt out". *Choice* is represented as a dichotomous variable taking the value of 1 for the chosen alternative and zero for both other alternatives. From Table 3.6 it is seen that respondent 1 chose alternative A in choice set 1, and alternative B in choice set 2.

Alongside DCE responses, information is collected about respondents' socio-economic characteristics such as *age*. Given each respondent has more than one row in the data set this information is copied on to each row related to an individual. From the example presented in Table 3.6 respondent 1 is 35 years old, while respondent 2 is 40 years old. Given socio-economic characteristics do not vary within a choice these can not be added into the model directly. Including interaction terms between respondent characteristics and attributes allows slope coefficients to differ across subgroups. For example, see Chapter 4 and Ryan (1999).

As an aside, most of the above can be set up before the data is collected. Often before administering a questionnaire to the sample, data are generated for the response variable. The model the researcher intends to use for estimation is then applied to this simulated data as a check that the data are correctly coded and the design allows the estimation of parameters of interest (see Section 3.1.2).

5. MODEL ESTIMATION AND INTERPRETATION

5.1. *Model Estimation*

Forty-nine respondents completed the questionnaire. Of these, 38 respondents completed all eight choices, 2 respondents completed seven choices, 3 respondents completed one choice and 6 respondents did not complete any of the choices. Thus, the number of individuals providing responses for the regression analysis is 43, providing responses to 321 completed choices and resulting in 963 observations.

Given respondents were asked to choose between three alternatives (two screening tests and no screening) data were analysed using an MNL model (see Chapter 1).

The command necessary for the estimation of this choice model in LIMDEP is as follows (LIMDEP, 2002):

```
NLOGIT
;lhs = choice,cset,alt
;choices = alt1,alt2,alt3
; model;
u(alt1) = B_simple*infos + B_comp*infoc + B_wait*wait + B_cost*cost/
u(alt2) = B_simple*infos + B_comp*infoc + B_wait*wait + B_cost*cost$
```

(Note U(alt3), the neither option, was normalised to zero, so it is not needed in the model specification.)

The first line specifies the NLOGIT package within LIMDEP, the second line tells the package the dependent variable and the variables LIMDEP requires to identify the choice sets (or which observations in choice "go together"). This form of the LIMDEP command specifies a utility function for each alternative. **B_simple, B_comp, B_wait,** and **B_cost** are the estimators, in this specification these are the same across the alternatives. This is not necessary and separate coefficient estimates could be obtained for each alternative. Note, within LIMDEP, it is important to end the command with the $.

The command necessary for the estimation of this choice model in STATA is as follows (Statacorp, 2005):

clogit choice infos infoc wait cost, group(c_id)

where clogit specifies the conditional logit model (this estimates McFadden's choice model and is interchangeable with the term MNL), the second object in the command (choice) is the dependent variable this is followed by the regressors. Other information required by STATA or options in the regression are separated from the model by a comma. In this case, it is required to tell STATA which observations to group together to represent one choice (c_id). Note: LIMDEP is not case or space sensitive and uses a comma delimiter, while STATA is case sensitive and uses a space delimiter.

5.2. Model Interpretation

Table 3.7 presents the results from the MNL model. In what follows, we look at how such information can be used at the policy level. Following Chapter 1, the goodness of fit of the model as explained by McFadden's R^2 is 0.146. The chi-squared statistic of 102.698, distributed with two degrees of freedom, indicates that the estimated model has improved explanatory power over a model where only constant terms were included.

5.2.1. Importance of attributes

When looking at the output of a DCE note whether the attributes are significant, and therefore having an impact on the probability of choosing an alternative. The negative and significant coefficients for the "waiting time" and "cost" attributes show respondents preferred these attributes to take lower levels. In other words, respondents were more likely to choose a prenatal test with a lower waiting time and

TABLE 3.7. *Results from multinomial logit model*

	Coefficient	t-statistic
Simple information (β_1)	1.965688	(8.21)
Comprehensive information (β_2)	2.251685	(8.93)
Waiting time (β_3)	−0.0513463	(−6.29)
Cost of screening (β_4)	−0.0028466	(−4.53)
Log-likelihood (at convergence)	−301.306	
Log-likelihood (constants only)	−352.655	
Chi-squared statistic (4-2 df)	102.698	
McFadden's R^2	0.146	
Adj McFadden's R^2	0.134	
Number of individuals	43	
Number of observations	963	

lower cost. These results were inline with expectations and provided support for the theoretical validity of the model. The positive and significant coefficients of "simple" information and "comprehensive" information indicated that respondents prefer having information to not having information, again providing support for the theoretical validity of the model. Further, given that the coefficient on "comprehensive" information is larger than that on "simple" information, then, *everything else equal*, respondents preferred "comprehensive" information to "simple" information.

5.2.2. Effect of attribute on utility
When interpreting these coefficients it is important to be aware of the unit of measurement: β_1 and β_2 show the change in utility in moving from having no information (i.e. not being screened) to having simple information (β_1) or comprehensive information (β_2). β_3 indicates the utility of a 1-day reduction in waiting time for results and β_4 the utility of a £1 reduction in cost.

5.2.3. Marginal rates of substitution
Trade-offs between attributes are calculated by the negative of the ratio of any two coefficients. It should be noted that the denominator is the measure that the trade-off is estimated in terms of. To calculate trade-offs in terms of waiting time, $-(\beta_1/\beta_3)$

would calculate how long the average respondent is willing to wait for "simple" information (rather than receiving no information), likewise $-(\beta_2/\beta_3)$ how long the average respondent is willing to wait for "comprehensive" information (rather than receiving no information).

The average respondent was willing to wait a maximum of 41 days for "simple" information $-(\beta_1/\beta_3)$ and 45 days for "comprehensive" information $-(\beta_1/\beta_3)$. If waiting times were longer than this for each of the tests, the average respondent would prefer not to be screened. This also implies that respondents required the "simple" information result 4 days sooner than the "comprehensive" information.

5.2.4. Marginal willingness to pay

When cost is included as the denominator in trade-off calculations, MWTP can be estimated. For example, *everything else equal*, respondents are willing to pay $-(\beta_1/\beta_4)$ for "simple" information and $-(\beta_2/\beta_4)$ for "comprehensive" information. Following this, the MWTP for comprehensive rather than simple, *everything else is equal*, is $-\{(\beta_2 - \beta_1)/\beta_4\}$ and the WTP for a day's reduction in waiting time is $-\{\beta_3/\beta_4\}$.

On average respondents MWTP for "simple" information is calculated be to £690.54 and for "comprehensive" information the MWTP = £791. The MWTP for the additional information contained in the "comprehensive" information over the "simple" information is £100.46 (£791–£690.54). The preference for lower waiting times, reflected by the MWTP of £18.03 $-(\beta_3/\beta_4)$ for a reduction in waiting time by one day.

5.2.5. Predicting clinic uptake rates

Consider two hypothetical screening services: *comprehensive* information where women wait 21 days for results and pay £10 and *simple* information where women wait 2 days for results and pay £5. Women also have the option of *no screening*. Equation 1.7 in Chapter 1 shows how the probability of take-up is estimated for any set of options. Before calculating the probability of uptake for each screening service, the indirect utility of each service is calculated:

$$
\begin{aligned}
V_{\text{comp}} &= 2.251685 + (-0.0028466 \times 10) + (-0.0513463 \times 21) \\
&= 2.25 - 0.028466 - 1.0782723 \\
&= 1.1449467 \\
V_{\text{simple}} &= 1.965688 + (-0.0028466 \times 5) + (-0.0513463 \times 2) \\
&= 1.965688 - 0.014233 - 0.1026926 \\
&= 1.8487621 \\
V_{\text{no screening}} &= 0
\end{aligned}
$$

Whilst the average respondent prefers comprehensive information, given the waiting time and cost of this screening programme the simple programme is preferred. This is indicated by the higher utility. Following this, the probability of uptake for screening *comprehensive, simple* and *no screening* are:

$$
\begin{aligned}
Pr\,(\text{comp}) &= e^{1.1449467}/e^{1.8487621} + e^{1.1449467} + e^{0} \\
&= 3.142273869/10.49422544 \\
&= 0.299428851
\end{aligned}
$$

$$Pr\,(\text{simple}) = e^{1.8487624}/e^{1.8487621} + e^{1.1449467} + e^0$$
$$= 6\,351951573/10.49422544$$
$$= 0.605280647$$
$$Pr\,(\text{no screening}) = e^0/e^{1.8487621} + e^{1.1449467} + e^0$$
$$= 1/10.49422735$$
$$= 0.095290501$$

Following the estimated utilities, while *comprehensive* information is preferred, *all other things equal*, for the average individual the uptake of the simple test is predicted to be higher. This is because it provides results faster and costs less.

Now consider a case where in addition to the *comprehensive* and *simple* screening tests presented above, a private clinic introduced a *new* prenatal screening test providing comprehensive information with a 14-day wait from screening to receiving results, and costing £15. The indirect utility of this *new* test is:

$$V_{new} = 2.251685 + (-0.0028466 \times 15) + (-0.0513463 \times 14)$$
$$= 2.251685 - 0.042699 - 0.7188482$$
$$= 1.4901378$$

Now individuals have four options, *comprehensive* and *simple* as before, the *new* service and *no* screening. The probability of taking each test will be altered:

$$Pr\,(\text{comp}) = e^{1.1449467}/e^{1.8487621} + e^{1.1449467} + e^{1.4901378} + e^0$$
$$= 3.142273869/14.93193243$$
$$= 0.210439866$$
$$Pr\,(\text{simple}) = e^{1.8487621}/\,e^{1.8487621} + e^{1.1449467} + e^{1.4901378} + e^0$$
$$= 6.351951573/\,14.93193243$$
$$= 0.425393806$$
$$Pr\,(\text{new}) = e^{1.4901378}/e^{1.8487621} + e^{1.1449467} + e^{1.4901378} + e^0$$
$$= 4.437706993/14.93193243$$
$$= 0.297195758$$
$$Pr\,(\text{no screening}) = e^0/e^{1.8487621} + e^{1.1449467} + e^{1.4901378} + e^0$$
$$= 1/14.93193243$$
$$= 0.066970568$$

If we compare these probabilities for take-up with those calculated when there were three alternatives, we can see the probability of all alternatives has changed. The introduction of the new comprehensive test has resulted in some respondents switching from the old comprehensive test. There has also been a reduction in the probability of respondents having the simple information test and the neither option.

5.3. Compensating Variation

In many cases the researcher is interested in the change in welfare that arises when a new policy or service is introduced. To calculate this we use the formula for compensating variation presented in Chapter 1, see Equation 1.14 (since respondents have the choice of comprehensive, simple or not being screened, and therefore we are not operating in a state of the world model). In the context of this example, suppose that we are interested in the change in welfare resulting from a reduction in the price of the original comprehensive test from £10 to £5. Firstly, the indirect utility of this test is calculated as:

$$V_{comp\_reduced} = 2.251685 + (-0.0028466 \times 5) + (-0.0513463 \times 21)$$
$$= 2.251658 - 0.014233 - 1.0782723$$
$$= 1.1591527$$

Intuitively, this is higher than the utility of the initial comprehensive test. Given the utility of the comprehensive test has changed, then the probability of being screened using this test will also change. Here, it is crucial to note that individuals may move from not being screened to having this cheaper comprehensive test or move from being screening with the simple test to being screened with the comprehensive test.

$$Pr\,(comp\_reduced) = e^{1.1591527}/e^{1.8487621} + e^{1.1591527} + e^0$$
$$= 3.18723159/6.351951573 + 3.18723159 + 1$$
$$= 3.18723159/10.53918316$$
$$= 0.302417326$$
$$Pr\,(simple) = e^{1.8487621}/e^{1.8487621} + e^{1.1591527} + e^0$$
$$= 6.351951573/6.351951573 + 3.185795429 + 1$$
$$= 6.351951573/10.53918316$$
$$= 0.60269866$$
$$Pr\,(no\ screening) = e^0/e^{1.8487621} + e^{1.1591527} + e^0$$
$$= 1/10.53918316$$
$$= 0.094884013$$

Probabilities have changed slightly here, but not greatly. This is because the proposed change of cost for the comprehensive service (a £5 reduction) is relatively low given the overall value of the service. There has, however, been a slight fall in the number of individuals taking up the simple and no screening options, and an associated increase in the number taking up the comprehensive test. To calculate the change in welfare we use the following equation presented in Chapter 1:

$$CV = 1/-\beta_{cos\,t}\left[\ln\left(\sum \exp(V_j^1)\right) - \ln\left(\sum \exp(V_j^0)\right)\right]$$

Where $\ln(\Sigma \exp(V_j^1))$ is welfare after the change and $\ln(\Sigma \exp(V_j^0))$ is welfare before the change.

$$CV = (1/0.0028466)\,[\ln(e^{1.8487621} + e^{1.1591527} + e^0) - \ln(e^{1.8487624} + e^{1.1449467} + e^0)]$$
$$= (351.2962833)\,[\ln(10.53918316) - \ln(10.49422544)$$
$$= (351.2962833)\,[2.355100041 - 2.350825148]$$
$$= £1.501754022$$
$$= £1.50$$

The important point to note here is that whilst the cost was reduced by £5 for the comprehensive test, the welfare change is not equal to this because only a proportion of the population will use the comprehensive test.

Using this method it is also possible to calculate the welfare associated with the introduction of the new private clinic screening test presented above:

$$
\begin{aligned}
CV &= (1/0.0028466)\,[\ln(e^{1.8487621} + e^{1.1449467} + e^{1.4901378} + e^{0}) - \ln(e^{1.8487621} + e^{1.1449467} + e^{0})] \\
&= (351.2962833)\,[\ln(14.93193243) - \ln(10.49422544)] \\
&= (351.2962833)\,[2.703502036 - 2.350825148] \\
&= 351.296833 \times 0.352676834 \\
&= 123.8942738 \\
&= £123.89
\end{aligned}
$$

Note that this differs from the MWTP for the new service compared to not being screening. Respondent's MWTP would be £538.47 – WTP for comprehensive information is £791, this is reduced by £18.03 for every day patients have to wait for the test results, in this case 14 days, thus £252.53. The compensating variation of the new clinic is £123.89 because this is the average welfare across all respondents. Not all individuals are screened using the new service. In the calculation, individuals screened using the new service have not necessarily moved from not having screening and the welfare gain to individuals moving to the new service from services A or B will be lower than the welfare gain to those individuals moving from no screening.

6. CONCLUSION

This chapter provided a discussion of practical issues involved in conducting a DCE. Particular attention was given to checking experimental design properties, data input, analysis and interpretation. The practitioner is encouraged to consider the properties of their chosen design. As noted by Street et al. in Chapter 2, this should be done on a case-by-case basis. In the Appendix, we consider the design properties of the experimental design presented in this chapter in more detail.

The data input for DCE studies is different to many survey techniques, since one individual represents a number of observations within the data, depending on the number of choice sets, and the number of alternatives within a choice set. The practitioner should be aware of the data requirements for the software they are using at the analysis stage. Data analysis was demonstrated for the simple MNL model, with consideration given to the many potential uses of the DCE results. Part 2 uses a number of case studies to show further how the DCE results can be used at the policy level.

Finally, whilst this chapter has focused on design, data input, analysis and interpretation, the importance of developing the questionnaire in a format that is understandable to respondents cannot be stressed enough. In this study, it was crucial that we worked with a geneticist and obstetrician to develop and explain the attributes and levels of interest. The best design and most complicated methods of analysis cannot compensate for a bad questionnaire. Practitioners should ensure that in developing the questionnaire they pilot the questionnaire, and follow the methods of good survey design. Qualitative research techniques are likely to prove useful here.

ACKNOWLEDGEMENTS

We are grateful to Jane Diack and Norman Smith for their contribution to developing and administering the empirical study within this chapter and to all women who completed the DCE questionnaire.

REFERENCES

Bradley, M. 1991. User's manual for the speed version 2.1 stated preference experiment editor and designer. Hague Consulting Group, Hague.

Dillman, D.A. 2000. Mail and Internet Surveys: The Tailored Design Method. New York: Wiley.

Hensher, D.A., Rose, J.M. and Greene, W.H. 2005. Applied Choice Analysis: A Primer. Cambridge: Cambridge University Press.

NLOGIT v3.0/LIMDEP v8.0, Econometric Software Inc. www.limdep.com

Louviere, J.J., Hensher, D.A. and Swait, J.D. 2000. Stated Choice Methods: Analysis and Application. Cambridge: Cambridge University Press.

Presser, S., Rothgeb, J.M., Couper, M.P., Lessler, J.T., Martin, E., Matrin, J. and Singer, E. 2004. Methods for Testing and Evaluating Survey Questionnaires. New York: Wiley.

Ryan, M. 1999. Using conjoint analysis to go beyond health outcomes: an application to in vitro fertilisation. *Social Science and Medicine*, vol 48, 535–546.

Ryan, M., Diack, J., Watson V. and Smith N. 2005. Rapid prenatal diagnostic testing for Down syndrome only or longer wait for full karyotype: the views of pregnant women. *Prenatal Diagnosis*, vol 25, 1206–1211.

Statacorp. 2005. Stata statistical software: Release 9. College Station, TX: StataCorp LP.

UK Department of Health. 2003. Our Inheritance, Our Future: Realising the potential of genetics in the NHS. London: Stationery Office.

APPENDIX

COMMENTS ON THE DESIGN OF THE CHOICE EXPERIMENT

LEONIE BURGESS AND DEBORAH J STREET

In this section, we focus on the properties of the design of the choice experiment used in the case study discussed in this chapter. In Chapter 2, we looked at ways to construct near-optimal choice experiments and also show how to calculate the efficiency of these designs. To begin with, we calculate the efficiency of the design in Table 3.2 and discuss the properties of this design. We then construct a design using the methods given in Chapter 2 and compare the efficiency and properties of this design with the design used in the case study in this chapter.

In order to calculate the efficiency of the choice sets in Table 3.2, we first need to construct the $B_{M,n}$, Λ_n and $C_{M,n}$ matrices, and for this design we denote the last two by $\Lambda_{n,ch3}$ and $C_{M,n,ch3}$. We then calculate the determinant of $C_{M,n,ch3}$ and the determinant of the optimal design. There are $k = 3$ attributes, with levels $l_1 = 2$, $l_2 = l_3 = 4$, and $m = 2$ options in each choice set plus a none option. The $B_{M,n}$ matrix will have seven rows for the main effects plus one row for the none option. There will be $L = 2 \times 4 \times 4 = 32$ columns for the treatment combinations in the complete factorial, plus one column for the none option. Because of its size, $B_{M,n}$ has been split into two smaller matrices B_1 and B_2, which are given in Table 3.8. So $B_{M,n} = [B_1 \ B_2]$.

Similarly, the $\Lambda_{n,ch3}$ matrix, which has $L + 1 = 33$ rows and columns, is split into four sub-matrices and these are given in Table 3.9. Note that

$$\Lambda_{n,ch3} = \frac{1}{72} \begin{bmatrix} \Lambda_{11,ch3} & \Lambda_{12,ch3} \\ \Lambda_{21,ch3} & \Lambda_{22,ch3} \end{bmatrix}$$

Then, we calculate the information matrix $C_{M,n,ch3}$ (also given in Table 3.10) and we find that $\det(C_{M,n,ch3}) = 3.25298 \times 10^{-14}$. Since $L = 32$ and $S_1 = S_2 = S_3 = 1$, and from Section 8 in Chapter 2, we find that $\det(C_{M,n})$ of the optimal design is given by

TABLE 3.8. B_1 and B_2 matrices for a $2 \times 4 \times 4$ factorial design where $B_{M,n} = [B_1\ B_2]$.

$$B_1 =$$

$$B_2 =$$

$$\Lambda_{11,\,ch3}=\begin{bmatrix} 0&0&0&0&0&0&0&0&0&0&0&0&0&0&0&0&0 \\ 0&2&0&0&0&0&0&0&0&0&0&0&0&0&0&0&0 \\ 0&0&0&0&0&0&0&0&0&0&0&0&0&0&0&0&0 \\ 0&0&0&0&0&0&0&0&0&0&0&0&0&0&0&0&0 \\ 0&0&0&0&2&0&0&0&0&0&0&0&0&0&0&0&0 \\ 0&0&0&0&0&2&0&0&0&0&0&0&0&0&0&0&0 \\ 0&0&0&0&0&0&0&0&0&0&0&0&0&0&0&0&0 \\ 0&0&0&0&0&0&0&0&0&0&0&0&0&0&0&0&0 \\ 0&0&0&0&0&0&0&0&0&0&0&0&0&0&0&0&0 \\ 0&0&0&0&0&0&0&0&0&2&0&0&0&0&0&0&0 \\ 0&0&0&0&0&0&0&0&0&0&2&0&0&0&0&0&0 \\ 0&0&0&0&0&0&0&0&0&0&0&2&0&0&0&0&0 \\ 0&0&0&0&0&0&0&0&0&0&0&0&0&0&0&0&0 \\ 0&0&0&0&0&0&0&0&0&0&0&0&0&0&0&0&0 \\ 0&0&0&0&0&0&0&0&0&0&0&0&0&0&0&2&0 \\ 0&0&0&0&0&0&0&0&0&0&0&0&0&0&0&0&2 \end{bmatrix},\ \Lambda_{12,\,ch3}=\Lambda_{21,\,ch3}^{T}=\begin{bmatrix} 0&0&0&0&0&0&0&0&0&0&0&0&0&0&0&0&0 \\ 0&0&0&0&0&0&0&0&-1&0&0&0&0&0&0&0&-1 \\ 0&0&0&0&0&0&0&0&0&0&0&0&0&0&0&0&0 \\ 0&0&0&0&0&0&0&0&0&0&0&0&0&0&0&0&0 \\ 0&0&0&0&0&0&0&0&0&0&0&0&-1&0&0&0&-1 \\ 0&0&0&0&0&0&0&0&0&0&0&-1&0&0&0&0&-1 \\ 0&0&0&0&0&0&0&0&0&0&0&0&0&0&0&0&0 \\ 0&0&0&0&0&0&0&0&0&0&0&0&0&0&0&0&0 \\ -1&0&0&0&0&0&0&0&0&0&0&0&0&0&0&0&-1 \\ 0&0&0&-1&0&0&0&0&0&0&0&0&0&0&0&0&-1 \\ 0&0&-1&0&0&0&0&0&0&0&0&0&0&0&0&0&-1 \\ 0&0&0&0&0&0&0&0&0&0&0&0&0&0&0&0&0 \\ 0&0&0&0&0&0&0&0&0&0&0&0&0&0&0&0&0 \\ 0&0&0&0&0&0&-1&0&0&0&0&0&0&0&0&0&-1 \\ 0&0&0&0&0&0&-1&0&0&0&0&0&0&0&0&0&-1 \end{bmatrix}$$

$$\Lambda_{22,\,ch3}=\begin{bmatrix} 2&0&0&0&0&0&0&0&0&0&0&0&0&0&0&0&-1 \\ 0&0&0&0&0&0&0&0&0&0&0&0&0&0&0&0&0 \\ 0&0&2&0&0&0&0&0&0&0&0&0&0&0&0&0&-1 \\ 0&0&0&2&0&0&0&0&0&0&0&0&0&0&0&0&-1 \\ 0&0&0&0&0&0&0&0&0&0&0&0&0&0&0&0&0 \\ 0&0&0&0&0&0&0&0&0&0&0&0&0&0&0&0&0 \\ 0&0&0&0&0&0&2&0&0&0&0&0&0&0&0&0&-1 \\ 0&0&0&0&0&0&0&2&0&0&0&0&0&0&0&0&-1 \\ 0&0&0&0&0&0&0&0&2&0&0&0&0&0&0&0&-1 \\ 0&0&0&0&0&0&0&0&0&0&0&0&0&0&0&0&0 \\ 0&0&0&0&0&0&0&0&0&0&0&0&0&0&0&0&0 \\ 0&0&0&0&0&0&0&0&0&0&0&0&0&0&0&0&0 \\ 0&0&0&0&0&0&0&0&0&0&0&0&2&0&0&0&-1 \\ 0&0&0&0&0&0&0&0&0&0&0&0&0&2&0&0&-1 \\ 0&0&0&0&0&0&0&0&0&0&0&0&0&0&0&0&0 \\ 0&0&0&0&0&0&0&0&0&0&0&0&0&0&0&0&0 \\ -1&0&-1&-1&0&0&-1&-1&-1&0&0&0&-1&-1&0&0&16 \end{bmatrix}$$

$$\det(C_{M,n,\,opt}) = \frac{m(L+1)}{L(m+1)^2} \prod_{q=1}^{k} \left[\frac{2S_q l_q + m(l_q-1)}{(m+1)^2(l_q-1)L} \right]^{l_q-1}$$

$$= \frac{2(32+1)}{32(2+1)^2} \times \left[\frac{2 \times 1 \times 2 + 2(2-1)}{(2+1)^2(2-1)32} \right]^{2-1} \times \left[\frac{2 \times 1 \times 4 + 2(4-1)}{(2+1)^2(4-1)32} \right]^{4-1}$$

$$\times \left[\frac{2 \times 1 \times 4 + 2(4-1)}{(2+1)^2(4-1)^{32}} \right]^{4-1}$$

$$= 8.64164 \times 10^{-14}$$

Hence, the efficiency of the design is

$$D - eff = \left[\frac{3.25298 \times 10^{-14}}{8.64164 \times 10^{-14}} \right]^{\frac{1}{8}} = 88.50\%.$$

We now look at the structure of $(C_{M,n,ch3})^{-1}$ in Table 3.10. As we discussed in Chapter 2, the C^{-1} matrix needs to be diagonal (or at least block diagonal) for the effects of interest to be uncorrelated. From the $(C_{M,n,ch3})^{-1}$ matrix we can see that all of the pairs of main effects are correlated. One problem with this design is that the 16 profiles in the FFD are not of resolution 3, which means that, for any two attributes, the combinations of pairs of levels do not appear with proportional frequencies (see Section 3 of Chapter 2). If the FFD were of resolution 3, we would expect each of the entries in Table 3.11 to be $(8 \times 4)/16 = 2$.

It is also worth noting that if the none option had not been included in the choice sets, $\det(C_M)$ would be equal to zero. This is because the main effects of the second and third attributes cannot be estimated at all without the none option present. If we consider the second attribute (*wait*), level "2" appears only with level "16", so the respondents never have to choose between levels "2" and "8", or "2" and "30". The same applies to the third attribute (*cost*).

So how would we construct a better design for this case study? Firstly, we need a $2 \times 4 \times 4$ FFD of resolution 3 and we start with the OMEP in Table 3.11. This OMEP has five attributes, each with four levels, so we collapse the levels of the first attribute to two levels by changing 2s to 0s and 3s to 1s. Then, together with this attribute, we take the last two four-level attributes to obtain the required OMEP. This is just one of many ways that we could have obtained the OMEP. The levels of the attributes are coded so that the two-level attribute has levels 0 and 1, and the four-level attributes have levels 0, 1, 2 and 3. The OMEP is given in Table 3.12.

Now that we have a starting design we can construct the choice sets. As noted in Section 8 of Chapter 2, the designs that are optimal for the estimation of main effects only are also optimal when a none option is included in the choice sets. Hence, we can use the method described in Section 6 of the same chapter to construct a near-optimal design. The treatment combinations in the OMEP become the profiles in alternative A and we then make systematic level changes to the OMEP to create the profiles in alternative B. For the first attribute we change 0s to 1s and 1s to 0s, and for the two four-level attributes we change 0s to 1s, 1s to 2s, 2s to 3s, and 3s to 0s. This is

TABLE 3.10. $C_{M,n,ch3}$ and $(C_{M,n,ch3})^{-1}$ matrices for the choice sets in Table 3.2

$$
C_{M,n,ch3} =
\begin{bmatrix}
\frac{1}{48} & \frac{-1}{96\sqrt{5}} & \frac{1}{192} & \frac{1}{192\sqrt{5}} & \frac{-1}{192\sqrt{5}} & \frac{1}{192} & \frac{-1}{96\sqrt{5}} & 0 \\[4pt]
\frac{-1}{96\sqrt{5}} & \frac{13}{720} & 0 & \frac{-1}{180} & 0 & 0 & 0 & 0 \\[4pt]
\frac{1}{192} & 0 & \frac{1}{48} & 0 & 0 & 0 & 0 & 0 \\[4pt]
\frac{1}{192\sqrt{5}} & \frac{-1}{180} & 0 & \frac{7}{720} & 0 & 0 & 0 & 0 \\[4pt]
\frac{-1}{192\sqrt{5}} & 0 & 0 & 0 & \frac{7}{720} & 0 & \frac{1}{180} & 0 \\[4pt]
\frac{1}{192} & 0 & 0 & 0 & 0 & \frac{1}{48} & 0 & 0 \\[4pt]
\frac{-1}{96\sqrt{5}} & 0 & 0 & 0 & \frac{1}{180} & 0 & \frac{13}{720} & 0 \\[4pt]
0 & 0 & 0 & 0 & 0 & 0 & 0 & \frac{11}{48}
\end{bmatrix}
$$

and

$$
C_{M,n,ch3}^{-1} =
\begin{bmatrix}
64 & \frac{32}{\sqrt{5}} & -16 & \frac{-16}{\sqrt{5}} & \frac{16}{\sqrt{5}} & -16 & \frac{32}{\sqrt{5}} & 0 \\[4pt]
\frac{32}{\sqrt{5}} & \frac{352}{5} & \frac{-8}{\sqrt{5}} & \frac{184}{5} & \frac{8}{5} & \frac{-8}{\sqrt{5}} & \frac{16}{5} & 0 \\[4pt]
-16 & \frac{-8}{\sqrt{5}} & 52 & \frac{4}{\sqrt{5}} & \frac{-4}{\sqrt{5}} & 4 & \frac{-8}{\sqrt{5}} & 0 \\[4pt]
\frac{-16}{\sqrt{5}} & \frac{184}{5} & \frac{4}{\sqrt{5}} & \frac{628}{5} & \frac{-4}{5} & \frac{4}{\sqrt{5}} & \frac{-8}{5} & 0 \\[4pt]
\frac{16}{\sqrt{5}} & \frac{8}{5} & \frac{-4}{\sqrt{5}} & \frac{-4}{5} & \frac{628}{5} & \frac{-4}{\sqrt{5}} & \frac{-184}{5} & 0 \\[4pt]
-16 & \frac{-8}{\sqrt{5}} & 4 & \frac{4}{\sqrt{5}} & \frac{-4}{\sqrt{5}} & 52 & \frac{-8}{\sqrt{5}} & 0 \\[4pt]
\frac{32}{\sqrt{5}} & \frac{16}{5} & \frac{-8}{\sqrt{5}} & \frac{-8}{5} & \frac{-184}{5} & \frac{-8}{\sqrt{5}} & \frac{352}{5} & 0 \\[4pt]
0 & 0 & 0 & 0 & 0 & 0 & 0 & \frac{48}{11}
\end{bmatrix}
$$

TABLE 3.11. *Profiles from the Initial OMEP
(a.16.5.4.2) from Sloan's website*

00000	10123	20231	30312
01111	11032	21320	31203
02222	12301	22013	32130
03333	13210	23102	33021

TABLE 3.12. *2 × 4 × 4 FFD of resolution 3*

000	123	031	112
011	132	020	103
022	101	013	130
033	110	002	121

equivalent to adding the generator 111 to the OMEP, where the addition is performed in mod 2 for the two-level attribute and mod 4 for the four-level attributes. The resulting design consists of 16 choice sets, which are 98.58% efficient and all effects are uncorrelated. Furthermore, we would get the same efficiency if we used any one of the generators 113, 131 or 133.

However, if we must limit the design to eight choice sets, we can pair the profiles in the OMEP in Table 3.12 in such a way that the profiles in alternative B are as close as possible to the profiles we would get if we added the generator 111 to the profiles in alternative A. We also try to ensure that for each pair of attributes each level of one attribute appears equally often with the levels of the other attribute.

The $B_{M,n} = [B_1 \ B_2]$ is the same as before and is given in Table 3.8. Once again the Λ_n matrix, which for this design we denote by $\Lambda_{n,SB}$, is split into four sub-matrices such that $\Lambda_{n,SB} = \frac{1}{72}\begin{bmatrix} \Lambda_{11,SB} & \#38; \Lambda_{12,SB} \\ \Lambda_{21,SB} & \#38; \Lambda_{22,SB} \end{bmatrix}$. These matrices are given in Table 3.14.

Then, we calculate the information matrix $C_{M,n,SB}$ and the variance–covariance matrix $(C_{M,n,SB})^{-1}$ (both are given in Table 3.15) and we find that $\det(C_{M,n,SB}) = 8.36672 \times 10^{-14}$. The design is 99.60% efficient relative to the optimal design and since the variance–covariance matrix is block diagonal, all of the pairs of main effects are uncorrelated.

TABLE 3.13. *Eight near-optimal choice sets for*
main effects only plus a none option

Alternative A	Alternative B
000	112
132	011
110	033
022	130
031	103
013	121
101	020
123	002

So how can we summarise our observations? The Street–Burgess designs are easy to construct and give designs that are optimal (or near-optimal) and they have variance–covariance matrices that allow for the independent estimation of main effects (in this case, and of the effects of interest in general). The ideas behind their construction can be used to get smaller ad hoc designs that also have a variance–covariance matrix with a good structure.

The designs considered in this appendix emphasise the importance of looking not only at the efficiency of a design, but also at its variance–covariance matrix. The problems that we saw here with the design discussed in Chapter 3 resulted from using a starting design that was not of resolution 3, and then creating pairs in which only two of the $l_q(l_q - 1)$ pairs of attribute levels appear in the design. This resulted in a design in which the main effects can not be estimated at all without the inclusion of a none option, and even then the effects can not be independently estimated.

TABLE 3.14. $\Lambda_{n,SB}$ sub-matrices for the choice sets in Table 3.13

$$A_{11,SB} =$$

$$A_{12,SB} = A_{21,SB}^T =$$

$$A_{22,SB} =$$

TABLE 3.15. $C_{M,n,SB}$ and $(C_{M,n,SB})^{-1}$ matrices for the choice sets in Table 3.13

$$C_{M,n,SB} = \begin{pmatrix} \frac{1}{48} & 0 & 0 & 0 & 0 & 0 & 0 & 0 \\ 0 & \frac{1}{60} & 0 & -\frac{1}{720} & 0 & 0 & 0 & 0 \\ 0 & 0 & \frac{5}{288} & 0 & 0 & 0 & 0 & 0 \\ 0 & -\frac{1}{720} & 0 & \frac{7}{480} & 0 & 0 & 0 & 0 \\ 0 & 0 & 0 & 0 & \frac{1}{60} & 0 & -\frac{1}{720} & 0 \\ 0 & 0 & 0 & 0 & 0 & \frac{5}{288} & 0 & 0 \\ 0 & 0 & 0 & 0 & -\frac{1}{720} & 0 & \frac{7}{480} & 0 \\ 0 & 0 & 0 & 0 & 0 & 0 & 0 & \frac{11}{48} \end{pmatrix}$$

and

$$C_{M,n,SB}^{-1} = \begin{pmatrix} 48 & 0 & 0 & 0 & 0 & 0 & 0 & 0 \\ 0 & \frac{1512}{25} & 0 & \frac{144}{25} & 0 & 0 & 0 & 0 \\ 0 & 0 & \frac{288}{5} & 0 & 0 & 0 & 0 & 0 \\ 0 & \frac{144}{25} & 0 & \frac{1728}{25} & 0 & 0 & 0 & 0 \\ 0 & 0 & 0 & 0 & \frac{1512}{25} & 0 & \frac{144}{25} & 0 \\ 0 & 0 & 0 & 0 & 0 & \frac{288}{5} & 0 & 0 \\ 0 & 0 & 0 & 0 & \frac{144}{25} & 0 & \frac{1728}{25} & 0 \\ 0 & 0 & 0 & 0 & 0 & 0 & 0 & \frac{48}{11} \end{pmatrix}$$

PART 2

CASE STUDIES IN VALUING HEALTH
AND HEALTH CARE

CHAPTER 4

USING DISCRETE CHOICE EXPERIMENTS TO GO BEYOND CLINICAL OUTCOMES WHEN EVALUATING CLINICAL PRACTICE

MANDY RYAN AND DIANE SKÅTUN

Health Economics Research Unit, University of Aberdeen, UK

KIRSTEN MAJOR

Director of Strategic Planning and Performance, NHS Ayrshire and Arran Health Board, Scotland, UK

1. INTRODUCTION

Until the 1990s benefit assessment in health economics was dominated by an assumption that health was the only important outcome from health care. This is evidenced by the large amount of research devoted to valuing health outcomes using quality-adjusted life years (QALYs) (Williams, 1985; Dolan, 1997). The 1990s saw a challenge to this assumption, arguing that concentration on health outcome fails to allow for the possibility that individuals derive benefit from other sources – non-health outcomes and process attributes – (Ryan and Shackley, 1995; Ryan and Hughes, 1997; Diener et al., 1998; Donaldson et al., 1998; Ryan, 1999; Donaldson and Shackley, 2003). Non-health outcomes refer to sources of benefit such as the provision of information, reassurance, autonomy and dignity in the provision of care. Process attributes include such aspects of care as waiting time, time in consultation, location of treatment and continuity of care and staff attitudes. While it should be recognised that some of these will have direct effects on health outcomes, they also have what can be regarded as pure non-health benefits. The debate about going beyond health outcomes led to the question of how such attributes can be valued. It became clear that QALYs would not be appropriate for valuing non-health outcome and process attributes. For example, it would not be realistic to ask individuals how many years at the end of their life they would be willing to give up to have waiting time reduced by 3 months; as would be required using the time–trade-off method.

Recently, it was argued that the National Institute of Health and Clinical Excellence (NICE) should use the discrete choice experiment (DCE) approach in their "patient centred" evaluations of technologies (Ryan, 2004). By adopting this approach factors beyond health outcomes can be considered and their valuation from the patient's perspective may lead to different recommendations to those based on the cost per QALY

101

M. Ryan, K. Gerard and M. Amaya-Amaya (eds.), Using Discrete Choice Experiments to Value Health and Health Care, 101–116.
© 2008 *Springer.*

approach. This is more likely to be the case when comparing technologies that differ with respect to factors beyond those measured in a QALY (Ryan, 2004), as well as to interventions that result in short-term QALY gains (Gafni and Zylak, 1990).

These points are clearly demonstrated in this chapter where we present the results of a DCE conducted following a randomised controlled trial (RCT) concerned with examining the effect of reducing waiting times on the health of patients referred for a non-urgent rheumatology opinion. The intervention compared a "fast-track" appointment (mean waiting time of 43 days between referral and seeing hospital doctor) with an "ordinary" appointment (mean waiting time of 105 days). No significant differences were found in health gains across the two arms of the trial 15 months after treatment (Hurst et al., 2000). The authors conclude that this finding suggests no benefit from fast-tracking. Further, they argue that given rationing by delay was not detrimental to either mental or physical health, expenditure of resources on waiting times is likely to be wasteful, and that additional resources should be directed at achieving the greatest clinical benefit. However, crucially, such an approach ignores the value that patients attach to reductions in waiting time. Related to this, it is likely that patients in the fast-track arm received benefit 6 weeks earlier. Whilst the RCT design did not collect data on the time course of health change, the small time gained means that the QALY is unlikely to be sensitive to the value of any health gain derived 6 weeks earlier. The QALY approach does not assign value to short-term QALY gains (Gafni and Zylak, 1990). The reason for this is that whilst the difference in health states may be significant, when this is multiplied by the length of time spent in the state, any effects then become negligible.

In the study presented in this chapter we apply the DCE methodology to estimate the monetary value of reducing waiting time. It is shown how the technique can be used to take a patient-centred approach that values all aspects of care important to patients. In Section 2 we describe the DCE methodology applied to value reductions in waiting time in the provision of routine rheumatology care. The results are discussed in Section 3. Section 4 discusses the policy relevance of the findings as well as the application of the DCE approach when providing patient-centred evaluations on health care interventions.

2. METHODOLOGY

2.1. Attributes, Levels, Experimental Design and Questionnaire

Following the results of the RCT by Hurst et al. (2000), this study was mainly concerned with the value of reducing waiting time in the management of routine rheumatology care. Two attributes included in the study were therefore waiting time and a price proxy such that willingness to pay (WTP) could be indirectly estimated. In addition, the study valued two other attributes of care that were identified as important by patients (Ryan et al., 2000). The attributes are shown in Table 4.1 together with the levels assigned to them. These attributes and levels gave rise to 96 possible scenarios.

Experimental design techniques were used to derive eight choices that were presented to respondents (Bradley, 1991). For each choice subjects were asked which clinic they would prefer, with possible responses being "clinic A", "clinic B" or

TABLE 4.1. *Attributes and levels*

Attributes	Levels of attributes (regression coding)
Length of time from referral by your GP to seeing a hospital doctor – WAIT	6 weeks, 12 weeks, 19 weeks, 28 weeks
Length of time you spend with a hospital doctor – TIME	15 min, 30 min, 45 min
Pain management service – PAINMAN	"Specialist team" – you receive input from a pain management specialist at a dedicated clinic on pain counselling and coping skills for your condition (coded as "1") "No specialist team" – you receive no service of this type (coded as "0")
Cost of clinic – PRICE	To assess value you place on these different options, you are asked how much you would be prepared to pay for them. Levels = £60, £120, £180, £240

Question 2	Clinic A	Clinic B
Length of wait	19 weeks	28 weeks
Time with doctor	30 minutes	15 minutes
Pain Management Service	No Specialist Team	Specialist Team
Cost to you	£60	£180

Which Clinic would you prefer (*tick one box only*)?	Prefer Clinic A	Prefer Clinic B	Neither
	☐	☐	☐

FIGURE 4.1. *Example of choice set*

"neither". The neither option can be interpreted as a patient instructing their general practitioner (GP) not to refer them to a rheumatology clinic or more simply non-attendance at a clinic. Figure 4.1 shows an example of the type of question presented to subjects.

Internal consistency was checked by testing the rationality of choices made, i.e. if one scenario is considered to be "better" than another, individuals are expected to choose that scenario. Two choices provided these consistency checks. These were based on the levels for the attributes cost and availability of a pain management service. It was assumed that respondents would prefer a lower cost clinic, all other things equal. Preferences concerning the availability of a specialist pain management service were determined by responses to a direct question asking respondents whether they would like access to a pain management service. To pass the consistency test, a respondent had to choose either the "better" or neither option. To allow for random error, only those who failed both consistency checks were dropped from the regression analysis.

The sample constituted all patients from the original clinical trial ($n = 138$). Of this subgroup, 53% were in the fast-track arm and 47% were in the standard treatment group. In addition, 124 patients who did not participate in the original trial, but who had received a rheumatology outpatient appointment and were participating in an audit study, were included in the DCE study. Increasing the sample size, the addition of this non-trial group facilitated the inclusion of a wider range of diagnostic groups (given that the original trial was restricted to non-urgent cases) and so is more representative of the total patient population, at whom waiting list initiatives are targeted. The questionnaire was mailed to all subjects, one reminder was sent 2 weeks after the initial mailing, and a telephone reminder followed this 1 week later.

Information was also collected in the questionnaire on a number of socio-economic, demographic and health characteristics of subjects included in the original sample. These included: age; gender; perceptions of physical and mental health status (assessed using the SF-12 [Ware et al., 1998]); EQ-5D utility scores (assessed using a visual analogue scale (Dolan, 1997)); diagnosis at clinic (inflammatory versus non-inflammatory); and deprivation based on the Carstairs deprivation score (Carstairs and Morris, 1991). These data were compared across respondents and non-respondents to test for respondent bias.

2.2. Nested Logit Model

The decision-making process in the DCE involves the individual comparing utility across each alternative, where utility is derived from the various combinations of the different levels of the attributes. In the question presented in this survey, individuals were asked to choose their preferred option from three alternatives on offer. The individual will choose the alternative giving them the highest utility. Chapter 1 outlined the benchmark model used when there are three or more alternatives on offer as the multinomial logit (MNL) model. Recall that the probability that individual n chooses alternative i from choice set C_n can be written as

$$P_{in} = \frac{\exp(V_{in})}{\sum_{j \in C_n} \exp(V_{jn})}. \tag{4.1}$$

However, as Chapter 1 has already discussed, the MNL model relies on the assumption of the independence of irrelevant alternatives (IIA). This assumption ensures that the odds ratio of one alternative over another stays constant, whatever other alternatives are introduced. This requires all alternatives to be competing equally with each other. We therefore must consider whether the choice set from which respondents are asked to choose will satisfy this assumption. The two clinic referral alternatives (clinic A and clinic B) may be considered to have more in common with each other than each of them individually has compared to the no clinic (neither) option. This pattern of cross elasticity of substitution indicates a violation of the IIA assumption. We therefore use the nested logit (NL) model in which we "nest" or group more similar alternatives together (Ryan and Skåtun, 2004). The NL model is a generalisation of the MNL where the nesting structure allows a partial relaxation of the IIA assumption; it holds within but not between nests. Figure 4.2 illustrates the alternative relationship between the three alternatives on offer. The tree diagram on the left indicates the standard MNL set-up with all three options equal competitors. The tree diagram on the right illustrates the two nests; referral to a clinic and no referral to a clinic. Within the no-referral nest there is only one alternative on offer, the attend no clinic option and within the referral nest there are two alternatives on offer, attend clinic A or attend clinic B. Note that the tree diagram of the nested model does not indicate a sequence in the decision making – it is a means of illustrating the potential groupings or nesting structure of the alternatives open to individuals.

The choice probabilities associated with the NL model are different from that of the logit model.[1] For individual n, the probability of choosing alternative i from within nest g is expressed as a product of the probability of alternative i coming from nest g and the probability of alternative i from nest g being chosen given nest g is chosen.

$$P_{i(g)n} = P\,(\text{nest } g) \cdot P\,(i, \text{given nest } g) \qquad (4.2)$$

This decomposition of the choice probability is often referred to as the upper and lower model where the upper model can be seen as the choice of nest and the lower model as a conditional model: conditioned on the choice of nest. The conditional choice probability of choosing alternative i given nest g is given by

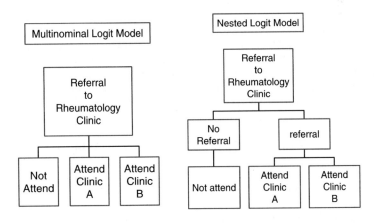

FIGURE 4.2. *Alternative decision-making processes and appropriate economic analysis*

$$P_{in \mid g} = \frac{e^{V_i}}{\sum_{k \in g} e^{V_k}} \qquad (4.3)$$

The probability that an alternative from nest g is chosen can also be expressed as a logit as follows:

$$P(g) = \frac{e^{\lambda_g IV_g}}{\sum_{g=1}^{G} e^{\lambda_g IV_g}} \qquad (4.4)$$

Where IV_g is the inclusive value for nest g and is given by

$$IV_g = \ln \sum_{j \in g} e^{V_j} \qquad (4.5)$$

This is also referred to as the expected utility from the choice of alternatives within nest g and is the link between the upper and lower model whereby the expected utility from nest g affects the probability of choosing an alternative within nest g. The parameter λ_g for each nest g is estimated within the model with $0 \leq \lambda_g \leq 1$. As we have already seen, λ is a measure of the correlation in unobserved factors within each nest g.[2] If $\lambda = 1$ for all nests, the model will collapse to a standard MNL model. It can be seen as the degree to which the expected utility from a nest feeds through to the probability of choosing that particular nest. If $\lambda_g = 1$ for all nests, this indicates that all alternatives are equal competitors as described above and a multinomial model is indicated.

2.3. Model Specification

The utility function V_i underlying the model is given in Equation 4.6. The four attributes in the DCE that characterise the alternatives refer to their status in relation to: WAIT, TIME, PAINMAN and PRICE (all as defined in Table 4.1). In addition, we can apply more information to this nesting structure in providing a model at the referral or no-referral decision level (clinic A/B versus neither). This will be based on information of the individual's characteristics and shown in Equation 4.7. Factors hypothesised to influence whether the respondent took up the referral (and therefore did not give a neither response) were: age (AGE), whether or not the respondent had an inflammatory diagnosis (INFLAM), deprivation score (DEPSCORE, ranging from −5 to +12 where a higher score indicates a higher level of deprivation), gender (GENDER, where 1 = female and 0 = male) and perceptions of physical (PHYSICAL) and mental health (MENTAL). For both PHYSICAL and MENTAL, a higher score indicated a better perception of health status.

$$V = \delta_1 WAIT + \delta_2 PRICE + \delta_3 PAINMAN + \delta_4 TIME + e \qquad (4.6)$$

$$\text{Attend} = \kappa + \beta_1 AGE + \beta_2 INFLAM + \beta_3 DEPSCORE + \beta_4 GENDER$$
$$+ \beta_5 PHYSICAL + \beta_6 MENTAL + u \qquad (4.7)$$

where V is the benefit (or utility) obtained from moving from one alternative to another and *attend* is whether or not a neither option was answered (1 represents neither, and 0 not choosing the neither option), κ, β_i (i = 1, 2, 3, 4, 5, 6) and

δ_j (j = 1, 2, 3, 4) are the parameters (coefficients) of the model to be estimated, e and u are the unobservable error terms and all other variables are as defined above.[3] Ninety-five percent confidence intervals (CIs) were estimated for the parameter estimates. Equation 4.6 is referred to as the basic model (as opposed to the segmented model, see below).

Equation 4.6 was used to indirectly estimate WTP for: a unit (week) change in length of time from referral by GP to seeing a hospital doctor (WAIT); a unit (minute) change in length of time spent with the doctor; and the introduction of a pain management service (PAINMAN).

LIMDEP was used for all data analysis.

2.3.1. Segmented model

To allow for non-random variation in coefficients (i.e. preferences for individual attributes may vary across sub-populations), segmentation analysis was carried out. Interaction terms were created between the attribute "PRICE" and respondent's income and the attribute "TIME" and actual waiting time experienced by respondents. Three income groups were created – income group 1 had income of up to £5,000 per year, income group 2 had £5,000–£10,000 and income group 3 had £10,000 plus. This resulted in the cost attribute being segmented into three groups: PRICE1, PRICE2 and PRICE3. A priori we would expect the highest income group (PRICE3) to have a lower marginal valuation of cost, resulting in a lower coefficient (see below). Given that waiting times for the non-trial respondents were not significantly different from the fast-track group (44 days compared to 53), these two groups were combined and compared to the standard group (who had a mean waiting time of 102 days). Two WAIT variables were therefore created: WAITFTN (preferences concerning waiting time for fast-track and non-trial respondents) and WAITS (preferences for waiting time for standard group). The utility function estimated was of the following form (with the attendance decision as defined above):

$$V = \alpha_1 \text{WAITFTN} + \alpha_2 \text{WAITS} + \alpha_3 \text{PRICE1} + \alpha_4 \text{PRICE2} + \alpha_5 \text{PRICE3} + \alpha_6 \text{PAINMAN} + \alpha_7 \text{TIME} + e \tag{4.8}$$

where all variables are as defined above. Mean WTP was estimated for all attributes within each income group. For WAIT, mean WTP was estimated for both the fast-track and non-trial groups and standard group. Ninety-five percent CIs were calculated for the parameter estimates.

3. RESULTS

3.1. Respondents

Of the 262 questionnaires mailed, 180 were sent to women and 82 to men. An overall response rate of 71.4% (n = 187) was achieved. The mean age of the group was 56.25 years (95% CI 50.81, 54.48). The mean heath status measure scores at baseline were SF12 (physical) 35.9 (95% CI 34.6, 37.1), SF-12 (mental) 44.3 (95% CI 42.8, 45.8) and EQ-5D utility 0.47 (95% CI 0.42, 0.52). The mean deprivation score for the whole group was −0.87 (−1.2, −0.54). Table 4.2 details a range of variables for respondents

TABLE 4.2. *Characteristics of respondents and non-respondents*

Variable	Respondents ($n = 187$)	Non-respondents ($n = 75$)	Mean difference (95% CI)	Significance
Mean age	53.96	49.37	4.59 (0.56, 8.62)	$p = 0.03$
Gender (% female)	71%	63%		$\chi^2 = 1.78$, $p = 0.18$
Study arm				$\chi^2 = 0.52$, $p = 0.77$
Fast-track (%)	28.8	25		
Standard (%)	25.1	24		
Non-trial (%)	45.9	50.6		
SF-12 physical	35.87	35.88	−0.02 (−2.77, 2.74)	$p = 0.99$
SF-12 mental	43.71	45.82	−2.11 (−5.33, 1.10)	$p = 0.20$
EQ-5D utility	0.45	0.51	−0.06 (−0.16, 0.05)	0.28
Clinical diagnosis				$\chi^2 = 3.57$, $p = 0.06$
Inflammatory (%)	56.1	43		
Non-inflammatory (%)	43.8	56.9		
Deprivation score	−1.09	−0.34	−0.75 (−1.49, −0.02)	$p = 0.05$

and non-respondents. As can be seen the only significant differences observed were for deprivation score and age, such that respondents tended to be older and more affluent than their non-respondent counterparts.

3.2. Regression Results

Only two respondents failed both consistency checks. The small numbers of those failing indicated that the respondents understood the questionnaire and were able to answer it in a meaningful way. Regression analysis was conducted on 185 consistent responses.

The results from the NL regression model are shown in Table 4.3. The estimated coefficient on the IV parameter is significantly different from one. This indicates some correlation in unobserved factors within the referral nest. This suggests that a change in one of the probabilities of choosing a clinic will have a disproportionate effect on the probability of choosing the alternative clinic as opposed to choosing the no clinic option. This is the advantage of the NL model, the ability of the property of identically distributed (IID) to be relaxed between nests.

3.2.1. Clinic Attendance: Basic Model

AGE has a negative effect on non-attendance indicating that as age increases, the individual is more likely to choose to attend a clinic and INFLAM has a negative sign which indicates that an individual diagnosed with an inflammatory condition is more likely to choose to attend a clinic. Neither deprivation score, gender or physical and mental health status were significant in predicting whether or not an individual would choose to attend a clinic.

3.2.2. Utility function attributes: basic model

The attributes of the utility function are all well defined (behave in line with a priori expectations and therefore provide support for the theoretical validity of the model) and are significant at the 1% level. The main findings are:

1.   The longer the waiting time between referral and clinic consultation, the lower the utility (benefit)
2.   The higher the cost of the clinic, the lower the utility
3.   A clinic with a pain management service gives a higher utility compared to a clinic with no pain management service available
4.   The longer the time spent with the clinic doctor, the higher the utility

3.2.3. Willingness to pay: basic model

The estimated monetary value of changes in the above attributes is shown in Table 4.4. Respondents were willing to pay £14.55 for a 1-week reduction in waiting time. Assuming a linear additive model, this implies a WTP of £130.95 for a 9-week reduction in waiting time (which the fast-track service offered in comparison with standard treatment). This compares to a value of £219 for the introduction of a pain management service. This suggests that respondents to the questionnaire would prefer to see the introduction of such a service compared to the introduction of fast

M. RYAN ET AL.

TABLE 4.3. *Results from the nested logit – basic model*

Variable	Coefficient	95% Confidence intervals		*p*-value
		Lower	Upper	
Decision of non-attendance (neither)				
Constant	0.092	−0.826	1.010	0.844
AGE (β_1)	−0.022	−0.032	−0.013	0.001
INFLAM (β_2)	−0.346	−0.602	−0.090	0.008
DEPSCORE (β_3)	−0.020	−0.069	0.028	0.410
GENDER (β_4)	−0.055	−0.341	0.231	0.705
PHYSICAL (β_5)	−0.003	−0.016	0.010	0.602
MENTAL (β_6)	0.001	−0.010	0.010	0.971
Utility function attributes				
WAIT (δ_1)	−0.110	−0.131	−0.088	0.001
COST (δ_2)	−0.0075	−0.009	−0.006	0.001
PAINMAN (δ_3)	1.653	1.424	1.881	0.001
TIME (δ_4)	0.016	0.004	0.027	0.007
IV parameter (clinic)	0.607	0.450	0.764	0.001
Number of observations	4,101			
McFadden *R*	0.32			
Chi-squared	1,036 ($p = 0.001$)			

tracking. The estimated monetary value of a 1 minute increase in the time spent in the clinic with the doctor is £2.09. Again, assuming a linear additive model, this would imply a WTP of £31.35 for a quarter of an hour increase in time with the doctor.

3.2.4. Segmented model
The attributes of the utility function are again well defined and significant at the 1% level (Table 4.5). Individuals who have not experienced shorter waiting times (i.e. those who receive standard treatment) have stronger preferences for reducing waiting

TABLE 4.4. *Willingness to pay for aspects of rheumatology outpatient clinic – basic model*

Attribute	Willingness to pay calculation $(\delta_i / -\delta_j)$	Willingness to pay estimate (£)[b]
1 week reduction in waiting time[a]	$\delta_1 / -\delta_2$	14.55[a]
Introduction of a pain management service	$\delta_3 / -\delta_2$	219
1 min increase in time spent with clinic doctor	$\delta_4 / -\delta_2$	2.09

[a] Whilst the ratios would result in a negative WTP, representing what individuals would need to be compensated for a 1 week *increase* in waiting time, the figures represented show the opposite i.e. WTP for a 1 week *reduction* in waiting time.
[b] Estimated ratios are based on non-rounded figures whilst rounded figures are reported in the Table.

time (as indicated by the higher coefficient). As expected, individuals on a higher income have a lower marginal valuation of the cost attribute (as indicated by the cost coefficient being smaller for the higher income groups). This again provides support for the theoretical validity of the technique.

3.2.5. Willingness to pay

The estimated monetary value of changes in the attributes for the segmented model is shown in Table 4.6. As expected, higher-income individuals are willing to pay more for improvements in all attributes compared to lower-income groups. For example, income group 3 from the fast-track and non-trial group are willing to pay £17.23 for a 1-week reduction in waiting time, compared to £12.66 for income group 2 and £11.06 for income group 1. Assuming a linear additive model, WTP for a 9-week reduction in waiting time is equal to £99.54 for income group 1, £113.94 for income group 2 and £155.07 for income group 3. These results provide further support for the theoretical validity of the technique.

Respondents who experienced standard care were willing to pay more for a reduction in waiting time than the fast-track and non-trial groups. Extrapolating to the value of a 9-week reduction in waiting time, income group 1 who receive standard care were willing to pay £126.63, income group 2 £144.90 and income group 3 £197.19.

The introduction of a pain management service was valued at £180 by income group 1, £207 by income group 2 and £281 by income group 3. In line with the results from the basic model, respondents to the questionnaire would prefer to see the introduction of a pain management service compared to the introduction of fast tracking.

The estimated monetary value of a 1 minute increase in the time spent in the clinic doctor is £1.66 for income group 1, £1.90 for income group 2 and £2.58 for income group 3. Again, assuming a linear additive model, this implies a WTP for a 15 minute increase in time with the doctor of £24.90 for income group 1, £28.50 for income group 2 and £38.70 for income group 3.

TABLE 4.5. *Results from the nested logit – segmented model*

Variable	Coefficient	95% confidence intervals		p
		lower	upper	
Decision of non-attendance (neither)				
Constant	−0.070	−1.004	0.864	0.883
AGE (β_1)	−0.023	−0.033	−0.013	0.001
INFLAM (β_2)	−0.309	−0.567	−0.051	0.019
DEPSCORE (β_3)	−0.027	−0.076	0.022	0.274
GENDER (β_4)	−0.061	−0.356	0.234	0.687
PHYSICAL (β_5)	−0.002	−0.015	0.012	0.821
MENTAL (β_6)	0.002	−0.008	0.012	0.703
Utility function attributes				
WAITFTN (α_1)	−0.101	−0.123	−0.079	0.001
WAITSD (α_2)	−0.128	−0.156	−0.101	0.001
COST1 (α_3)	−0.0091	−0.012	−0.006	0.001
COST2 (α_4)	−0.0080	−0.010	−0.006	0.001
COST3 (α_5)	−0.0058	−0.008	−0.004	0.001
PAINMAN (α_6)	1.644	1.415	1.872	0.001
TIME (α_7)	0.015	0.004	0.026	0.009
IV parameter (clinic)	0.628	0.468	0.789	0.001
Number of observations	4,101			
McFadden R^2	0.32			
Chi-squared	1,047 ($p = 0.001$)			

TABLE 4.6. *Willingness to pay for aspects of rheumatology outpatient clinic – segmented model*

Attribute	Willingness to pay calculation $(\alpha_i/-\alpha_j)$	Willingness to pay estimate (£)[b]
1 week reduction in waiting time		
Fast-track and non-trial[a]		
Income 1	$\alpha_1/-\alpha_3$	11.06
Income 2	$\alpha_1/-\alpha_4$	12.66
Income 3	$\alpha_1/-\alpha_5$	17.23
Standard		
Income 1	$\alpha_2/-\alpha_3$	14.07
Income 2	$\alpha_2/-\alpha_4$	16.10
Income 3	$\alpha_2/-\alpha_5$	21.91
Introduction of a pain management service		
Income 1	$\alpha_6/-\alpha_3$	180
Income 2	$\alpha_6/-\alpha_4$	207
Income 3	$\alpha_6/-\alpha_5$	281
1 min increase in time spent with clinic doctor		
Income 1	$\alpha_7/-\alpha_3$	1.66
Income 2	$\alpha_7/-\alpha_4$	1.90
Income 3	$\alpha_7/-\alpha_5$	2.58

[a] Whilst the ratios would result in a negative WTP, representing what individuals would need to be compensated for a 1 week *increase* in waiting time, the figures represented show the opposite i.e. WTP for a 1 week *reduction* in waiting time.
[b] Estimated ratios are based on non-rounded figures whilst rounded figures are reported in the Table.

4. DISCUSSION AND CONCLUSION

Following the results of an RCT showing no difference in clinical outcomes 15 months post-treatment when waiting time is reduced, this study used the DCE methodology to value the reduction in waiting time to patients. Consideration was also given to the value of introducing a pain management service and extra minutes spent with the consultant. Whilst the trial showed no value in terms of clinical outcomes when reducing waiting time, patients valued a 9-week reduction in waiting time at £131. However, it is worth noting that the introduction of a pain management service would be of more value to respondents.

The conclusions regarding the reduction of waiting times as outlined in Hurst et al. (2000) are clearly more complex when issues beyond clinical measures are captured and a reduction of waiting times by 9 weeks is clearly of value to patients. A comparison of the findings regarding the value of reducing waiting time with the policy-based cost estimates of strategies such as waiting time reductions would facilitate a more efficient allocation of resources and potentially a greater level of benefit for potential patients.

An interesting finding from this study is that the reduction in waiting time was not valued as highly as the introduction of a pain management service. The reduction of waiting times is a central plank of National Health Service (NHS) policy (Hamblin, 1998). However, to date, there is very little work looking at either the value of this reduction to users of the service, or the relative importance of reductions vis-à-vis other improvements in care that may take place. The results from this study are encouraging in terms of using DCEs to address such policy issues.

In proposing the use of the DCE methodology it is important to ensure that respondents understand the task they are confronted with, and complete it in a rational manner. Within this study only two respondents failed the consistency checks, and evidence of theoretical validity was found, with the coefficients of the utility function behaving in line with a priori expectations. These results are in line with other studies applying DCEs to health care issues (Ryan and Gerard, 2003). Whilst there are a number of methodological issues that need to be addressed in the application of DCEs to value health care interventions, including the external validity of responses to hypothetical questions and the generalisability of results from one context to another (Viney et al., 2002; Ryan and Gerard, 2003), the DCE approach is likely to be a useful economic technique for promoting patient-centred care. Further, it may well result in conclusions that differ from the cost per QALY approach. It is clear from this study that if patient-centred care is to be provided, NICE will have to go beyond the cost per QALY approach.

ACKNOWLEDGEMENTS

Alison Lochhead is thanked for her administration of the questionnaire to all respondents. Pete Lock and John Forbes are thanked for input during the inception of this study and their contribution and comments throughout. Finally, all those individuals who completed the questionnaire are thanked for their time and the information they imparted.

ENDNOTES

[1] Thanks to Mabel Amaya for providing the relevant links and associated probabilities from Chapter 1.

[2] For a nest with only one alternative the IV parameter is set to 1.

[3] Given that respondents were told to assume that all aspects of the service, other than those specified in the questionnaire, were identical, there was no constant term in Equation 4.3 (Ryan and Hughes, 1997).

REFERENCES

Bradley, M. 1991. Users manual for the Speed Version 2.1 Stated Preference Experiment Editor and Designer. The Hague: Hague Consultancy Group.

Carstairs, V. and Morris, R. 1991. Deprivation and Health in Scotland. Aberdeen: Aberdeen University Press.

Diener, A., O'Brien, B. and Gafni, A. 1998. Health care contingent valuation studies: a review and classification of the literature. *Health Economics*, vol 7, 313–326.

Dolan, P. 1997. Modelling valuation for Euroqol health states. *Medical Care*, vol 35, 351–363.

Donaldson, C. and Shackley, P. 2003. Willingness to pay for health care. In: Advances in Health Economics. Scott, A., Maynard, A. and Elliott, R. (eds). London: Wiley.

Donaldson, C., Hundley, V. and Mapp, T. 1998. Willingness to pay: a method for measuring preferences for maternity care? *Birth*, vol 25, 33–40.

Emery, D. and Barron, F. 1979. Axiomatic and numerical conjoint measurement: an evaluation of diagnostic efficacy. *Psychometrika*, vol 44, 195–210.

Gafni, A. and Zylak, C.J. 1990. Ionic versus non-ionic contrast media: a burden or a bargain? *Canadian Medical Association Journal*, vol 143, 475–478.

Hamblin, R. 1998. The wrong target. *Health Services Journal*, vol 108, 28.

Hurst, N., Lambert, C., Forbes, J., Lochhead, A., Major, K. and Lock, P. 2000. Does waiting time matter? A randomised controlled trial of non-urgent rheumatology outpatients referrals. *Rheumatology*, vol 39, 369–376.

Pearmain, D., Swanson, J., Kroes, E. and Bradley, M. 1991. Stated preference techniques: a guide to practice. The Hague: Steer Davies Gleave and Hague Consulting Group.

Ryan, M. 1999. Using conjoint analysis to go beyond health outcomes and take account of patients preferences: an application to in vitro fertilisation. *Social Science and Medicine*, vol 48, 535–546.

Ryan, M. 2004. Discrete choice experiments in health care. *British Medical Journal*, vol 328, 60–61.

Ryan, M. and Gerard, K. 2003. Using discrete choice experiments to value health care: current practice and future prospects. *Applied Health Economics and Policy Analysis*, vol 2, 55–64.

Ryan, M. and Hughes, M. 1997. Using conjoint analysis to assess women's preferences for miscarriage management. *Health Economics*, vol 6, 261–273.

Ryan, M. and Shackley, P. 1995. Assessing the benefits of health care: how far should we go? *Quality in Health Care*, vol 3, 207–213.

Ryan, M. and Skåtun, D. 2004. Modelling non-demanders in discrete choice experiments. *Health Economics Letters*, vol 13, 397–402.

Ryan, M., Major, K. and Ryan, M. 2000. Outpatient queuing and clinical prioritisation in rheumatology: health outcomes and economic consequences. Report submitted to the Chief Scientist Office of the Scottish Executive Health Department, K/OPR/2/2/D315 (supplementary report).

Viney, R., Lancsar, E. and Louviere, J. 2002. Discrete choice experiments to measure preferences for health and health care. *Expert Review Pharmacoeconomics Outcomes Research*, vol 2, 319–326.

Ware, J.J., Kosinski, M. and Keller, S. 1998. SF-12: How to Score the SF-12 Physical and Mental Health Summary Scales. 3rd edn. Lincoln, RI: Quality Metric.

Williams, A. 1985. The value of QALYs. *Health and Social Services Journal*, vol 8 (Suppl).

CHAPTER 5

USING DISCRETE CHOICE MODELLING TO INVESTIGATE BREAST SCREENING PARTICIPATION

KAREN GERARD

Faculty of Medicine, Health and Life Sciences, University of Southampton, UK

MARIAN SHANAHAN

National Drug and Alcohol Research Centre, University of New South Wales, Australia

JORDAN LOUVIERE

School of Marketing, University of Technology Sydney, Australia

1. INTRODUCTION

The aim of this chapter is to show how discrete choice experiments (DCEs) can be applied to examine the preferences of women reinvited for breast screening and to use the results in developing breast screening participation enhancement strategies.

Typically, a population-based breast screening programme aims to achieve target participation rates because it is assumed that participation levels and the population benefit achieved (i.e. breast cancer mortality reduction) are directly proportional. However, for population benefits to be demonstrated, regular participation at the recommended screening frequency is necessary. Evidence suggests that while long-term participation does not reach programme target rates the information to assist in addressing how to improve uptake remains inadequate (Rimer et al., 1989; Scaf-Klomp et al., 1995; Horton Taylor et al., 1996; Cockburn et al., 1997a, b; Viney et al, 1999). It was felt that given there are likely to be a number of competing factors which influence a women's decision to participate; hence, information on stated preferences would be important to shed light on the relative importance of, and marginal trade-offs between, key attributes. This information then could be used to show how marginal changes to the delivery of a service are likely to impact the probability of participation and identify more feasible participation enhancement strategies. This chapter focuses on a study of the intended decisions of women invited to reattend an Australian breast screening service.

M. Ryan, K. Gerard and M. Amaya-Amaya (eds.), Using Discrete Choice Experiments to Value Health and Health Care, 117–137.
© 2008 *Springer.*

1.1. Some Received Wisdom

The function of a typical breast screening service is to recruit eligible, usually well, women in each screening cycle and to manage them from the point of screening up to, and including histological or cytological diagnosis of breast cancer. This process involves a series of stages: screening, assessment, notification of results, referral for treatment if necessary, and regular reinvitation and rescreening (Slaytor and Ward, 1998). Along the screening pathway the service provider may choose to influence participation choices by impacting how the service is delivered. However, it is important to recognise that as the beneficiary of breast screening is asymptomatic at the time of screening it may be argued that regular breast screening participation is a decision to invest in information about current health status and process of care received as much as it is about improving health. For this reason it is important that decision makers examine women's preferences for breast screening and intended behaviour towards it more closely to learn more about key factors of a breast screening service which are amenable to change and influence participation.

Each individual woman's decision to be screened will depend upon a complex interaction between her perception of screening value, how well informed she is, how able and willing she is to make her own participation decisions about screening and the attributes of the screening service. From consumer satisfaction surveys we understand that high satisfaction with a given attendance for breast screening strongly influences future attendance (Bakker et al., 1998). Other behavioural studies suggest that improved promotional materials might enhance participation by communicating realistic views of screening, including that most women do not find the procedure particularly painful, steps taken to minimise embarrassment; and clarifying misconceptions about perceived risk of breast cancer (Munn, 1993; Cockburn et al., 1997a; Baines et al., 1990; Kee et al., 1992). They may also be used to encourage individuals who did not "get around to it" last time, those who thought they did not need to reattend because they had a clear result previously (Kaye et al., 1996), or who could not attend previously due to poor health (Elwood et al., 1998).

In addition, some non-attenders have found existing breast screening services inconvenient, lacked the time to do it or found travel distances excessive (Rimer et al., 1989; Baines et al., 1990). Thus, there is potential to investigate ways to reduce these barriers by improving location, frequency and timing of sessions.

Many of these previous studies provide helpful insights into behaviour, but they are somewhat limited in terms of their usefulness for policy and management decision making. Limitations include many studies do not quantify the change or show the strength of preference required to enhance participation while others focus only on factors the service provider cannot directly manipulate. The study described in this chapter uses a DCE approach to illustrate how the health care decision maker can use it as a tool to predict the impact of reconfiguring existing services in ways that are compatible with the preferences of women invited for screening and that will enhance participation.

2. METHODS

2.1. A Model of Breast Rescreening

Hypothetical yet realistic scenarios for breast screening services were presented to respondents. Respondents were asked a series of dichotomous choices of the form whether or not they would reattend for screening in the future if the service was as described. Each "yes/no" decision for each scenario was then modelled as a binary discrete choice where "yes" indicated the subject would accept screening, and "no" indicated that they would not accept. A "yes" response indicated that the utility of accepting a particular screening scenario i was greater than the utility of rejecting it. This binary choice model is a simplification of the multiple choice model discussed in Chapter 1 and is specified as follows:

$$U_i = V_i + \varepsilon_i \qquad (5.1)$$

Where U_i is the latent utility of a choice option for consumer n and is assumed random, V_i is the systematic (explainable) component of utility and ε_i is the random disturbance.

In the case of a "yes/no" response to a single choice scenario, a "yes" response indicates that the utility of accepting is greater than the utility of rejecting, as specified below:

$$\text{Probability } (Y \mid Y,N;X) = \text{probability } (U^{\text{yes}}_i \geq U^{\text{no}}_i) \qquad (5.2)$$

where Y is choose the "yes" scenario; N is choose the "no" scenario; X is a design matrix that describes scenarios as combinations of attribute levels and U_i is true utility of the ith choice.

Assuming the individual obtains no utility when she says "no" to scenario i (i.e. probability ($U^{\text{no}}_i = 0$)) we have

$$\text{Probability } (Y) = \text{probability } (U^{\text{yes}}_i > 0) \qquad (5.3)$$

The utility that individual n obtains from a particular scenario i in choice situation t ($t = 1, 2, \ldots, T$ choices) was specified as:

$$U_{int} = V_{int} + \varepsilon_{int} = \beta'X_{int} + \gamma'Z_{int} + \varepsilon_{int} \qquad (5.4)$$

where, in line with most literature, systematic utilities V_{nit} are assumed linear in parameters and a function of a matrix of attributes and their levels pertaining to the breast screening service (X_{int}) and a matrix of other covariates Z_{int} pertaining to socio-demographics (age, employment), health status and health service experience such as previous experience of screening and whether breast cancer is at the forefront of the individual's thinking. β' and γ' are the vectors of coefficients associated with X_{int} and Z_{int}. Given that multiple observations, which are unlikely to be independent, were obtained from each individual, an error components assumption was made about the disturbances whereby disturbances are decomposed as $\varepsilon_{int} = v_{int} + u_{in}$; where v_{int} embodies an individual-specific component and u_{in} denotes the remainder random error. It is assumed that v_{int} are independent and normally distributed with zero mean and constant conditional variance, σ_v^2 and that they are orthogonal (uncorrelated) to the u_{in} and the explanatory variables X_{int} and Z_{int}. This implies that the correlation between two successive error terms for the same individual is a constant (*Rho*). This random effects specification allows one to test for correlations across the different responses obtained from each individual (Greene, 1999). The random errors u_{in} are assumed to follow an EV type I or Gumbel distribution.

2.2. Screening Pathway, Attributes and Levels

In the current study, we focused on attributes relating to core elements of the screening pathway, i.e. the common (generic) aspects of any breast screening service. These core elements were: "recruitment", "screening", "notification of screening results" and screening outcome.

Perhaps not surprisingly, we found there was a long list of potentially important attributes identified in the literature that could be used to characterise breast screening services (Cockburn and White, 1994; Knowles et al., 1996). With help from collaborators directly involved in service delivery (at state and local levels) a reduced set containing ten key attributes was identified. Nine related to different aspects of the screening process and one to the outcome. Two attributes-concerned aspects of the recruitment phase, six focused on the screening phase and one each reflected aspects of notification of results and outcome (see Table 5.1).

In selecting these attributes, levels and units of measurement, we tried to reflect, as closely as possible, the key drivers of the woman's choice to rescreen whilst at the same time reflect aspects of the way the service is delivered that could be manipulated by the provider. Published minimum national screening standards (CDHS&H, 1994) were helpful sources for assigning attribute levels to certain aspects of the screening process and consultation with service providers also helped to ensure sufficient variation of levels was represented.

2.2.1. Selecting the attribute and levels for screening outcome

There continues to be considerable debate in the literature over how to define and measure screening outcomes (e.g. Sox, 1998; Cockburn et al., 1995; Woloshin et al., 2000; Raffle, 2001). For our purpose it was adequate to use sensitivity of screening (i.e. true cancer detection rate) to indicate screening outcome. At the time it was shown that a sizeable proportion of Australian breast screening programmes (26%), including our study site, used this measure in promotional leaflets to inform women of screening benefit (Slaytor and Ward, 1998). Therefore, whilst we acknowledge this measure is unlikely to provide an accurate account of screening outcome as it misses out specificity (i.e. those screened negative who truly do not have the disease), it was a definition that we could expect our sample to be familiar with and not confused by. We do, however, recognise the importance of conducting future work to assess the impact of a broader concept of screening benefit, including the specificity of screening.

TABLE 5.1. *Enumeration of attributes and levels*

Screening pathway	Attribute (variable name(s))	Attribute level (design code)
Recruitment	Method of inviting women for rescreening (HINFFX0, HINFFX1, HINFFX2, HINFFX3)	Personal reminder letter from the local service [0]
		Personal reminder letter and recommendation by your GP [1]
		A media campaign [2]
		A recommendation from your family or friends [3]
	Information included with invitation (ISHT)	Sheet about the procedure, benefits and risks of breast cancer screening [0]
		No information sheet [1]
Screening	Time to wait for an appointment (WAPPT)	1 week [0]
		4 weeks [1]
	Choice of appointment times (APPCH)	Usual office hours [0]
		Usual office hours, one evening per week, Saturday morning [1]
	Time spent travelling (TTFX0, TTFX1, TTFX2, TTFX3)	Not more than 20 min [0] Between 20 and 40 min [1] Between 40 and 60 min [2] Between 1 and 2 h [3]
	How staff at the screening service relate to you (STAFF)	"Welcoming" manner [0] "Reserved" manner [1]
	Attention paid to privacy (PRIV)	Private changing area [0]
		Open changing area [1]
	Total spent attending for mammogram (SCTTFX0, SCTTFX1, SCTTFX2, SCTTFX3)	20 min [0] 30 min [1] 40 min [2] 50 min [3]
Results notification	Time to notification of results (WRFX0, WRFX1, WRFX2, WRFX3)	8 working days [0]
		10 working days [1]
		12 working days [2]
		14 working days [3]
Screening outcome	Level of accuracy of the screening test (ACCFX0, ACCFX1, ACCFX2, ACCFX3)	70% [0] 80% [1] 90% [2] 100% [3]

Definition of the screening outcome levels also requires further clarification. We opted to use four levels of accuracy: 70%, 80%, 90% and 100%. In Chapter 1 it was noted that, when choosing levels for the attributes, the analyst must decided how far to stretch the imagination of the respondent yet at the same time convey information which is treated credibly. In this study, there is an issue in setting an accuracy level of 100%.

Whilst it is highly unlikely that breast screening is 100% accurate, the inclusion of this level results in trade-offs that are easier to understand and differences in levels that are large enough for subjects to perceive real differences. The literature on risk shows that individuals have difficulty in understanding risk information. Individuals view events as more likely if they are familiar; and they respond to risk information differently if presented as relative risks compared with absolute risks (Lloyd, 2001). Furthermore, risk attributes have been incorporated in DCE instruments in a variety of ways with little exploration of what is most appropriate for the study in question. We felt the best approach for this study was to look for evidence that the estimated utilities were systematically related to the accuracy levels. Such evidence would suggest that we can use the estimated utility function to extrapolate an estimate of part-worth (or marginal) utility for a more realistically attainable maximum level of accuracy.

2.3. Experimental Design and Survey Instrument

The next step in the DCE was to create an experimental design to generate combinations of attribute levels that describe the breast screening scenarios to be evaluated. All possible combinations of the attribute levels is given by a complete factorial, which in this case was five attributes with four levels and five with two levels, i.e. there are $4^5 \times 2^5$ (= 32,768) possible combinations, which is too large for use in an empirical study. A smaller, orthogonal fractional factorial design was used instead; this design can independently estimate three two-attribute interaction effects as well as all ten main effects independently of one another (see Section 2.5 for more discussion on this issue). (The design was created by JL.) The design produced 32 breast screening scenarios. In order to reduce the number of scenarios that any one respondent evaluated, we blocked the design into two versions of 16 scenarios each using an extra two-level column in the design (see Hensher et al., 2005 for a fuller discussion of this issue). A typical choice scenario is shown in Table 5.2.

A self-complete postal return questionnaire was handed out to women attending for screening that contained the DCE. The survey used simple, clear and informative language throughout. In addition to the choice scenarios, other questions were included to: provide a "warm up" example, obtain important demographic information about the participants and assess validity; these measures represent covariates that are included in the choice model.

2.4. Participants

The study was conducted in Sydney, Australia, at a local metropolitan breast screening and assessment service. Participants were a convenience sample of women

TABLE 5.2. *Example of a breast screening choice (scenario)*

	Screening service
How you are informed	A personal letter and recommendation by your GP
Information sheet provided with invitation	No information sheet
Wait for an appointment	1 week
Appointment choices	Usual office hours, one evening per week and Saturday mornings
Time spent travelling (one way)	Between 20 and 40 min
How staff relate to you	Welcoming manner
Privacy	Private changing area
Time spent having screen	20 min
Time waiting for results	12 working days
Accuracy of results	100%

Imagine that your next invitation to be screened is approaching, would you choose to attend this particular screening service or not? (tick one box only)   YES❑   NO❑

who were in the process of attending for breast screening. They were asked to provide their preferences for future screening experiences. A total of 180 questionnaires were randomly distributed during June and August 1999. Women who attended with an interpreter or were unwilling to participate were excluded from the study.

2.5. Model Refinement and Estimation Procedure

Before the model represented by Equation 5.4 could be specified, we needed to make two methodological decisions. The first one was to decide which attributes would be assigned to the columns in the design that allow their interactions to be estimated. A significant interaction implies that the utility derived from one attribute depends on the level of the second attribute, for example, the response to the cost of screening may depend on the accuracy level. At lower accuracy levels, women may be more sensitive to cost levels than at higher accuracy levels. As noted in Louviere et al. (2000), while interaction terms often are ignored in practice, this does not mean that they do not matter. If one's research objective is to better understand respondent's behaviour (rather than merely predict responses to one or more changes in attributes), it may be important to estimate key interactions of interest. This subsequently begs the question of how to decide which interactions to include in the experiment. In some cases theory or prior empirical evidence may help one decide; in other cases there may be little basis for deciding other than intuition, practicality and plausibility, which was the case in the current study.

The design allowed us to estimate two interaction terms: two 2×2 interactions and one 4×2 interaction. It seemed reasonable a priori that the length of time waiting for a screening appointment (WAPPT) and the time of day of the appointment (APPCH) would jointly relate to ease of accessing breast screening. It was also felt that the privacy of the service (PRIV) and staff manner (STAFF) also might interact; i.e. a service committed to privacy is more likely to offer a "welcoming" staff manner. Interaction terms are represented in the statistical analyses as simple cross products where the attributes are effects-coded (referring to Equation 5.5 below these were represented by the variables WATT_APP and STAFF_PR, respectively). The third interaction involved the impact of method of invitation and whether or not women had access to an information sheet. Women may react more strongly to an information sheet combined with a personal reminder letter from the local service (HINFFX0) and, also possibly, with a personal reminder letter and recommendation by the general practitioner (GP) (HINFFX1) than the remaining levels of invitation method (either population based in nature or reliant on word of mouth). However, it is important to note that these interaction terms are (a) not exhaustive and (b) there may be other interpretations of the interactions than the examples we provided. Other interactions also could have been considered, and one might want to include them in future research on this issue.

The second methodological decision concerns how best to represent the attribute effects in econometric terms (i.e. based on the data matrix described in Chapter 3). In this study, there are five qualitative and five quantitative attributes. One can decide to retain the actual measurement units for the quantitative attributes and use dummy coding for qualitative attributes (see, e.g. Chapter 3). Another possibility is to use effects codes to represent some or all attributes. Both coding approaches allow one to capture non-linear attribute effects. Dummy coding confounds the level chosen to represent the baseline with the constant term (or grand mean), whereas effects coding orthogonalises the attribute effects to the intercept (grand mean). A second advantage of effects codes is that the attribute interaction effects can be independently estimated; whereas, dummy coding results in artificially high correlations of interactions and main effects. Hence, there are pros and cons to using either (see Louviere et al., 2000; Bech and Gyrd-Hansen, 2005 for more discussion). We chose to use effects coding in order to be able to visualise all the attribute effects, and because as previously noted, we were concerned about using an unobtainable level of maximum accuracy. We also wanted to visualise the relationship between utility and time (i.e. attributes involving travel time, screen time and time waiting for results) to determine whether typical assumptions of linearity are justified. Because subsequent interpretations of the analysis hinges on this assumption, we decided to explore its relevance in this study. By doing this we hoped to better understand (and represent) breast screening behaviour, not merely to predict the impact of changes.

TABLE 5.3. *Example of effects coding for attribute "accuracy"*

Attribute: "accuracy"	Effects code variables		
	ACCFX0	ACCFX1	ACCFX2
Level 1 – 70%	1	0	0
Level 2 – 80%	0	1	0
Level 3 – 90%	0	0	1
Level 4 (base level) 100%	−1	−1	−1

This is important if one wants to design and implement well-informed participation strategies.

Effects coding all attributes increases the number of effects to be estimated. In particular, each L-level attribute has L-1 effects (or dummy) codes. Thus, our study required 20 effects to be estimated for main effects ($5^*3 + 5^*1$) and a further five effects for the interaction terms. As noted earlier, a key difference between dummy and effects coding involves interpretation of the intercept term ($\beta 0$). With dummy coding the omitted level (i.e. the level used as the reference) is confounded with the intercept, whereas with effects coding the reference level is defined as the negative sum of the L-1-estimated coefficients, and so is identified.[1] In turn, effects coded estimates of part-worth or marginal utilities can be presented graphically and used as a starting point for deciding whether or not to introduce non-linearities in main effects and interactions into the choice model. Table 5.3 illustrates how one of the attributes, namely accuracy of test, was effects coded.

It follows then that the full specification of the utility model to be estimated is:

$$U_{in} = \beta 0 + \beta 1 * \text{HINFFX0} + \beta 2 * \text{HINFFX1} + \beta 3 * \text{HINFFX2} + \beta 4 * \text{ISHT}$$
$$+ \beta 5 * \text{WAPPT} + \beta 6 * \text{APPCH} + \beta 7 * \text{TTFX0} + \beta 8 * \text{TTFX1} + \beta 9 * \text{TTFX2}$$
$$+ \beta 10 * \text{STAFF} + \beta 11 * \text{PRIV} + \beta 12 * \text{SCTTFX0} + \beta 13 * \text{SCTTFX1}$$
$$+ \beta 14 * \text{SCTTFX2} + \beta 15 * \text{WRFX0} + \beta 16 * \text{WRFX1} + \beta 17 * \text{WRFX2}$$
$$+ \beta 18 * \text{ACCFX0} + \beta 19 * \text{ACCFX1} + \beta 20 * \text{ACCFX2} + \beta 21 * \text{ISHHINFX0}$$
$$+ \beta 22 * \text{ISHHINFX1} + \beta 23 * \text{ISHHINFX2} + \beta 24 * \text{WATT\_APP} + \beta 25 * \text{STAFF\_PR} + \gamma'Z \ (5.5)$$

where: $\beta 0$ is a constant (intercept) term; $\beta 1$–$\beta 20$ are estimates of main effect attribute levels (see Table 5.1 for identification of each one – note following standard econometric convention L-1 attribute levels are required for model estimation, which in this case means all the Lth (i.e. 4th) level attributes are omitted in the model above[2]); $\beta 21$–$\beta 25$ are estimates of interaction effects; Z is the set of covariate terms of interest (see bottom right in Table 5.5) and γ' the set of estimates for these covariate terms. All other terms as previously defined.

2.6. Expected Relationships

Given the specified model with effects-coded variables, expected relationships can be identified to support the validity of the model (see notes accompanying Table 5.5 for further details of coding used). In particular, we expected utility to be negatively related to estimates for time travelled, screened, wait time for results and waiting time for an appointment, and utility should be positively related to test accuracy, privacy and how staff related to the screenee. Expected relationships with remaining effects either were more speculative or, simply, unknowable; hence, cannot contribute to establishing model validity.

2.7. Analysis

Consistent with the accepted wisdom reported in Chapter 1, we analysed the response data using a binary logit model, although in the case of binary choices, there is little difference in practice between results from probit and logit models, which should be similar up to scale (Ben-Akiva and Lerman, 1985).[3]

Equation 5.1 was estimated using a random effects binary logit regression. The probability that an individual says "yes" to a scenario i in choice situation t is

$$\text{Probability}\,(Y \mid Y, N; X) = \text{probability}\,(U_i^{\text{yes}} \geq U_i^{\text{no}}) \hspace{2cm} (5.6)$$
$$= P\left(\exp^{V\text{yesi}/}\sum \exp(^{V\text{yesii}+V\text{noi}})\right) = 1/1 + e^{-V\text{int}}$$

where V_{int} is defined as in Equation 5.5.

LIMDEP 8.0 (NLOGIT 3.0) was used to estimate the binary logit model. Estimation results and summary statistics for model performance are reported. As in Chapter 1, these statistics relate to (a) overall model significance (χ^2); (b) goodness of fit; and (c) predictive capability (percentage of correctly predicted responses). We also provide the within-subject correlation coefficient (Rho). In addition, we graph part-worth utility estimates against their levels to visually assess their functional form.

Choice probabilities also are calculated to provide a way to convey DCE results to decisions makers that is more easily understandable. We present these results in the form of a Christmas tree or "tornedo" graph[4] to illustrate the marginal effect of varying attribute levels on the predicted probability of uptake. The comparisons are made by varying one attribute level at a time from a base case, holding all other attributes constant. This approach provides insights into the way in which each attribute systematically affects choices relative to a base case scenario. The "base case" used in this study represents current local practice where the DCE survey was administered, and represents choice probabilities associated with the "typical" woman attending for screening (reflecting modal socio-demographic and other information from the DCE survey). These results allow one to inform policy analysis by evaluating any number of alternative options for reconfiguring a local breast screening service compared with current practice.

3. RESULTS

3.1. Response Rate and Survey Characteristics

Eighty-seven useable surveys were returned, for an overall response rate of 48%. The total number of choice observations was 1,392 (86×16). Responses from all individuals were judged to be consistent (a simple dominance test was embedded in the design, for more details see Gerard et al., 2003). A summary of the personal characteristics of the sample is shown in Table 5.4.

3.2. Regression Analysis

Logit regression results are in Table 5.5. The statistical significance Rho ($Rho = 0.41$, $P < 0.000$) implies that there is significant unobserved correlation over the multiple responses obtained from each individual, suggesting that a random effects specification is appropriate. The model in Table 5.5 is statistically significant ($\chi^2 = 54.23$) and fits the data reasonably well (pseudo R^2, 0.174). It also predicted 76% of the responses correctly.

The signs of the coefficients for attribute main effects were as expected, suggesting that the model is consistent with a priori expectations; one exception was attribute levels for waiting time for results (WRFX0, WRFX1, WRFX2 and WRFX3), which produced counter-intuitive results, but were not statistically significantly different from zero. The attribute "method of invitation" only exhibited one significant effect, namely for the level "media campaign" (HINFFX2), and the sign on this coefficient indicates that if a media campaign were the only invitation received for screening, it would have a negative impact (i.e. fewer women would choose to return for screening by this method). For two of the time attributes TTFX0, TTFX1, TTFX2, TTFX3 and SCTFX0, SCTFX1, SCTFX2, SCTFX3, as time levels increased women were less likely to screen in the future. Similarly, as accuracy of results (ACCFX0, ACCFX1, ACCFX2, ACCFX3) improved, women were more likely to choose to rescreen. Respondents also were more likely, *ceteris paribus*, to choose to rescreen if the service had private changing areas and provided information about screening benefits.

Of the remaining attributes the choice of appointment waiting time, appointment slot and how staff related to the woman were not statistically significant predictors of choice. Also, no interaction effects were significant. Of the various covariate terms investigated the only ones to reach statistical significance were if the typical respondent thought a lot about breast cancer and if his or her age was greater than 69 years.[5]

TABLE 5.4. *Personal characteristics of women surveyed*

Personal characteristics	Level	$n\,(N = 87)$
Health status	Excellent	29
	Good	47
	Fair or poor	11
How often do you think about breast cancer?	None of the time	14
	A little of the time	50
	Less than little	23
Has anyone close to you had breast cancer?	Yes	43
	No	44
How often do you examine your breasts?	At least every 2 months	33
	At least every 6 months	33
	Never	21
How many breast screens have you had previously?	First or second	15
	Third or more	72
How many invitations or reminders did you receive?	One	61
	More than one	26
How painful was your mammogram?	Not painful	24
	A little painful	45
	More than a little painful	18
Marital status	Currently not married	23
	Currently married/ defacto	64
Age	Less than 50 years	24
	50–69 years	55
	>69 years	8
Main activity	Work full-time	30
	Work part-time	25
	Not working	29

TABLE 5.5. Random effects logit model: main and selected interaction effects with screenees' personal characteristics

Variable	β	SE	P value	Variable	β	SE	P value
Constant	0.161	0.000	1.000	Accuracy of test 70% (ACCFX0)	-1.287	0.163	0.000
Main effects				Accuracy of test 80% (ACCFX1)	-0.414	0.163	0.011
Personal letter from service (HINFFX0)	0.227	0.191	0.234	Accuracy of test 90% (ACCFX2)	0.231	0.148	0.119
Personal letter from service and GP recommendation (HINFFX1)	0.252	0.167	0.130	Accuracy of test 100% (ACCFX3)[6]	1.469	0.0167	0.000
Media campaign (HINFFX2)	-0.348	0.192	0.070	*Interaction effects*			
Recommended by family (HINFFX3)[7]	-0.131	0.020	0.475	ISHT * HINFFX0 (ISHHINFX0)	0.009	0.149	0.952
Information sheet included (ISHT)[8]	0.196	0.074	0.008	ISHT * HINFFX1 (ISHHINFX1)	-0.070	0.175	0.690
Appointment waiting time (WAPPT)[9]	-0.083	0.093	0.373	ISHT * HINFFX2 (ISHHINFX2)	-0.064	0.159	0.689
Choice of appointment (APPCH)[10]	0.172	0.120	0.151	WAPPT * APPCH (WATT_APP)	0.062	0.121	0.608
Travel time 20 min (TTFX0)	0.402	0.126	0.001	STAFF * PRIV (STAFF_PR)	0.111	0.083	0.179
Travel time 30 min (TTFX1)	0.337	0.125	0.007	*Covariates*			
Travel time 50 min (TTFX2)	0.002	0.134	0.989	Never think of bc (GETBC0)	0.539	0.000	1.000

(continued)

TABLE 5.5. (continued)

Variable	β	SE	P value	Variable	β	SE	P value
Travel time 90 min (TTFX3)[11]	−0.741	0.013	0.000	Sometimes think of bc (GETBC1)	−0.033	0.000	1.000
How staff relate (STAFF)[12]	0.172	0.109	0.112	Think of bc a lot (GETBC2)[13]	−0.506	0.000	0.000
Privacy of changing facilities (PRIV)[14]	0.410	0.088	0.000	No. of screens (VISITFRE)[15]	−0.557	0.506	0.271
Screening time 20 min (SCTFX0)	0.275	0.138	0.047	No. of reminder letters (LETFREQ)[16]	−0.241	0.462	0.602
Screening time 30 min (SCTFX1)	0.226	0.129	0.079	Marital status (MARITAL)[17]	−0.251	0.379	0.508
Screening time 40 min (SCTFX2)	−0.056	0.158	0.722	Less than 50 years old (AGE0)	−0.320	0.386	0.407
Screening time 50 min (SCTFX3)[18]	−0.444	0.015	0.002	Aged between 50 and 69 years (AGE1)	−0.436	0.270	0.106
Results in 8 working days (WRFX0)	−0.096	0.166	0.564	More than 69 years old (AGE2)[19]	0.757	0.035	0.021
Results in 10 working days (WRFX1)	−0.091	0.147	0.539	Full-time employment (ACT0)	−0.111	0.295	0.706
Results in 12 working days (WRFX2)	0.150	0.145	0.302	Part-time employment (ACT1)	0.211	0.273	0.440
Results in 14 working days (WRFX3)[20]	0.037	0.016	0.809	Not employed (ACT2)[21]	−0.099	0.030	0.727
				Rho	0.410	0.038	0.000

Log-likelihood, −570; number of individuals, 87; number of observations, 1,392; percentage 1s and 0s predicted correctly, 76.43%; pseudo R^2, 0.174, $\chi^2 = 54.23$, $P < 0.00$

3.3. Assessing the Assumption of Linearity in Key Attributes

The attribute "accuracy of the test" was of particular interest for reasons mentioned previously. The effects coding allows us to look more closely at the relationship between estimated part-worth utility and the test accuracy levels to visualise the relationship with estimated utilities. Figure 5.1 clearly shows a positive linear relationship between utility and accuracy, which in turn suggests that a linear assumption would have been reasonable in this case. Had the finding been different the graphical information may have provided insights into the form of an alternative, more appropriate relationship to fit (e.g. quadratic or logarithmic forms).

This finding also supports the view that it is feasible to identify a lower, more realistic, maximum level of accuracy than the 100% level used. We can use the linear assumption to quantify utility for a more attainable maximum level of accuracy, say 95%, by extrapolating the value from the graph.

Similarly, we can do the same graphical analysis for any of the other four-level attributes. For reasons of expediency we only present the graphical plot for screening time. In this instance, we argue that there is weaker evidence of a negative linear relationship between level and part-worth utility. Figure 5.2 clearly reveals that the relationship between the utility estimates and the attribute levels for screening time is not linear. Despite this, we chose to represent the relationship as linear for parsimony reasons. Also, the design we used was an orthogonal main effects plan (OMEP) that requires us to assume that ALL unobserved effects equal zero; and as only one level in the graph is associated with the non-linearity, this could be due to omitted variable bias. As noted by Louviere et al. (2000), this is a major disadvantage of using OMEPs to design DCEs that unfortunately also means that we cannot estimate alternative specifications that do not assume linearity. Thus, we assumed that this relationship was linear over the range of levels SCTFX0, SCTFX1, SCTFX2 and SCTFX3. Even if this is incorrect, a linear relationship still will approximate the relationship reasonably well over the range.

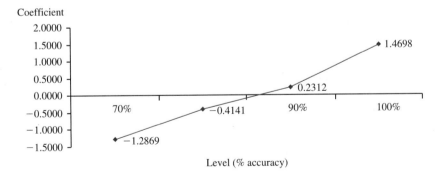

FIGURE 5.1. Plot of part-worth estimates for accuracy of test by level

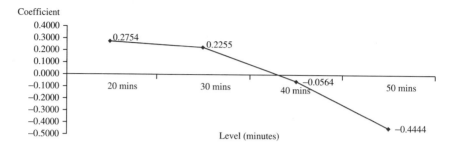

FIGURE 5.2. *Plot of part-worth estimates for screening time by level*

Overall, we inferred from this analysis that it appeared justifiable to assume linearity in the (statistically significant) parameters.

3.4. Estimating Probability of Participation: Policy Analysis

We estimated the probability of participation for the base case, which was defined in terms of the variables identified in Table 5.5; a variable was coded equal to "1" if the variable applied and "0" if it did not. These values effectively switched on or off (as appropriate) the coefficient value assigned to the respective variable, allowing us to estimate the overall utility of the base case. Next, Equation 5.6 was used to predict the probability of participation in the next rescreening round at the local service, which was approximately 65%, a participation level significantly below the target rates set at the time (75% of initial screens required to be rescreened at the first rescreening round; and 90% of these rescreened in subsequent rounds (CDHS&H, 1994)). Naturally, this begs the question of how best to raise participation.

Figure 5.3 graphs the marginal changes in the predicted probability of participation associated with each attribute level in the choice model compared to the base case (indicated as zero change in the probability of the x-axis). Presenting information in this way allows a policy maker to quickly glean detailed information about how important these attributes are in terms of their separate influence on participation, and to evaluate the size of the effect of each attribute with respect to improvements in predicted participation probability.

Significant attributes are of particular interest to service providers (all attribute levels are included because the overall model was significant). Horizontal bars on the left-hand side of the base case represent reductions in the probability of participation; bars on the right-hand side represent positive effects. The attribute that would provide the greatest leverage to a provider is accuracy, which exhibits the widest range in marginal probabilities (a rise from base case accuracy, i.e. from 90% to 100%, increases the probability of participation by 21%, a fall to 70% accuracy reduces participation by 36%). Accuracy rates can be affected by some of the attributes such as who is invited, the screening frequency and method of reading mammograms. As another example of using this information as part of a decision tool, the data suggest that if women think

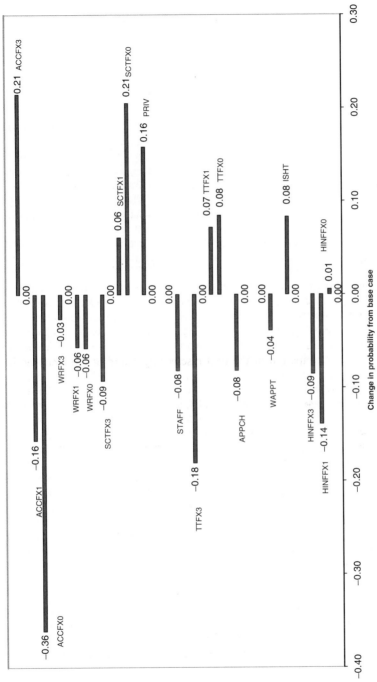

FIGURE 5.3. Marginal probabilities in predicted probability of participation

the time spent being screened is as quick as possible (i.e. 20 min), this can increase participation by 21%. Again, there are a number of ways to configure the service to reduce screening time (e.g. overhauling the appointment system, available staffing levels). Thus, this type of marginal probability information can be used to assess which attributes may be most effective as part of a participation enhancement strategy.

4. DISCUSSION

This chapter demonstrated the feasibility of using the DCE technique to elicit preferences for breast screening services from women eligible for screening. In setting up the experiment, we explored two methodological issues. The first was how to incorporate interaction terms into the model, and there is little guidance in the literature as to how practitioners should do this. Our approach was pragmatic and explicit, but it seems clear that more research in this area is needed. The second issue challenged naïve assumptions of linearity in attributes by undertaking a visual assessment of the implied relationships that was more systematic than most previous work in this area in health economics. Effects coding was able to provide useful insights into screening behaviour, but it also raised issues as to how meaningful unit changes in marginal rates of substitution might be if linearity is not satisfied.

Subject to some caveats our results suggest that the estimated model was consistent with a priori expectations, and non-health attributes and the accuracy of screening influenced the probability of screening uptake. Attributes that were particularly important were screening time, travel time, information about screening benefits and the desire for privacy. This lends weight to the argument that it is advisable that decision makers consult eligible screenees directly before embarking on strategies to improve participation.

Of course our study has a number of limitations (see Gerard et al., 2003 for further details). A key limitation mentioned at the outset was that we recognise the importance of conducting future work to assess the impact of a broader concept of screening benefit, including the specificity of screening.

In summary, while we showed that DCEs can be an economic tool to help decision makers identify the most feasible participation enhancement strategy in screening services like breast screening, the knowledge and experience of the provider remains paramount in determining which aspects of the service are amenable to change, including consideration of barriers to change, supply constraints and costs. Finally, it is important to remember that although a DCE approach would allow decision makers to predict the impact of a new service or reconfiguration of existing services, any proposed change would still require rigorous economic evaluation.

ACKNOWLEDGEMENTS

Thanks to: the staff and women at BreastScreen NSW, North Sydney and Lower Central Coast screening and assessment service for their participation; BreastScreen NSW State coordination Unit and Northern Sydney Area Health Service; and our colleagues Madeleine King, Denzil Fiebig, and Angela Yeoh for their contributions. Financial support was provided by The University of Sydney.

ENDNOTES

[1] See Hensher, Rose and Green (2005) and Bech and Gyrd-Hansen (2005) for a discussion of dummy and effects codes.

[2] Coefficients for missing levels can be calculated retrospectively, see how in note 5.

[3] The probit model was used for the published paper Gerard et al. (2003).

[4] See pp 280–281 of Louviere et al. (2000) for further details.

[5] As this is a binary choice model covariates do not need to be interacted with attributes, but generally this would be the case in multiple choice models.

[6] As L-1 levels are estimated in the model, the missing level can be calculated using the following equation, $\beta_4 = (-1 * \beta_1) + (-1 * \beta_2) + (-1 * \beta_3)$. The standard deviation for the missing level is the average of the estimated attribute levels and P-values are found in standard T-tables. For example, see web site http://www.anu.edu.au/nceph/surfstat/surfstat-home/tables/normal.php (last accessed 29 November 2006).

[7] As note 5 above.

[8] Two levels coded as 0 = no information sheet, 1 = information sheet.

[9] Two levels coded as 0 = 1 week, 1 = 4 weeks.

[10] Two levels coded as 0 = usual hours, 1 = usual hours plus some weekends/evenings.

[11] As note 5 above.

[12] Two levels coded as 0 = "reserved" manner, 1 = "welcoming" manner.

[13] As note 5 above.

[14] Two levels coded as 0 = open, 1 = private.

[15] Two levels coded as 0 = 1st or 2nd visit, 1 = 3 or more.

[16] Two levels coded as 0 = one letter, 1 = more than one letter.

[17] Two levels coded as 0 = not married, 1 = married.

[18] As note 5 above.

[19] As note 5 above.

[20] As note 5 above.

[21] As note 5 above.

REFERENCES

Baines, C.J., To, T. and Wall, C. 1990. Women's attitudes to screening after participation in the National Breast Screening Study. A questionnaire survey. *Cancer*, vol 65, 1663–1669.

Bakker, D.A., Lightfoot, N.E., Steggles, S. and Jackson, C. 1998. The experience and satisfaction of women attending breast cancer screening. *Oncology Nursing Forum*, vol 25, 115–121.

Ben-Akiva, M. and Lerman, S. 1985. *Discrete Choice Analysis: Theory and application to travel demand.* Cambridge, MIT Press.

Bech, M. and Gyrd-Hansen, D. 2005. Effects coding in discrete choice experiments. *Health Economics*, vol 14, 1079–1083.

Cockburn, J. and White, V. 1994. Review of Australian research into behavioural aspects of screening mammography. Centre for Behavioural Research into Cancer, University of Melbourne, Melbourne, Australia.

Cockburn, J., Redman, S., Hill, D. and Henry, E. 1995. Public understanding of medical screening. *Journal of Medical Screening*, vol 2, 224–227.

Cockburn, J., Schofield, P., White, V., Hill, D. and Russell, I. 1997a. Predictors of returning for second round screening at a population based mammographic screening programme in Melbourne, Australia. *Journal of Epidemiology and Community Health*, vol 51, 62–66.

Cockburn, J., Sutherland, M., Cappiello, M. and Hevern, M. 1997b. Predictors of attendance at a relocatable mammography service for rural women. *Australian and New Zealand Journal of Public Health*, vol 21, 739–742.

Commonwealth Department of Human Services and Health (CDHS&H). 1994. National Accreditation Requirements, National Program for the Early Detection Breast Cancer. Canberra: Australian Government Publishing Service.

Elwood, M., McNoe, B., Smith, T., Bandaranayake, M. and Doyle, T.C. 1998. Once is enough–why some women do not continue to participate in a breast cancer screening programme, *New Zealand Medical Journal*, 111:1066, 180–183.

Gerard, K., Shanahan, M. and Louviere, J. 2003. Using Stated Preference Discrete Choice Modelling to inform health care decision-making: a pilot study of breast screening participation. *Applied Economics*, vol 35, 1073–1085.

Greene, W. 1999. Econometric Analysis. Upper Saddle River, NJ: Prentice Hall.

Hensher, D., Rose, J. and Greene, W.H. 2005. Applied Choice Analysis: A Primer. Cambridge: Cambridge University Press.

Horton Taylor, D., McPherson, K., Parbhoo, S. and Perry, N. 1996. Response of women aged 65–74 to invitation for screening for breast cancer by mammography: a pilot study in London, UK. *Journal of Epidemiology and Community Health*, vol 50, 77–80.

Kaye, F., King, A., Ryan, R. and Sadler, G. 1996. Reasons for failure to re-attend for repeat screening mammography in women aged 50–69 years of age in Western Australia, Perth, University of Western Australia.

Kee, F., Telford, A.M., Donaghy, P. and O'Doherty, A. 1992. Attitude or access: reasons for not attending mammography in Northern Ireland. *European Journal of Cancer Prevention*, vol 1, 311–315.

Knowles, S., Dawes, V.P. and Wiese, S.M. 1996. Client Satisfaction Survey 1995. Women's Cancer Screening Service, Occasional Paper 81. University of Western Australia, Perth.

Lancaster, K. 1966. A new approach to consumer theory. *Journal of Political Economy*, vol 74, 134–157.

Lloyd, A. 2001. The extent of patients' understanding of the risk of treatments. *Quality in Health Care*, vol 10 (Suppl), i14–i18.

Louviere, J., Hensher, D. and Swait, J. 2000. Stated Choice Methods: Analysis and Application. Cambridge: Cambridge University Press.

Munn, E.M. 1993. Nonparticipation in mammography screening: apathy, anxiety or cost? *New Zealand Medical Journal*, vol 106, 284–286.

Raffle, A.E. 2001. Information about screening – is it to achieve high uptake or to ensure informed choice? *Health Expectations*, vol 4, 92–98.

Rimer, B.K., Kasper Keintz, M., Kessler, H.B., Engstrom, P.F. and Rosan, J.R. 1989. Why women resist screening mammography: patient-related barriers. *Radiology*, vol 172, 243–246.

Scaf-Klomp, W., van Sonderen, F.L., Stewart, R., van Dijck, J.A. and van den Heuvel, W.J. 1995. Compliance after 17 years of breast cancer screening. *Journal of Medical Screening*, vol 2, 195–199.

Slaytor, E.K. and Ward, J.E. 1998. How risks of breast cancer and benefits of screening are communicated to women: analysis of 58 pamphlets. *British Medical Journal*, vol 317, 263–264.

Sox, H.C. 1998. Benefit and harm associated with screening for breast cancer. *New England Journal of Medicine*, vol 338 (1), 145–146.

Viney, R., De Abreu Lorenco, R., Kitcher, D. and Gerard, K. 1999. NSW Breast and Cervical Screening Program Review. Report for NSW Department of Health, Centre for Health Economics Research and Evaluation, Sydney, Australia.

Woloshin, S., Schwartz, L., Byram, S.J., Sox, H., Fischoff, B. and Welch, G. 2000. Women's understanding of the mammography screening debate. *Archives of Internal Medicine*, vol 160, 1434–1440.

CHAPTER 6

PREFERENCES FOR HEALTH CARE PROGRAMMES

Results from a general population discrete choice survey

STIRLING BRYAN AND TRACY ROBERTS

Health Economics Facility, School of Public Policy,
University of Birmingham, UK

1. INTRODUCTION

With the rapid growth in the development of new health care technologies, including both drugs and devices, health care decision makers worldwide are facing the challenge of making technology coverage decisions. Decisions have to be made concerning which technologies to fund, and these decisions have to be made in both public and private insurance settings. In order to ensure that health care resources are used in the most appropriate manner health care decision makers need to adopt robust processes for setting priorities. Recent developments in the UK, such as the launch of the National Institute for Health and Clinical Excellence (NICE), have encouraged a more open debate about the principles and issues concerned in health care resource allocation decisions (Entwistle et al., 1996; New, 1996; Rawlins, 1999). However, the appropriate criteria that should be used in setting priorities in a publicly funded health care system are far from clear. From a health economics perspective, one criterion that might be considered as part of the decision-making process when setting health care priorities is the maximisation of quality-adjusted life years (QALYs). A QALY-maximisation approach would then involve the targeting of resources towards health care interventions and services that were expected to deliver the largest gain in QALYs, for every dollar (or pound, euro, etc.) spent.

The QALY combines two forms of outcome of health care interventions, namely health-related quality of life and survival (Williams, 1985). Survival is adjusted to reflect the fact that it may not be experienced at full health, using weightings or utilities assigned to health states. If an individual lives 4 years at full health, he or she will experience four QALYs, whilst an individual who lives for 4 years in a health state considered to be 50% of full health will enjoy only two QALYs, assuming no discounting. This allows the two outcomes (survival and quality of life) to be combined into a

M. Ryan, K. Gerard and M. Amaya-Amaya (eds.), Using Discrete Choice
Experiments to Value Health and Health Care, 139–152.
© 2008 *Springer.*

single index number which is then used as a means of making comparisons between interventions in terms of levels of benefit experienced by patients.

In considering the expected benefits of health care programmes where many patients or potential patients are targeted, the QALY calculation would typically take account of at least four features or characteristics: the number of patients receiving the programme; the probability of the treatment being successful; the survival gain if successful; and the gain in quality of life if successful. It has been argued that the QALY potentially represents a poor measure of health-related utility since only one aspect of its constituent parts, that relating to quality of life, is based upon preferences (Nord, 1994; Dolan, 1998). Thus, all other things equal, a programme treating 100 patients generates twice as many QALYs as one serving 50 patients, a 0.5 probability of treatment success leads to twice as many QALYs as a 0.25 probability, and 10-year survival generates twice the number of QALYs as 5 years (again assuming no discounting). The absence of explicit consideration of broader preferences in QALY calculations has important implications for the adoption of a QALY-maximisation criterion for use in health care resource allocation.

The objective of the study reported here was to investigate the extent to which a QALY-maximisation approach, with its proportionality assumptions relating to number of patients, success probability and length of life, is supported by members of the public. This was done through an empirical investigation of public preferences using a discrete choice experiment (DCE). In addition, the trade-offs between different components of health care programmes were also explored. A fuller account of this research is reported in Bryan et al. (2002).

2. METHODS

A general population survey was conducted, using face-to-face interviews, in order to explore preferences for the key components of the programme QALY calculation. Respondents were presented with health programme scenarios and asked to make a series of choices. Other DCE studies conducted in health care have focused on specific clinical questions (Ryan and Hughes, 1997; Bryan et al., 1998) but few studies have adopted a DCE framework for eliciting broad public preferences in health care decision making. In what follows, we describe attribute identification and level assignment, scenario presentation, data collection and data analysis.

2.1. Attribute Identification and Level Assignment

The four attributes selected to allow investigation of the core components of the QALY-maximisation model are: number of people (N); chance of success (C); survival (S); and quality of life (Q). In order to limit the number of variables to be presented to respondents, for the quality of life attribute a decision was made to focus only on two of the five components of the EQ-5D measure (EuroQol Group, 1990), namely usual activities and depression or anxiety. The focus for the study was on more challenging decisions and so the selection of attribute levels needed to represent as many realistic situations as possible where there were lower chances of success, relatively small numbers of patients and short survival periods. However, the four health states that were included represent a relatively wide range of health descriptions. The overall number of attributes and levels that could be investigated in the study was limited by the need to ensure that the task respondents were asked to consider was manageable.

2.2. Scenario Presentation and Preference Elicitation

A maximum of 96 combinations of attributes and levels were possible from the defined attributes. A subset of 16 of these were identified for use in the survey, using an orthogonal main effects design. The use of the orthogonal main effects design found the optimal spread of scenarios to cover a broad range of alternatives. This was achieved using the software package SPEED (Bradley, 1991). Given our desire to keep the questionnaire simple and relatively short, it was important to limit the number of scenarios to present and so no interaction terms were specified in the design.

The 16 scenarios (defined as A–P) were randomly paired to form eight discrete choices. This procedure was carried out three times to generate three separate questionnaires (I, II and III), and so overall there was a total of 24 choices. The justification for using three separate questionnaires was simply in order to increase the number of different choices, and so trade-offs between attributes, presented. It should, however, be noted that the sample of information from the full factorial was not increased by this, as the same 16 scenarios were used for all three questionnaires. Summary details of the scenarios presented are given in Table 6.1 and the content of the choices is shown in Table 6.2.

Members of the research team identified a suitable clinical situation for each scenario from the published literature. Specific clinical conditions and interventions were constructed for each choice presented to participants in the questionnaires. This enabled the research team, interviewers and respondents to be confident that the information presented reflected clinical scenarios that might face the health service and where their views, as stakeholder would be of legitimate concern. Details of the clinical scenarios, however, were not included in the final questionnaire. This decision was taken because there was no significant difference in the level of engagement with the study between the three groups in the pilot: those who received full clinical information; those given clinical information only when they requested it; and those given no additional clinical information (Roberts et al., 1999).

The choices to be presented to respondents were always between scenarios involving the *same* financial cost. A decision was made not to include cost as a further attribute for two reasons: first, to avoid adding to the complexity of the cognitive task, and second, because different levels of cost for each scenario within each choice would leave respondents uncertain about the opportunity cost associated with their choices.

2.3. Data Collection

A random sample of the adult (i.e. over 16 years) population within the boundary of East and North Hertfordshire Health Authority was identified. The size of the sample was a trade-off between achieving as high a degree of precision as possible whilst living within project financial constraints.

Data collection was undertaken using structured face-to-face interviews conducted by a public survey company (MORI) who used experienced interviewers. Each interview had three sections:

TABLE 6.1. Summary details of scenarios

Scenario	Number of individuals	Chance of success (%)	Survival (years)	Quality of life (weight)	QALY score*
A	100	50	5	No problems with usual activities; not anxious or depressed (1.00)	250
B	10	50	5	Unable to perform usual activities; extremely anxious or depressed (0.401)	10.025
C	1	50	1	Some problems in performing usual activities; moderately anxious or depressed (0.893)	0.4465
D	10	50	1	Unable to perform usual activities; moderately anxious or depressed (0.566)	2.83
E	10	1	1	No problems with usual activities; not anxious or depressed (1.00)	0.1
F	100	1	1	Unable to perform usual activities; extremely anxious or depressed (0.401)	0.401
G	10	1	5	Some problems in performing usual activities; moderately anxious or depressed (0.893)	0.4465
H	1	1	5	Unable to perform usual activities; moderately anxious or depressed (0.566)	0.0283

(continued)

TABLE 6.1. (continued)

Scenario	Number of individuals	Chance of success (%)	Survival (years)	Quality of life (weight)	QALY score*
I	1	10	1	No problems with usual activities; not anxious or depressed (1.00)	0.1
J	10	10	1	Unable to perform usual activities; extremely anxious or depressed (0.401)	0.401
K	100	10	5	Some problems in performing usual activities; and moderately anxious or depressed (0.893)	44.65
L	10	10	5	Unable to perform usual activities; moderately anxious or depressed (0.566)	2.83
M	10	0.1	5	No problems with usual activities; not anxious or depressed (1.00)	0.05
N	1	0.1	5	Unable to perform usual activities; extremely anxious or depressed (0.401)	0.002005
O	10	0.1	1	Some problems in performing usual activities; moderately anxious or depressed (0.893)	0.00893
P	100	0.1	1	Unable to perform usual activities; moderately anxious or depressed (0.566)	0.0566

*QALY score for scenario A $= 100 \times 0.5 \times 5 \times 1.00 = 250$

TABLE 6.2. *QALY maximisation and public choices: results*

	QALY difference between scenarios (undiscounted)	QALY-maximising programme	Number (proportion) of respondents who choose QALY-maximising programme
Questionnaire I			
D vs K	−41.820	K	211 (0.75)
C vs G	0.000	−	−
I vs O	0.091	I	217 (0.77)
L vs H*	2.802	L	255 (0.90)
E vs F	−0.301	F	116 (0.40)
B vs P	9.968	B	210 (0.75)
J vs M	0.351	J	104 (0.63)
A vs N*	249.998	A	283 (0.97)
Questionnaire II			
G vs C	0.000	−	−
P vs J	−0.344	J	190 (0.66)
K vs M	44.600	K	220 (0.75)
H vs A*	−249.972	A	285 (0.97)
D vs B	−7.195	B	201 (0.67)
E vs F	−0.301	F	103 (0.36)
O vs L	−2.821	L	238 (0.83)
N vs I	−0.098	I	253 (0.88)
Questionnaire III			
H vs P	−0.028	P	110 (0.42)
F vs B	−9.624	B	216 (0.79)
D vs E	2.730	D	165 (0.60)
A vs K*	205.350	A	242 (0.85)
I vs G	−0.347	G	147 (0.54)
C vs O	0.438	C	224 (0.79)
J vs N	0.399	J	235 (0.85)
L vs M	2.780	L	196 (0.70)

*Indicates a choice where one scenario was "dominant"

- Socio-demographic questions (e.g. age, gender, occupation, employment status and household characteristics)
- Questions concerning the respondent's current health status, experience of long-standing illness and recent use of health services (i.e. selected questions taken from the General Household Survey)
- Choices relating to priority setting in health care (core element of the interview)

Information was elicited from respondents by the presentation of the series of choices involving two alternative health care scenarios. The context described to respondents was one of a Health Authority facing a situation where it was unable to fund all it would wish to and so a series of difficult choices had to be made. Each respondent was asked to express a preference for one of the two programmes for every choice. The interviewer read out the scenario descriptions to respondents who were able to view a showcard that contained only the summary information about the choice. Questionnaires I, II and III were used at random throughout the survey in order that approximately one third of participants responded to each version.

2.4. Data Analysis

Data analysis was conducted using STATA. There were three principal components of data analysis. The first involved an investigation of response patterns by establishing the extent to which respondents were engaged in the exercise and were trading between attributes. The second component established the level of public support for QALY maximisation in general terms. Finally, the data were analysed using a random effects probit model which was used to explore the trade-offs being made between scenario attributes.

2.4.1. Investigation of response patterns

The process of pairing scenarios to define the choices to present, led to some choices with a dominant scenario (defined as a scenario with a "better" level on at least one attribute and no "worse" level on all other attributes). Questionnaire I contained two such choices and questionnaires II and III each contained one. These dominated choices were included in order to assess the internal consistency of respondents. Respondents who "failed" the internal consistency test by choosing the non-dominant scenario were identified and defined as "inconsistent respondents". Comparison was then made of the characteristics of inconsistent and consistent respondents using chi-square and chi-square trend tests for comparisons of proportions, and student's t-tests for comparisons involving continuous data (Altman, 1991).

2.4.2. Level of support for QALY maximisation

The choice patterns of respondents were reviewed in order to identify the broad level of support for a QALY maximisation objective. For each programme within each choice, the expected QALY score was calculated and a QALY maximisation response was defined as a preference for the programme with the higher expected QALY score (Table 6.2). For each respondent, the number of choices in line with QALY maximisation was identified and presented as a frequency distribution.

2.4.3. Probit model

The DCE data were analysed using a probit model where the dependent variable is binary, taking the value 0 if the left-hand programme was chosen and the value 1 if the right-hand programme was chosen. The independent variables represent the differences between levels on attributes within the choices and were coded such that where there was a "better" level on the right-hand programme this gave a negative value for the difference. An aggregate model was estimated that drew on data from all survey respondents since the focus of this work was on public preferences, and so it was important that the methods provide results that have broad public policy relevance.

Given that each individual provided eight data points there was the potential problem of correlation between observations from the same respondent. This leads to the presence of non-independent errors in the model which may be correlated within respondents due to variation in tastes and preferences between respondents (Bates, 1988). As highlighted in Chapter 1, the presence of these non-independent errors potentially have serious implications for the use of standard regression techniques: the coefficient standard errors are likely to be underestimated with the consequence of overstating statistical significance (Permain et al., 1991; Vick and Scott, 1998). In this study, the problem was addressed through the adoption of a probit model with random effects (Propper, 1991; Greene, 1997; Ryan, 1999; Gossen et al., 2000).

The design (i.e. the use of paired comparisons) required the estimation of a difference model, such that the main independent variables were the *differences* in levels between scenarios presented within the choices for the four core attributes: number of patients, chance of success, survival and quality of life. The functional form for the basic model was:

$$y_{iq} = \alpha_0 + \alpha_1 N_q + \alpha_2 C_q + \alpha_3 S_q + \alpha_4 Q_q + v_{iq} + u_i \qquad (6.1)$$

where $i = 1, \ldots, 909$, the number of respondents to the survey

$q = 1, \ldots, 24$, the number of choices posed

y = the difference in the deterministic component of random utility between the two scenarios presented within a choice

N, C, S, Q = the *difference* in levels within each choice for the number of patients, chance of success, survival and quality of life attributes, respectively

$\alpha_0, \ldots, \alpha_4$ = the model coefficients

v_{iq} = is the random error term due to differences amongst observations

u_i = is the disturbance due to differences amongst respondents resulting from measurement error.

The model was specified with a constant term in order to investigate the presence of a systematic tendency to choose left or right (Ryan and Hughes, 1997). Given that each attribute has quantitative levels where the direction of preference is clear, it is possible to predict the expected signs on each attribute coefficient. The a priori expectation was that the coefficients on all attributes would be negative (i.e. a larger number of patients to receive treatment would be preferred to a smaller number).

3. RESULTS

3.1. Sample Size and Characteristics

A sample of 1,762 households in Hertfordshire was initially identified for inclusion in the survey. Attempts were made to contact all households but no response was obtained from 462 (26.2%), while 391 (22.2%) actively refused to participate in the survey. Thus, 909 interviews were successfully completed, representing an overall response rate of 51.6%. The sample were evenly distributed across the three versions of the questionnaire (I respondents = 305; II respondents = 309; III respondents = 295). On average, the interviews lasted 20 min (standard deviation: 4.3 min), with the longest taking 62 min and the shortest only 10 min. The characteristics of the sample are given in Table 6.3. The sample is highly representative of the population of Hertfordshire in terms of gender, age and social class groupings.

3.2. Response Patterns

A total of 88 respondents (9.7% of the total sample) were defined as inconsistent. The characteristics of the inconsistent and consistent respondents were compared. Inconsistent responders tended to be significantly older and a significantly larger proportion was in lower social class groups (C2, D and E). In addition, the

TABLE 6.3. *Characteristics of sample*

Characteristics	Levels	N	(%)
Gender	Female	523	57.5
	Male	386	42.5
Age (years)	Mean (SD)	49	18.12
	Range (IQ range)	16–91	34–63
Working status	Working (FT and PT)	490	53.9
	Retired	250	27.5
	Carer	92	10.1
	Student	23	2.5
	Others	54	5.9
Social class	A	38	4.2
	B	181	19.9
	C1	280	30.8
	C2	196	21.6
	D	92	10.1
	E	122	13.4
Health in general	Very good	291	32.0
	Good	382	42.0
	Fair	183	20.1
	Bad	45	5.0
	Very bad	8	0.9
Experience of long-standing illness	Personally	294	32.5
	Family or friends	342	38.0

self-reported health status of inconsistent responders was worse: a significantly lower proportion of inconsistent responders, compared to consistent responders, reported their health either as "very good" or "good".

The number of apparent non-trading respondents was 268 (29.5%): 43 for number of patients treated, 96 for chance of success, 80 for survival and 52 for quality of life. The random pairing of scenarios led to a situation where for one version of the questionnaire (i.e. questionnaire II) it was not possible for us to distinguish between respondents who were non-trading for number of patients and survival – three respondents fell into this category. In terms of personal characteristics there was no statistically significant differences between the trading and non-trading respondents ($p > 0.05$).

3.3. Level of QALY Maximisation Support

Only a small minority of respondents ($n = 77$; 8.5%) chose in a manner that was always in line with a QALY maximisation objective. Figure 6.1 shows the number of respondents choosing in line with QALY maximisation across the three questionnaires. Given the differential exposure, it was not possible for respondents to questionnaire I and II to respond in a QALY-maximising manner to all eight choices. It is clear from Figure 6.1 that across all three questionnaires, the majority of respondents made choices that could be interpreted as supporting a QALY maximisation line for over half of the choices posed. The average number of choices in line with QALY maximisation was 4.58 (SD 1.56) for questionnaire I, 4.82 (SD 1.64) for questionnaire II and 5.20 (SD 1.87) for questionnaire III. These results are supported by findings shown in Table 6.2 – when the difference in QALY scores between the alternative programmes was reasonably large, the vast majority of respondents chose the QALY-maximising programme.

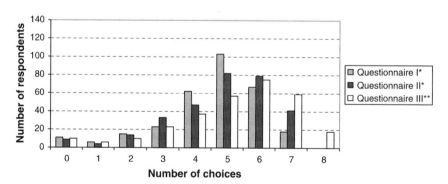

* Respondents exposed to 7 choices where a QALY maximising option existed
** Respondents exposed to 8 choices where a QALY maximising option existed

FIGURE 6.1. *Frequency distribution of number of choices in line with QALY-maximisation*

3.4. Probit Model

Table 6.4 reports the results of the random effects probit model. DCE data were available for 880 respondents and due to some missing data for a small number of questions we have 6,801 data points. As we are seeking to estimate a model reflecting the "average" preferences for all citizens (and not just the trading citizens), data from all respondents has been used in the estimation. The correlation of observations within individuals (ρ) is quite low but significant, indicating that a random effects specification was appropriate. Also the model seems to fit the data reasonable well in terms of the model χ^2.

The coefficients relating to all four attributes are highly significant indicating that, in general, the choices respondents made were sensitive to variation in the levels for these factors. In addition, the negative sign on the coefficient for all four attributes is as expected and is a result of the way the data in a probit model is coded. For example, other things being equal, the larger the number of patients receiving treatment in scenario r within a choice (i.e. the right-hand programme), the more negative was the value on the difference variable and the more likely were respondents to choose that programme. As indicated above, the conventional interpretation of the constant term in such models is the propensity to choose programme r over programme l (or the propensity to choose right rather than left), all other things remaining equal. The negative sign suggests a general tendency to choose the right-hand programme within the choice. Similar results were found when inconsistent respondents were excluded from the analysis.

The ratio of coefficients on any two attributes in the probit model gives an estimate of the trade-off between the attributes in question. If we consider the trade-off between average survival and the number of patients in the programme, the ratio of coefficients (i.e. $-0.1010/-0.0033 = 30$) indicates that people were, on average, willing

TABLE 6.4. Results from the probit model with random effects

Explanatory variables	Coefficient (SE)
Number of patients (N_q)	−0.0033 (0.00030)*
Chance of treatment success (C_q)	−1.2735 (0.0625)*
Quality of life (Q_q)	−0.8258 (0.0461)*
Survival (S_q)	−0.1010 (0.0062)*
Constant	−0.1167 (0.0216)*
ρ	0.1114 (0.0157)*
Number of observations	6,801
Number of groups	8,80
Log-likelihood	−4078
Likelihood ratio test (χ^2)	71.15*
Average number of observations per group	7.73

*$p < 0.01$

to see the programme size be smaller by 30 people in order that the average survival increased by 1 year. Similarly, the trade-off between survival and quality of life (i.e. $-0.1010/-0.8258 = 0.12$) suggests that, on average, people were prepared to accept a reduction of 0.12 in quality of life gain in order that survival increased by 1 year.

4. DISCUSSION

Given that QALYs are increasingly being portrayed as a measure of societal value, in the sense of a measure of society's preferences for different health outcomes (Dolan, 1998), it is important to explore the appropriateness of this interpretation. The central question addressed by the research described here was the extent to which there is public support for the QALY-maximisation model. In general, for many (but certainly not all) respondents this assumption is broadly supported by the data reported here, but people appear willing, on average, to make trade-offs between different components of the QALY construction. The use of a DCE approach allows the quantification of these trade-offs and provides policy makers with an indication of the treatment programme characteristics valued most highly by citizens. For example, people responded in a manner that suggests a willingness to support programmes targeted at a small number of potential recipients so long as the gains in terms of survival and/or quality of life were reasonably substantial. This has policy relevance to the orphan drug debate where decisions have to be made on the appropriateness of using public money to invest in use of high-cost medicines for very rare conditions.

This research represents a novel approach to eliciting public preferences for health care programmes: DCE methods have not been utilised in this way previously. However, positive findings regarding test–retest reliability of the DCE approach have been found in a different health care setting (Bryan et al., 2000) where the focus was on estimating the strength of preference for benefits associated with the use of magnetic resonance imaging in patients with knee injuries. In addition, there are many reasons to believe that the data collected and the results obtained are reliable and robust. The sample from which data were collected is large and highly representative of the population of Hertfordshire, and the use of face-to-face interviews rather than postal questionnaires allowed the opportunity to ensure that respondents fully understood the nature of the exercise they were being asked to undertake.

Some caution should, however, be exercised in the interpretation of the findings of this study. One reason for caution concerning the results of our study is that the broad conclusion, of some support for a QALY-maximisation position, runs counter to the finding of a qualitative study by Dolan and Cookson (2000) which elicited preferences in the context of discussion groups. They found that whilst "capacity to benefit" is important to people in health care resource allocation (a finding consistent with our data), concerns relating to equality of access were more important. One possible explanation for the difference in findings is the fact that respondents in our survey were not actively encouraged to reflect at length or discuss the issues being raised by the survey before they responded to the interviewer's questions. The work of Dolan et al. (1999) questions the value of surveys that do not allow time or opportunity for reflection. Another possible explanation for the difference is the fact that the "numbers game" nature of the DCE approach had the effect, when used in this context, of luring respondents away from an egalitarian position.

A further potential limitation of this study is the limited range explored for each attribute. In order to ensure that the task was manageable for respondents and to allow the use of a DCE approach, it was necessary to limit the range for attributes explored with the consequence that the results hold only within the actual ranges utilised and predictions outside the range would be inappropriate (Bryan and Dolan, 2004). Therefore, the data reported here provide no indication of the level of support for QALY-maximisation when programmes include many thousands of patients.

In addition, a study weakness is that the experiment had only three levels for the "number of patients" attribute. This is clearly a small number and, the simplicity of the design overall (only four attributes between second and fourth levels) represents a limitation of the experiment. A potentially fruitful extension to work of this kind, not undertaken as part of this project, would be to take the DCE forward qualitatively by investigating further the factors defined as important, and finding out in more depth the reality of the trade-offs people are willing to make and accept.

In conclusion, the public preference data from this study, in themselves, are not much at odds with a QALY-maximisation approach. The data are, however, at odds with reports from previous studies and so further work is required to explore the reasons for the differences between our conclusions and those of others. Such work might adopt more of a qualitative component through the use in-depth interviews, and should explore preferences in different groups of respondents and for broader health care programmes.

ACKNOWLEDGEMENTS

Particular thanks go to our collaborators, Chris Heginbotham and Alison McCallum. In addition, we thank Erik Nord who has provided very helpful and extensive comments on earlier drafts of this paper. We are grateful to our colleagues at the Health Services Management Centre, University of Birmingham, who have discussed this project with us, notably Pelham Barton, and also we acknowledge Sue Cashmore's help in preparation of the manuscript. Source of funding: East and North Hertfordshire Health Authority.

REFERENCES

Altman, D. 1991. Practical Statistics for Medical Research. London: Chapman & Hall.

Bates, J. 1988. Econometric issues in SP Analysis. *Journal of Transport Economics and Policy*, vol 22 (1), 59–70.

Bradley, M. 1991. User's manual for SPEED version 2.1 sated preference experiment editor and designer. The Hague: Hague Consulting Group.

Bryan, S. and Dolan, P. 2004. Discrete choice experiments in health economics: for better or for worse? *European Journal of Health Economics*, vol 5 (3), 199–203.

Bryan, S., Buxton, M., Sheldon, R. and Grant, A. 1998. Magnetic resonance imaging for the investigation of knee injuries: an investigation of preferences. *Health Economics*, vol 7, 595–604.

Bryan, S., Gold, L., Sheldon, R. and Buxton, M. 2000. Preference measurement using conjoint methods: an empirical investigation of reliability. *Health Economics*, vol 9, 385–395.

Bryan, S., Roberts, T., Heginbotham, C. and McCallum, A. 2002. QALY-maximisation and public preferences: results from a general population survey. *Health Economics*, vol 11, 679–693.

Dolan, P. 1998. The measurement of individual utility and social welfare. *Journal of Health Economics*, vol 17, 39–52.

Dolan, P. and Cookson, R. 2000. A qualitative study of the extent to which health gain matters when choosing between groups of patients. *Health Policy*, vol 51, 19–30.

Dolan, P., Cookson, R. and Ferguson, B. 1999. Effect of discussion and deliberation on the public's views of priority setting in health care: focus group study. *British Medical Journal*, vol 318, 916–919.

Entwistle, V.A., Watt, I.S., Bradbury, R. and Pehl, L.J. 1996. Media coverage of the Child B case. *British Medical Journal*, vol 312, 1587–1591.

EuroQol Group. 1990. EuroQol – a new facility for the measurement of health-related quality of life. *Health Policy*, vol 16, 199–208.

Gosden, T., Bowler, I. and Sutton, M. 2000. How do general practitioners choose their practice? Preferences for practice and job characteristics. *Journal of Health Services Research and Policy*, vol 5 (4), 208–213.

Greene, W. 1997. Econometric Analysis. 3rd edn. Englewood Cliffs, NJ: Prentice Hall.

New, B. 1996. The rationing agenda in the NHS. *British Medical Journal*, vol 312, 1593–1601.

Nord, E. 1994. The Qaly – a measure of social value rather than individual utility? *Health Economics*, vol 3, 89–93.

Permain, D., Swanson, J., Kroes, E. and Bradley, M. 1991. Stated preference techniques: a guide to practice. The Hague: Steer Davies Gleave and Hague Consulting Group.

Propper, C. 1991. Contingent value of time spent on NHS waiting lists. *Economic Journal*, vol 100, 193–199.

Rawlins, M. 1999. In pursuit of quality: the National Institute for Clinical Excellence. *The Lancet*, vol 353, 1079–1082.

Roberts, T., Bryan, S., Heginbotham, C. and McCallum, A. 1999. Public involvement in health care priority setting: an economic perspective. *Health Expectations*, vol 2, 235–244.

Ryan, M. 1999. Using conjoint analysis to take account of patient preferences and go beyond health outcomes: an application to in vitro fertilisation. *Social Science and Medicine*, vol 48, 535–546.

Ryan, M. and Hughes, J. 1997. Using conjoint analysis to assess women's preferences for miscarriage management. *Health Economics*, vol 6, 261–273.

Vick, S. and Scott, A. 1998. Agency in health care. Examining patients' preferences for attributes of the doctor–patient relationship. *Journal of Health Economics*, vol 17, 587–605.

Williams, A. 1985. Economics of coronary artery bypass grafting. *British Medical Journal*, vol 291, 326–329.

CHAPTER 7

EXAMINING THE PREFERENCES
OF HEALTH CARE PROVIDERS

An application to hospital consultants

ANTHONY SCOTT

Melbourne Institute of Applied Economic and Social Research, The University of Melbourne, Australia

CRISTINA UBACH

Consorcio para el Desarrollo de Tecnologia Avanzada de Imagen Medica, Spain

FIONA FRENCH AND GILLIAN NEEDHAM

NHS Education for Scotland, Aberdeen, UK

1. INTRODUCTION

The aim of this chapter is to show how discrete choice experiments (DCEs) can be applied to examine the preferences of health care providers. Health care providers comprise health care organisations and health professionals employed within them. Health professionals make decisions about their supply of labour in addition to clinical decisions. A key policy issue across many developed and developing countries is shortages of health professionals, particularly doctors and nurses. Although a number of policies are being introduced and have been suggested to reduce these shortages, there is little empirical evidence on what factors influence the labour market behaviour of doctors and nurses. Evidence on the relative impact of pay and remuneration on job choices and labour supply has shown that pecuniary factors do matter, but that their effect may be moderate. This raises the issue of what non-pecuniary job characteristics might be altered by policy to increase recruitment and retention. Existing "revealed preference" administrative and survey data do not collect good information on these non-pecuniary job characteristics. DCEs are a method that can be used to inform this issue (Scott, 2001). This chapter focuses on the labour market decisions of hospital consultants in the UK.

153

M. Ryan, K. Gerard and M. Amaya-Amaya (eds.), Using Discrete Choice Experiments to Value Health and Health Care, 153–171.
© 2008 *Springer.*

1.1. Using DCEs to Examine Labour Market Behaviour

It is important to first of all examine why stated, rather than revealed, preference methods are suitable to use in this labour market.[1] The first reason is that data on actual job choices and mobility is not available, and even it were, turnover amongst consultants is quite low compared to the general labour market. The second reason is that data on discrete job choices could not be used to estimate the monetary values of job characteristics. Most studies in labour economics that have attempted to estimate the monetary value of non-pecuniary job characteristics have used survey or administrative data to estimate hedonic wage models. Empirical studies have regressed job characteristics (and other factors) on market wages of workers to estimate worker's willingness to pay (WTP) for reduction in the risk of death or injury at work. (Herzog and Schlottmann, 1990; Kniesner and Leeth, 1991; Viscusi, 1993; Gronberg and Reed, 1994). Based on the theory of compensating wage differentials, these models have assumed long-run equilibrium of labour markets and that any differences in the non-pecuniary advantages or disadvantages of jobs are reflected in the equilibrium wage (Rosen, 1986). To attract and retain workers in a job or geographical area that is relatively unattractive (e.g. shift work, dangerous jobs, deprived areas, high cost of living), employers will pay more to compensate the employee for these unattractive attributes. This assumes that labour markets are free of transactions costs, that wages are set competitively and can be altered by employers, and that there is perfect information on job offers.

If there is disequilibrium in the labour market, the observed wages will not capture the value of job characteristics to employees. This is likely to be the case when examining specific labour markets or occupations. In these situations, observed wage differentials are more likely to reflect institutional rigidities, rather than reflecting workers' preferences for job characteristics (Marin and Psacharopoulos, 1982). The key point here is that in these labour markets revealed preference data might be available on wages, job choices and job characteristics, but they cannot be used to estimate the monetary value (employee's WTP) of job characteristics.

This is likely to be particularly important in some public sector labour markets, and particularly in health professionals' labour markets in the UK. In UK National Health Service (NHS), there are several reasons why wage differentials are unlikely to reflect doctors' WTP for job characteristics. First, hospital consultants are paid a salary plus bonuses, both of which are determined at a national level through negotiation between the government and the British Medical Association (BMA), mediated by the Doctors and Dentists Review Body (Blair, 2002). A recent new contract for hospital consultants was rejected by the profession who voted on a contract previously agreed by the government and BMA (Department of Health, 2001). This suggests that the BMA does not reflect the preferences of its members and that bargaining was inefficient. Within this structure, the local NHS employers of hospital consultants, NHS Hospital Trusts, have no influence on pay setting and so cannot compensate for differences in workplace disamenities. Even bonuses[2] are determined at a regional level. Where hospitals do compete for doctors, it is likely to be on the basis of a range of non-pecuniary factors such as the quality of clinical care and the availability of technology.

There are positive transactions costs of switching jobs for hospital consultants. Turnover is lower than in the general labour market (Booth and Francesconi, 1999; Elliot et al., 2002) and tenure with current employer is much higher. Since hospital consultants are specialists in a particular clinical area, this makes their skills less transferable to consultant jobs in other specialties. There are also restrictions on supply in terms of the length of undergraduate medical training, and on the ability to practise as a specialist. In situations of excess demand, which in the NHS is evidenced by persistent waiting lists, neither wages nor supply is able to adjust to clear the market. This is compounded by the fact the NHS is a monopsony buyer of medical labour in the UK. There is a small private sector, and NHS consultants are allowed to devote some of their time to non-NHS work. For these reasons, data on "market" wages are unlikely to reflect consultants' preferences for job characteristics and so reveals little about the determinants of their labour market behaviour.[3]

2. METHODS

2.1. A Model of Job Choice

Consultants are assumed to be choosing a job in which to work. It is assumed that the utility function is defined over bundles of job characteristics (z) and leisure activities (L), with each bundle of job characteristics representing a particular job in which the consultant could potentially work. Consultants can only choose one bundle of job characteristics given that they can only choose one job at a time, and so the alternatives in the choice set are mutually exclusive, with z exogenous at the time the choice is made.[4] The utility function is an indirect utility function, i.e. given the constraints on choice and therefore the alternatives in the feasible choice set, which bundle of job characteristics maximises utility (Peitz, 1995; Truong and Hensher, 1985). Each job in the choice set therefore comprises a bundle of job characteristics (z) faced by the nth consultant. With two jobs, i and j, a consultant will choose job j if:

$$U_j(z_j, s) > U_i(z_i, s) \tag{7.1}$$

and if U^* is positive, where

$$U^* = (z_j, s) - (z_i, s) \tag{7.2}$$

and is the difference in utility between jobs i and j, with s representing personal and socio-economic characteristics of the consultant. Using random utility theory, the indirect utility of each job is given by:

$$U_i = V_i + \varepsilon_i \quad \text{and} \quad U_j = V_j + \varepsilon_j \tag{7.3}$$

where $V = f(z, s)$ and is the deterministic component of utility, and ε is the random component. Consultants choose the job with the highest utility.

2.2. Development of DCE Questions

The DCE was part of a larger questionnaire used in a study of flexible working in NHS Scotland, from the perspectives of non-training grade doctors. The experiment presented each respondent with several choices between different types of job that mirror the choice process outlined in Figure 7.1. The included job characteristics were derived using data from existing literature, interviews with 14 consultants and four focus groups with consultants (Table 7.1). Realistic levels for each job characteristic were assigned to each attribute and are shown in Table 7.1. Change in total hours of work per week was used rather than absolute level of hours or sessions worked. This was to avoid non-trading as the gap between the levels might be too large. Using the change in hours is more realistic and capable of being traded off for those working both long and short hours. The attributes also referred to hours worked in total, i.e. including those outside of the NHS. This was to enable the elicitation of the marginal value of leisure. On-call work was included as a separate attribute as its measurement is more problematic. This is an important issue for consultants, although complex and difficult to quantify. The amount of on-call assigned and the real number of hours worked when on call depends on the specialty, the geographical area and the amount of staff available. Two important features of on-call were distilled from the focus groups: the location of on-call and the intensity of workload. The change in total NHS income was used rather than absolute levels because differences between levels would be too large for respondents to trade. Instead, the percentage change in annual net income was used. This was expressed in terms of percentages to ensure that it could be interpreted by those with different contracts and hours of work. Respondents were asked to trade off potential increases in income as it is unlikely that an actual reduction in income for doctors would be viewed as realistic. Opportunities to do non-NHS medical work were also included. At the time of the survey, consultants on whole-time contracts are allowed to work for the private sector as long as they earn <10% of their NHS salary. A maximum part-time contract enables the doctor to earn unlimited private income, as well as ten sessions per week for the NHS. Working relations with staff were also important in the focus groups, in addition to the amount of staff at work. Both of these attributes reflect other aspects of the working environment, atmosphere and relationships with others that featured strongly in the focus groups.

2.3. Scenario Pairing

The scenarios were organised into pairs (see, e.g. Figure 7.1). If all combinations of levels were used, it would result in a full factorial design of 576 possible scenarios. We reduced this to a more manageable level of 16 scenarios by using a fractional factorial experimental design, derived from SPEED (Bradley, 1991). It was assumed that two-way interactions between attributes were non-significant. These were placed in pairs by having the same scenario appear in each pair (a constant scenario) and pair this with every other scenario, resulting in 15 choices.

The properties of the experimental design were examined. Simple checks such as correlation matrix of the design's attribute levels[5] and frequency count of levels were

Which job would you prefer?	Job A	Job B
Working relations with staff	Fair	Good
Amount of staff at work	Enough	Enough
Change in total hours of work per week (including NHS and non-NHS but excluding on call)	0	-10
On call	Home-not busy	Home-very busy
Change in total NHS-income (after tax)	+10%	+10%
Opportunities to do non-NHS work	None	Unlimited

Prefer job A   Prefer job B

☐ *(tick one box only)* ☐

FIGURE 7.1. *Example of a choice presented in the questionnaire*

TABLE 7.1. *Attributes and levels used for the questionnaire*

Attributes	Levels	Regression coding
Working relations with staff	Good	1
	Fair	0
Amount of staff at work	Enough staff	0
	Shortage staff	1
Change in actual hours of work per week	−10	−10
	−5	−5
	0	0
	+5	+5
On call[a]	Home–not busy	0
	Home–very busy	1
	Residential–not busy	1
	Residential–very busy	1
Change in total NHS income	No change	0
	+10%	−10
	+20%	+20
Opportunities to do non-NHS medical work[b]	None	0
	Some	1
	Unlimited	1

[a]Coded as a dummy variable relative to "home–not busy"
[b]Coded as a dummy variable relative to no opportunities to do non-NHS work

conducted in order to reassure the key design properties. The pairing was undertaken to ensure that the statistical properties were satisfied such that the results did not depend on the way scenarios were paired (Zwerina et al., 1996; Carlsson and Martinsson, 2003). The three properties of orthogonality, level balance and minimal overlap were considered. There were 15 possible of choices sets and each was examined in terms of these criteria. Orthogonality was assessed by examining the correlations between attribute differences for the 15 different sets of pairs.[ii] Level balance was assessed by checking the frequencies of the levels of each attribute for the 15 different sets of pairs. Minimal overlap was assessed by checking the amount of zeros in the differences of levels per choice. The design property of utility balance was not examined given that a priori the utility of each scenario was not known. One set of the 15 original choice sets was chosen, on the basis of these criteria, to use in the questionnaire.

The face and content validity of the questionnaire was tested in an initial pilot survey that was sent to all consultants who participated in the interviews and focus groups. A new constant scenario was chosen because there was insufficient variation in the responses (shown in Figure 7.1 as job A). A second pilot questionnaire was sent to a random sample of 56 consultants. Previous face-to-face piloting suggests that 15 choices may lead to respondent fatigue, so they were divided across three versions of the questionnaire such that all attribute levels occurred with approximate equal frequency in each version. An extra choice was added to each version of the questionnaire to test for internal consistency. This involved presenting a choice with levels such that everyone should choose the same job. Each questionnaire therefore contained six pairs of scenarios. The questionnaire also contained other questions on workload, contractual details, income and family circumstances. Demographic information was also collected in the questionnaire.

2.4. Participants

The questionnaire was posted to all 2,923 hospital consultants in Scotland, except for those who had completed the pilot questionnaire and those who were known to have retired or died. The sample was obtained from the Information and Statistics Division of the Scottish Executive Health Department. The three versions of the questionnaire were randomly allocated to consultants. The questionnaire was posted in July 2001, followed by one reminder.

2.5. Analysis of Data

The form of the econometric models that were estimated is shown below. y_n^* is a latent variable representing the difference in utility between the jobs being compared for the nth respondent. Since it is the choice that is observed rather than the difference in utility, y_n^* is binary reflecting whether the respondent chose job A (0) or job B (1). Therefore:
$y_n = 1$ if $y_n^* > 0$ and 0 else, and

$$y_n^* = \left(\alpha + \beta z_i + \partial s_n + \varepsilon_{in}\right) - \left(\alpha + \beta z_j + \partial s_n + \varepsilon_{jn}\right) \tag{7.4}$$

where α, β and ∂ are coefficients, s is socio-economic characteristics reflecting influences on tastes and ε is the random component of utility accounting for the analyst's inability to accurately observe individual's behaviour (McFadden, 1974a, b; Manski and McFadden, 1977). The subscripts i and j refer to each scenario in the pairwise choice. Further, assume that there are taste variations, such that the marginal utility of z depends on s:

$$\beta = \pi + \lambda s_n \qquad (7.5)$$

This gives:

$$y_n^* = \left(\alpha + \pi z_i + \lambda s_n z_i + \partial s_n + \varepsilon_{in} \right) - \left(\alpha + \pi z_j + \lambda s_n z_j + \partial s_n + \varepsilon_{jn} \right) \qquad (7.6)$$

The DCE used to estimate the model presents each consultant with several pairs of scenarios. Multiple observations from each consultant means that errors are not independent and so an error term μ_n capturing random variation across consultants is included:

$$y_n^* = \left(\alpha + \pi z_i + \lambda s_n z_i + \partial s_n + \varepsilon_{in} + \mu_n \right) - \left(\alpha + \pi z_j + \lambda s_n z_j + \partial s_n + \varepsilon_{jn} + \mu_n \right) \qquad (7.7)$$

Taking differences for each pairwise choice (k), the equation to be estimated becomes:

$$y_{kn}^* = \pi z_k + \lambda s_n z_k + \varepsilon_{kn} \qquad (7.8)$$

Terms common to both indirect utility functions drop out of the model (i.e. α, ∂s_n and μ_n). However, the inclusion of a constant term (α) and error term across respondents (μ_n) can be used to test for misspecification due to unobservable attributes and unobservable interaction terms between consultants' socio-economic characteristics and attributes. The constant term can be interpreted as the difference in the average utility of scenario i and j, caused by the use of a constant scenario, left/right bias or an omitted dummy variable that is a function of other included attributes. The model to be estimated then becomes:

$$y_{kn}^* = \alpha + \pi z_k + \lambda s_n z_k + \varepsilon_{kn} + \mu_n \qquad (7.9)$$

Three separate regression models were estimated using a probit model with random effects. The first included the six main job characteristics only: a main effect only model. The second model examined how preferences varied according to respondents' demographic and family characteristics, and the third model examined how preferences varied across specialties and location. The second and third models included the six main attributes and several interaction term variables that multiplied each job characteristic with each variable of interest (such as hours worked × gender). This measures the extent to which the preference for hours of work (e.g. the regression coefficient in the first model) depends on gender. For the second and third models a backward stepwise approach was used and variables with the highest p-values ($p > 0.1$) were excluded from the model, one at a time.

The monetary valuation of each attribute or price is given by the trade-offs between income and each job characteristic that are implicit when respondents make choices. If consultants had several job offers, or even one job offer where they are making comparisons to their current post, they would be willing to forgo an amount of one characteristic in one job offer to have more of another characteristic in another job. The DCE is designed to replicate the decision-making process when consultants actually choose a job. The trade-offs are quantified by dividing each regression coefficient by the regression coefficient for income. This gives the equivalent amounts of income respondents are prepared to give up or accept for a change in the level of another characteristic. LIMDEP was used to analyse the results.

3. RESULTS

The final response rate was 61% (1,793:2,923). Thirty eight respondents were excluded who did not answer the DCE questions. Of the 1,755 remaining questionnaires, there were 105 inconsistent responses (5.9%). This left a final sample for analysis of 1,650 consultants. These were evenly distributed across each version of questionnaire and were broadly representative in terms of gender, specialty and geographic location.

Table 7.2 shows the results of the regression analysis of the main effects only model. The significant value of Rho suggests that a random effects specification was appropriate and that the five responses from individual consultants were correlated. The negative and significant constant term indicates a general preference for job A, which may reflect "left" bias or a preference for an unobserved attribute correlated with job A. It also reflects the base categories of the dummy variables. Consultants prefer a job with fewer hours at work, good rather than fair relations with staff, enough staff rather than a shortage, high increase in annual income, and opportunities to do non-NHS work. These broadly confirm the theoretical validity of the technique. For on-call commitment for the same location consultants prefer "not busy" to "very busy", and for the same amount of work, they prefer to be at home rather than in hospital.

The characteristic with the highest monetary value per unit of change was on call. Since the income attribute was defined in terms of the percentage change in income, the second column is calculated by dividing the coefficient of each variable by the income coefficient. If consultants' on call changed from "home–not busy" to "residential–very busy", they would need to be compensated by the equivalent of 29.9% (1.22/0.04) of their current NHS income. This was converted to a money value based on the average net income of the sample: £60,333 × 0.299 = £18,057 per year. For a change from "home–not busy" to "home–very busy", they would require remuneration of about £13,422 or 22% of their income. A move from "home–not busy" to "residential–not busy" was valued at £12,148 or 20% of their current income.

The next most important characteristic was the opportunity to undertake non-NHS work. Consultants would need to be compensated £7,361–9,730 (12–16% of their current average net income) if they could no longer do non-NHS work. Having good relationships with staff and enough staff at work were also important, with consultants willing to accept £7,060 (11.7% of their income) to compensate them for fair

TABLE 7.2. *Main effects model*

Explanatory variable	Regression coefficient (SE)	Monetary value of job characteristics (% of income) (95% CI)[a]	Monetary value of job characteristics (£) % × mean income[b]
Constant	−0.98 (0.083)*		
Working relations with staff	0.48 (0.048)*	−11.7% (−8.6 to −14.8)	−7,060
Amount of staff	−0.44 (0.047)*	10.81% (13.4–8.2)	6,520
Change in hours of work per week	−0.04 (0.004)*	0.93% (1.2–0.6)	562
On call (home– very busy)[c]	−0.91 (0.064)*	22.25% (27.7–17.5)	13,422
On call (residential– not busy)[c]	−0.82 (0.070)*	20.14% (24.4–15.9)	12,148
On call (residential– very busy)[c]	−1.22 (0.078)*	29.93% (35.7–24.1)	18,057
Change in annual NHS income	0.04 (0.003)*	–	–
Some opportunities to do non-NHS work[d]	0.50 (0.054)*	−12.20% (−8.9 to −15.5)	−7,361
Unlimited opportunities to do non-NHS work[d]	0.66 (0.052)*	−16.13% (−12.6 to −19.7)	−9,730
Rho	0.38 (0.023)		
Log-likelihood	−3,110	% 1s predicted correctly	22%
Number of individuals	1,650	% 0s predicted correctly	97%
Number of observations	8,199	Pseudo R^2	0.19

* $p < 0.001$
[a] Confidence intervals (in parentheses) were calculated from a Taylor series approximation to the variance of a function of random variables (see Propper, 1995).
[b] £60,333 based on midpoints of income bands.
[c] Coded as a dummy variables relative to home-not busy.
[d] Coded as a dummy variable relative to no opportunities to do non-NHS work.

rather than good working relations and £6,520 (10.8%) to compensate them for a shortage of staff rather enough staff.

Consultants would require an extra £562 a year (0.9% of their current net income) or £11.70 a week to compensate them for working one extra hour a week, indicating that working extra hours is less important than the other characteristics. However, the importance depends on the number of extra hours worked. For hours worked to become more important than the amount of staff at work, consultants would need to work an extra 11 h a week (£6,520/£562).

Preferences (and prices) for these characteristics differed depending on consultants' own circumstances, such as gender, age and health, whether they work part-time, family circumstances, specialty, income and location. Table 7.3 shows the regression results for the interactions with the consultants' personal characteristics.

The interaction term with partners and children dropped out of the estimated model during the backward stepwise elimination of variables, as it was not statistically significant. Thus, the preferences of consultants who had partners and children were no different from those of consultants who did not have partners or children, indicating that having a family does not influence the relative importance of job characteristics. Thus, the value of working an extra hour (or giving up an hour of leisure time) was the same for consultants with families as it was for those without.

Preferences varied by age. For the on-call attribute, where the reference category is "on call home–not busy", the main effect variable (with coefficient −1.43) suggests that consultants preferred "on call home–not busy" to "on call home–very busy". The negative sign indicates they preferred the reference category. The interaction term with age (coefficient of 0.01) suggests that older consultant's "preferred" being on call at home and being very busy, compared to "on call home–not busy". This implies that younger consultants prefer less onerous on-call duties and that the price for younger consultants for on-call would be higher than for older consultants as they need to be compensated more for undertaking on-call. The coefficient on the interaction term refers to the effect of one additional year of age as age is a continuous variable. The average consultant would need to be compensated £9,062 to do on-call. A consultant who is 1 year older would therefore require £80 (see formula in the notes of Table 7.3) less (£8,982) to be on call "home–very busy". It can therefore be inferred that a 35-year-old consultant would need to be compensated £1,200 more to be "on call at home–busy" compared to a 50-year-old consultant ((50 − 35) × £80).

Younger consultants were more likely to value an increase in annual income compared with older consultants. Consultants who reported better health placed a higher valuation on good relations with staff. Those who reported poorer health were likely to prefer working fewer hours a week and placed a lower weight on unlimited opportunities to do non-NHS work.

Preferences also differed by gender. Female consultants (gender was coded as a dummy variable with 1 = female and 0 = male) placed more weight than male consultants on having good relations with staff and having enough staff. The positive sign on the main effects coefficient for relations with staff (0.69) indicates that respondents preferred good to fair working relations. The positive coefficient on the interaction term with gender (0.42) suggests that women value this more highly than males. For

TABLE 7.3. *Main effects plus interactions with consultants' personal characteristics*

Variable	β	SE	Extra money value[a,b]	Total money value, specific subgroup
Constant	−1.04****	0.090		
Relations with staff	0.69****	0.104	4,373	
Relations with staff * health	−0.10***	0.037	−632	3,741
Relations with staff * female	0.42***	0.143	2,660	7,033
Amount of staff	−0.40****	0.547	−2,509	
Amount of staff * female	−0.32***	0.112	−2,041	−4,550
Change hours of work per week	−0.04***	0.014	−272	
Change hours of work per week * household income	0.00***	0.000	2	−269
Change hours of work per week * health	−0.01**	0.004	−59	−330
Change hours of work per week * female	−0.04***	0.012	−228	−499
On call home–very busy	−1.43****	0.322	−9,062	
On call home–very busy * age	0.01*	0.008	80	−8,982
On call home–very busy * female	−0.43**	0.173	−2,724	−11,786
On call residential– not busy	−1.33***	0.332	−8,436	
On call residential– not busy * age	0.01*	0.007	76	−8,360
On call residential– not busy * female	−0.32*	0.169	−2,022	−10,458
On call residential– very busy	−1.67****	0.166	−10,572	
On call residential– very busy * household income	0.01**	0.002	38	−10,534
On call residential– very busy * female	−0.36*	0.190	−2,294	−12,866
Annual income increase	0.09****	0.022		

(continued)

TABLE 7.3. (continued)

Variable	β	SE	Extra money value[a,b]	Total money value, specific subgroup
Annual income increase * age	−0.00**	0.001	−6	588
Some opportunities to do non-NHS work	0.40***	0.136	2,534	
Some opportunities to do non-NHS work * household income	0.00*	0.001	19	2,553
Some opportunities to do non-NHS work * female	−0.43***	0.144	−2,686	−152
Unlimited opportunities to do non-NHS work	0.46**	0.201	2,894	
Unlimited opportunities to do non-NHS work * household income	0.01****	0.001	40	2,937
Unlimited opportunities to do non-NHS work * health	−0.10*	0.055	−626	2,269
Unlimited opportunities to do non-NHS work * female	−0.68***	0.168	−4,297	−1,402
Rho	0.39****	0.025		
Log-likelihood	−2,739	% 1s predicted correctly		20.9%
Number of individuals[c]	1,497	% 0s predicted correctly		97.2%
Number of observations	7,447	Pseudo $R^{2\,d}$		0.21

*$0.1 > p \geq 0.05$
**$0.05 > p \geq 0.01$
***$0.01 > p \geq 0.0001$
****$p < 0.0001$
[a] Compared to reference category
[b] Calculated using the formula MRS = $\beta_j/(\beta_i + (\beta_{ia}*-1.54))$, where β_j is the coefficient of the variable, β_i is the rescaled coefficient of "change in annual income" attribute, β_{ia} is the coefficient of the "change in annual income*age" interaction term, and −1.54 is the mean of this latter interaction term. The denominator therefore calculates the coefficient for the whole sample. This gives the percentage, so it is then multiplied by the mean of income for the sample £60,375 per year to arrive at the money value. Coefficients in the table have been rounded.
[c] After the deletion of missing values for the characteristics that form interactions
[d] Percentage fall in LL compared to random effects model with constant term only

the amount of staff, the negative sign on the main effect (−0.40) indicates that respondents preferred "enough" to a "shortage" of staff ("enough" was in the constant job A, and negative sign indicates they preferred the constant scenario). The interaction term (−0.32) indicates that females had a stronger preference for this than males. Women preferred to work fewer hours a week and so would need to be compensated more (an additional £228 per annum or £4.30 per hour) to work an extra hour per week than their male colleagues. Women were less likely to want to undertake non-NHS medical work, preferred less on-call, and placed less weight on opportunities to do non-NHS work. These results were independent of the effect of having to care for children and imply that as the proportion of female consultants increase in the future it will be more difficult to maintain the current level of hours worked and on-call commitments without increases in remuneration. Consultants who preferred to work longer hours had higher household incomes, as did those who preferred "very busy" residential on-call and those who preferred to undertake non-NHS work. This does not necessarily imply a positive preference for longer working hours, but that consultants prefer what they do now.

The model with the interactions between the main attributes and specialty and geographic location are shown in Table 7.4.

The weight placed on attributes, and their prices, also differed across specialties and geographical areas (Table 7.4). Compared with those working in general medicine (the reference category), surgeons placed more importance on opportunities to undertake non-NHS work, whereas paediatricians placed less importance on such opportunities. Compared with consultants in general medicine, consultants in surgery, anaesthetics, obstetrics and gynaecology, oral medicine, and emergency medicine also had stronger preferences for "very busy residential on call". This suggests that these consultants view a high and residential on-call workload as an important part of their jobs. Compared with consultants in general medicine, consultants working in anaesthetics, obstetrics and gynaecology, oral medicine and emergency medicine have stronger preferences for an increase in income. Those working in anaesthetics also placed a lower weight on having good relations with staff. The importance of having enough staff did not differ across specialties.

There were no differences in the strength of preferences for job characteristics between urban and rural areas. Compared with consultants working in major cities, consultants working in towns placed less weight on having good relations with staff and preferred to work fewer hours a week. This is likely to reflect the preferences of consultants working in teaching and non-teaching hospitals. Finally, consultants' current income did not influence the monetary valuations of job characteristics.

4. DISCUSSION

This chapter has shown that DCE can be used to examine the preferences of health care providers. In occupations where there is substantial labour market regulation, DCEs provide an opportunity to examine workers' WTP for job characteristics.

Aspects of being on call were found to be the most important characteristics of the job. The value of a high on-call workload was £18,000, interpreted as the extra amount they would need to be paid. Compensation of up to £9,700 would be required

TABLE 7.4. *Main effects plus interactions with specialty and hospital location*

Variable	β	SE	Extra money value[a]	Total money value, specific subgroup
Constant	−0.962****	0.0840		
Relations with staff	0.567****	0.0563	11,504	
Relations with staff * anaesthesia	−0,176**	0.0863	−3,568	7,936
Relations with staff * town	−0.164**	0.0639	−3,327	8,177
Amount of staff	−0.446****	0.0487	−9,054	
Change hours of work per week	−0.031****	0.0049	−620	
Change hours of work per week * town	−0.017***	0.0064	−353	−973
On call home– very busy	−0.895****	0.0663	−18,166	
On call residential– not busy	−0.883****	0.0732	−17,909	
On call residential– not busy * oral medicine	0.577***	0.2027	11,716	−6,193
On call residential– not busy * A&E	1.182***	0.3159	23,981	6,072
On call residential– very busy	−1.518****	0.1020	−30,804	
On call residential– very busy * General surgery	0.315**	0.1370	6,34	−24,420
On call residential –very busy * Anaesthesia	0.691****	0.1403	14,016	−16,787

(continued)

TABLE 7.4. (continued)

Variable	β	SE	Extra money value[a]	Total money value, specific subgroup
On call residential–very busy * Gynaecology	0.525**	0.2474	10,654	−20,150
On call residential–very busy * Oral Medicine	0.920***	0.2465	18,668	−12,136
On call residential–very busy * A&E	1.927****	0.3652	39,089	8,286
Annual income increase	0.034****	0.0039		
Annual income increase * anaesthesia	0.025***	0.0082	497	1,190
Annual income increase * obstetric & gynaecology	0.034**	0.0137	695	1,388
Annual income increase * oral medicine	0.033**	0.0147	663	1,355
Annual income increase * A&E	0.056**	0.0226	1,129	1,822
Some opportunities to do non-NHS work	0.389****	0.0590	7,899	
Some opportunities to do non-NHS work * general surgery	0.549****	0.1061	11,132	19,032

(continued)

TABLE 7.4. (continued)

Variable	β	SE	Extra money value[a]	Total money value, specific subgroup
Unlimited opportunities to do non-NHS work	0.581****	0.0604	11,781	
Unlimited opportunities to do non-NHS work * general surgery	0.477****	0.0995	9,687	21,469
Unlimited opportunities to do non-NHS work * paediatrics	−0.582**	0.2316	−11,805	−23,520
Rho	0.369****	0.0249		
Log-likelihood	−3,029.898	% 1s predicted correctly		28.8%
Number of individuals	1,650	% 0s predicted correctly		95.7%
Number of observations	8,199	Pseudo $R^{2\,b}$		0.21

*$0.1 > p \geq 0.05$
**$0.05 > p \geq 0.01$
***$0.01 > p \geq 0.0001$
****$p < 0.0001$
[a] Compared to reference category

to forgo opportunities to undertake non-NHS work. Consultants would be willing to accept £7,000 in compensation for fair rather than good working relationships with staff and £6,500 to compensate them for a shortage of staff. The least important characteristic was hours of work, with £562 per year required to induce consultants to work one extra hour per week.

Given a priori expectations, the results are plausible and support the theoretical validity of the technique. DCEs have generally been shown to be reliable and valid, although this does depend on the context (Ryan and Gerard, 2002). However, the choices presented to the consultants were hypothetical, and further research needs to compare these results with results based on actual behaviour. Nevertheless, the hypothetical nature of the exercise has its advantages over using actual data as the researcher has complete control over the experimental design and this ensures statistical robustness. DCEs also allow the inclusion of characteristics that do not exist yet, such as having no opportunities to do non-NHS work and residential on-call. Two studies have suggested that monetary values from DCEs are sensitive to the range of monetary attributes included in the choices (Ratcliffe, 2000; Skjoldborg and Gyrd-Hansen, 2003). Other studies have suggested that respondents may not "trade off" attributes but use more simple decision heuristics (Scott, 2002; Lloyd, 2003). These are important topics of ongoing research. The money values should therefore be interpreted with these issues in mind. One issue is the possibility of combing revealed and stated preference data (see Chapter 11 for an in-depth discussion), and this should be considered in future studies where data on actual job choices are available.

The questionnaire was designed before the new consultant contract was introduced in 2004. However, the results still have important implications for the remuneration of consultants. From the first ballot of consultants across the UK about the new contract it was evident that English consultants were more concerned with the implication that managers would ask them to work extra antisocial hours. Working an extra hour a week was the least important characteristic for Scottish consultants, although the importance changed as the number of extra hours increased. However, the DCE did not examine the importance of working additional antisocial hours, although on-call was the most important attribute.

On-call is the attribute that consultants value most highly. It is difficult to measure the burden of on-call because it is necessary to account for frequency, intensity, location, time of day and subsequent time off. To maintain simplicity we included only intensity and location. The contract proposals indicate that those who are on an on-call rota with a high frequency should receive a supplement of up to 8% of their basic salary. Our results show that consultants would require at least 20% of their net NHS income for "very busy" on call. Although these two figures are not directly comparable, the figure of 8% seems too low.

The contract proposals also outlined several measures that will help to ensure that NHS work will be given priority over non-NHS work. Our results show that any reductions in opportunities to undertake non-NHS work would require consultants to be compensated by up to 16% of their net income. Scottish consultants undertake less private work than English consultants, and so this value may be comparatively low. However, they may still value the option to undertake such work in so far as it reflects professional autonomy.

The pricing of the various elements of the consultant contract will ultimately be the result of negotiation, and prices generated from DCEs should act as estimates of such prices, given the caveats of the study. We have shown how it is possible to derive such prices that are based on consultants' own preferences between different hypothetical jobs. The results also have implications for the recruitment and retention of consultants because if negotiated national prices are lower than individual consultants' valuations, the consultant is likely to remain dissatisfied with work and seek "compensation" in other ways, such as doing more private work, working part-time or leaving. The proposed contract also introduced flexibility for local employers to pay recruitment and retention premiums. These results may be useful to local employers in setting such premiums. Given the importance of NHS workforce policy in meeting NHS goals, the paucity of research on this issue is surprising.

ACKNOWLEDGEMENTS

Thanks to the other members of the research team: Morag Awremenko, Linda Leighton-Beck, Jill Mollison, Helen Coutts, Kim Walker and Jane Andrew. This study was funded by the Scottish Council for Postgraduate Medical and Dental Education (now NHS Education for Scotland). The Health Economics Research Unit is funded by the Chief Scientist Office of the Scottish Executive Health Department. The views in this paper are those of the authors. The results contained in this paper were first published in the British Medical Journal.

ENDNOTES

[1] See Chapter 1 for a general discussion and also Chapter 11 for discussion of the potential and circumstances under which revealed preference data and stated preference data can be combined.

[2] There are four levels of distinction award, the highest of which can almost double a consultant's salary.

[3] Further, hedonic wage models encounter econometric problems of the endogeneity of observed job characteristics that are not an issue within a DCE (Ekeland et al., 2002).

[4] z becomes endogenous only *after* the general practitioner (GP) has chosen the job in which they want to work.

[5] Note this definition of orthogonality (correlation between attributes) is different to that used by Street et al. in Chapter 2, and Burgess and Street in the Appendix to Chapter 3 (where correlation between estimates obtained from the choice experiment is investigated).

REFERENCES

Blair, M. 2002. Review body on doctors' and dentists' remuneration. Thirty-first report. London: Stationery Office.

Booth, A. and Francesconi, M. 1999. Job mobility in 1990s Britain: does gender matter? Working papers of the Institute for Social and Economic Research. Colchester: University of Essex.

Bradley, M. 1991. User's manual for SPEED version 2.1 sated preference experiment editor and designer. The Hague: Hague Consulting Group.

Carlsson, F. and Martinsson, P. 2003. Design techniques for stated preference methods in health economics. *Health Economics*, vol 12, 281–294.

Department of Health. 2001. The NHS Plan. Proposal for a new approach to the consultant contract. London: Department of Health.

Ekeland, I., Heckman, J.J. and Nesheim, L. 2002. Identifying hedonic models. *The American Economic Review*, vol 92, 304–309.

Elliot, R., Mavromaras, K., Scott, A., Bell, D., der Pol, M. and Gerova, V. 2002. Labour markets and NHS Scotland. Final Report to Scottish Executive Health Department, Aberdeen.

Gronberg, T.J. and Reed, W.R. 1994. Estimating workers marginal willingness to pay for job attributes using duration data. *Journal of Human Resources*, vol 29, 911–931.

Herzog, H.W. and Schlottmann, A.M. 1990. Valuing risk in the workplace: market price, willingness to pay, and the optimal provision of safety. *Review of Economics and Statistics*, vol 72, 463–470.

Kniesner, T.J. and Leeth, J.D. 1991. Compensating wage differentials for fatal injury risk in Australia, Japan, and the United States. *Journal of Risk and Uncertainty*, vol 4, 75–90.

Lloyd, A.J. 2003. Threats to the estimation of benefit: are preference elicitation methods accurate? *Health Economics*, vol 12, 393–402.

Manski C.F. and McFadden D. (eds). 1977. Structural Analysis of Discrete Data with Econometric Applications. Cambridge, MA: MIT Press.

Marin, A. and Psacharopoulos, G. 1982. The reward for risk in the labour market: evidence from the United Kingdom and a reconciliation with other studies. *Journal of Political Economy*, vol 90, 827–853.

McFadden, D. 1974a. The measurement of urban travel demand. *Journal of Public Economics*, vol 3, 303–328.

McFadden, D. 1974b. Conditional logit analysis of qualitative choice behaviour. In: Frontiers in Econometrics. Zarembka, P. (ed.). New York: Academic Press.

Peitz, M. 1995. Utility maximisation in models of discrete choice. *Economics Letters*, vol 49, 91–94.

Propper, C. 1995. The disutility of time spent on UK National Health Service waiting lists. *Journal of Human Resources*, vol 30 (4), 677–700.

Ratcliffe, J. 2000. The use of conjoint analysis to elicit willingness to pay: proceed with caution? *International Journal of Technology Assessment in Health Care*, vol 16, 270–290.

Rosen, S. 1986. The theory of equalising differences. In: Handbook of Labor Economics, vol 1. Ashenfelter, O. and Layard, R. (eds). Amsterdam: Elsevier, pp 641–692.

Ryan, M. and Gerard, K. 2002. Using discrete choice experiments in health economics: moving forward. In: Advances in Health Economics. Scott, A., Maynard, A. and Elliott, R. (eds). Chichester, UK: Wiley.

Scott, A. 2001. Eliciting GPs' preferences for pecuniary and non-pecuniary job characteristics. *Journal of Health Economics*, vol 20, 329–347.

Scott, A. 2002. Identifying and analysing dominant preferences in discrete choice experiments: an application in health care. *Journal of Economic Psychology*, vol 23, 383–398.

Skjoldborg, U.S. and Gyrd-Hansen, D. 2003. Conjoint analysis. The cost variable: an Achilles' heel? *Health Economics*, vol 12, 479–492.

Truong, T.P. and Hensher, D.A. 1985. Measurement of travel time values and opportunity cost from a discrete choice model. *The Economic Journal*, vol 95, 438–451.

Viscusi, W.K. 1993. The value of risks to life and health. *Journal of Economic Literature*, vol 31, 1912–1946.

Zwerina, K., Huber, J. and Kuhfeld, W. 1996. A general method for constructing efficient choice designs. Durham, NC: Fuqua School of Business, Duke University.

PART 3

METHODOLOGICAL ISSUES

CHAPTER 8

THE PRICE PROXY IN DISCRETE CHOICE EXPERIMENTS: ISSUES OF RELEVANCE FOR FUTURE RESEARCH

DORTE GYRD-HANSEN

Institute of Public Health, University of Southern Denmark, and Danish Institute for Health Services Research, Denmark

ULLA SLOTHUUS SKJOLDBORG

Institute of Public Health, University of Southern Denmark, Denmark

1. INTRODUCTION

The price proxy plays a distinct role in discrete choice experiments (DCEs) since the inclusion of a price proxy makes it possible to indirectly obtain willingness to pay (WTP) estimates for the good in its entirety or for a change in an attribute level. Marginal rates of substitution (MRS) between the price proxy and other programme attributes constitute these "part-worth" values. Thus, under the assumption of a linear additive utility function marginal WTP can be calculated as follows[1]:

$$\text{MWTP} = \beta_x i / - \beta_{\text{price}} \qquad (8.1)$$

where MWTP is the marginal willingness to pay for an extra unit of attribute β_{xix}.

To avoid misinterpretation of data it is, however, important that individuals trade between attributes (i.e. perform compensatory decision making) in order for the analyst to correctly assume a smooth continuous indifference curve. If such decision-making behaviour is incorrect, it can lead to misspecification of the regression model, subsequent misinterpretation of results which may in turn lead to erroneous conclusions. Although non-trading is an issue that may be related to all types of attributes, the issue is especially relevant in relation to the attribute that represents a price proxy as this signifies the opportunity costs associated with obtaining the good or service. Hence, the relative weighting of the price attribute may, in some instances, and/or amongst some subgroups be extremely high or extremely low. We may also observe protest bidding in which case respondents react against the mode of payment or cannot accept payments

M. Ryan, K. Gerard and M. Amaya-Amaya (eds.), Using Discrete Choice Experiments to Value Health and Health Care, 175–193.
© 2008 *Springer.*

above a certain threshold. If this is the case we may as analysts fail in obtaining preferences based on compensatory decision making.

In what follows, we discuss some key challenges associated with analysis and interpretation of a price proxy attribute within a DCE. We note this is also an important issue debated in the contingent valuation (CV) literature, but there the focus has been different. Within the CV literature the empirical evidence of the payment vehicle impact has generally been based on observed differences in magnitude of elicited WTP values. DCEs may, however, be a valuable tool in disclosing exactly *how* the payment vehicle influences respondents' choice behaviour. For this reason, we focus only on the DCE, using it to explore both the role of the payment vehicle and the influence of the price proxy attribute on elicited preferences. Both issues were recently highlighted as being poorly understood in a review paper by Ryan and Gerard (2003), which covered empirical studies published up to the year 2000. A more recent search of all health and social-related databases available at the library of the University of Southern Denmark revealed little further progress had been made on these issues. Indeed, only one new study was found fulfilling our search criteria; namely, one undertaken by the authors, which investigated the interpretation of WTP values elicited using DCE in two choice contexts; choice of hospital and choice of health care system (Slothuus Skjoldborg and Gyrd-Hansen, 2003). The lack of available research suggests a need for a greater focus on potential problems related to the price variable and use of different payment vehicles when applying DCE is required.

The aims of this chapter are to: consider issues raised in relation to the interpretation of the price proxy (and thus estimated [indirect] WTP) in DCEs; and illustrate how to analyse the data in more detail in order to avoid misinterpretation. We investigate possible lexicographic preferences for price and whether choice of payment vehicle may affect not only the relative weighting of the price proxy variable vis-à-vis the remaining attributes, but also the relative weighting of the non-monetary attributes. There are three remaining sections of the chapter. Section 2 summarises key aspects of the theory underpinning DCEs and existing evidence. Section 3 explains the empirical investigation of price in a Danish study of hospital choice. The methods used for testing the impact of vehicle payment, lexicographic preferences and comparing MRS across models are presented first. This is followed by presentation of the empirical findings. Conclusions are drawn in Section 4. Most importantly, we stress the need for future research within this area. Such research could provide valuable insight of relevance to both the CV and DCE literature.

2. THEORY AND EVIDENCE

2.1. Random Utility Theory

One of the important assumptions in DCE is that respondents are willing to trade amongst the attributes in the choice sets. Respondents are expected to be willing to accept more of one attribute as compensation for less of another attribute. This is known as compensatory decision making and is founded in microeconomic theory of consumer preferences (Deaton and Mullbauer, 1989). Random utility theory (RUT) assumes that the individual maximises utility and chooses the alternative, which constitutes the highest level of utility. As the researcher cannot observe the true utility function a probabilistic utility function is used in the estimation. The indirect utility function is decomposed into:

$$U_i = V_i + \varepsilon \tag{8.2}$$

where U_i is the true but unobservable utility for alternative i, V_i is the observable systematic component of utility and ε_i is unobservable to the researcher and treated as a random component (Hanemann, 1984).

Reasons for the random element ε may be threefold: heterogeneity in preference structures across the sample population, omitted explanatory variables in the model and/or factors influencing the respondent's decision making such as bounded rationality or random error (Train, 2003). The latter reason for randomness does not coincide with the fundamental axioms of RUT. Neoclassical theory builds on a series of additional axioms. It is assumed that individuals have complete, stable and consistent preferences and that the indifference curve is continuous. The continuity assumption does not allow for lexicographic preferences and the assumption of the utility maximising individual rules out the possibility of individuals applying heuristics in order to simplify the choice exercise. There is evidence, which suggests that these axioms may not always be fulfilled.

2.2. Lexicographic Preferences

A lexicographic preference structure violates the assumptions of continuous, differentiable and convex preferences (Payne et al., 1993). When individuals have lexicographic preference structures this entails that they do not make decisions based on all information simultaneously, but perform stepwise decisions in which they focus on the more important attributes before they consider other good characteristics. Recent studies have attempted to disclose the existence of lexicographic preference orderings in relation to preferences for health care programmes by identifying dominant preferences (Scott, 2002; Cairns et al., 2002). Dominant preferences appear when the respondent consistently chooses the scenario with the better level of a particular attribute while disregarding any potential trade-off between this attribute and other programme attributes (Keeney and Raiffa, 1976). It is worth noting, however, that preference dominance may appear only within a certain range of attribute values. There may exist a threshold value or aspiration level beyond which the respondent may exhibit compensatory decision making (Keeney and Raiffa, 1976; Nakaruma, 1997).

In the context of the issues discussed in this chapter one type of lexicographic preference is protest bidding which reflects the situation where a zero bid does not express zero valuation of the good, but rather a reaction to the notion of paying. This could be a reaction against paying more in tax or a principle opposition towards user charges in a specific context. Valid zero bids will reflect a genuine trade-off between the goods characteristics and the opportunity costs associated with paying for the good. Protest bidding is a form of lexicographic preference since the respondent focuses on whether the payment is greater than zero or not and makes a decision irrespective of the levels of the remaining attributes. Protest bidding is, however, only one type of lexicographic preference. Another type we may observe is where individuals are unwilling to pay any amount for small quality improvements but beyond a certain threshold are willing to trade monetary units for improvements on quality attributes, or vice versa. Yet another type may be based on pre-specified budgetary constraints. Individuals may, for example, operate with more or less explicit predetermined budgets for different types of goods. Hence, individuals may initially focus on the magnitude of payment in order to determine whether the cost is acceptable, i.e. whether the level of payment lies within the preset budgetary constraint. Only if the level of payment is acceptable will the respondent consider the other attributes, but with no consideration of costs. In this case, there may be very few protest bidders, but all respondents will be demonstrating lexicographic preferences. In this case, the threshold for acceptable level of payment is positive rather than zero. A fourth type of lexicographic preference could be the situation where individuals are inclined to always choose the cheaper of the two options irrespective of the gain on other attributes.

2.3. Heuristics

Especially within the psychology literature there is substantial evidence that individuals employ heuristics in order to simplify tasks they are presented with (Lloyd, 2003). This implies that respondents may ignore some of the information that is presented to them and they may make decisions that are not considered rational in the economic sense. Different cognitive short cuts may be applied depending on the presentation of the question. The axiom of completeness is also questioned implying the people do not have existing preferences for all goods, but may construct these in the course of the elicitation procedure (Ryan and San Miguel, 2002). To the extent that respondents' preferences are incomplete there is a significant danger that the elicited preferences are a function of the elicitation technique and the manner in which the question is formulated (framing effect) (see, e.g. Slovic, 1995). In the context of the present discussion such a framing effect may be induced by the payment vehicle (e.g. income tax, ear-marked tax, insurance premium or user charge) and differences in preference structures may arise due to the impact different payment vehicles have on the formation of preferences.

2.4. Payment Vehicle

Evidence shows that WTP values derived for particular commodities are not neutral to the payment vehicle employed (Brookshire et al., 1980; Greenley et al., 1981; Slothuus Skjoldborg and Gyrd-Hansen, 2003). There has been considerable debate in the CV literature on how to deal with differences in the WTP of respondents due to differences in payment vehicles. It has been argued that it is appropriate to see the payment vehicle as forming a part of the market context, as inextricably linked to the programme being valued. This entails that no unique programme value exists, but the elicited value is a function of the particular payment vehicle applied in the study. One intrinsic problem associated with payment vehicle is the extent to which it provokes protest bids. Hence, it is normally recommended that the most relevant payment vehicle should be applied in order to minimise bias (Posavac, 1998).

It has also been argued that insurance-based payment vehicles (i.e. increases in tax or risk premiums) should be applied because such vehicles yield "option value" in an *ex ante* situation (Dolan et al., 2003). The argument is that if individuals are paying to insure themselves against future incidents (e.g. a public health insurance context) it is the *ex ante* valuations, which should create the basis for prioritisation. Neumann and Johannesson (1994) demonstrated that WTP for in vitro fertilisation differed depending on whether the CV question was formulated as an *ex ante* or an *ex post* scenario.

3. EMPIRICAL INVESTIGATION OF PRICE ISSUES

In Section 2, we discussed how the price proxy attribute and payment vehicle may affect elicited preferences and estimated WTP values. In this section, we address how discrete choice data may be analysed to investigate these effects.

3.1. Overview of Method

The data upon which the analyses are based were collected in Denmark in 2000. A sample of 1991 non-institutionalised Danes aged 20–74 years participated in personal interviews. The aim was to elicit preferences for the hospital characteristics: payment level; travel time; direct access to accident and emergency; length of waiting lists;, receiving up-to-date treatment; and quality of treatment. Hospital A was a fixed alternative which involved zero additional payment, whereas hospital B had various characteristics including payment either as increases in income tax or user charges. In any given scenario only one payment vehicle was used. An example of a choice question and a listing of attribute levels are shown in Tables 8.1 and 8.2, respectively.

TABLE 8.1. *Example of choice question*

Which of these two types of hospitals would you prefer?

Attributes	Hospital A	Hospital B
Travel time to hospital when driving by car	35 min	35 min
Admission to accident and emergency	Open for everyone	A referral from the emergency doctor is required
Average waiting time for non-acute surgery	6 months	3 months
Frequency of treatment without complications	Less than average	Higher than average
Introduction of up-to-date treatment regimes has priority	No	Yes
The patient is primarily attended by the same physician	Yes	Yes
Number of beds per ward	4	4
Out-of-pocket payment per hospitalisation (Danish Kroner (DKK))	0 DKK	5,000 DKK
Or		
Extra tax payment per year (DKK)	0 DKK	2,500 DKK

TABLE 8.2. *The different attribute values used in the hospital model*

Attributes/variables	Hospital A	Hospital B	B–A; encoding
Travel time to hospital when driving by car (per minute)	35 min	• 15 min • 35 min • 60 min	• −20 • 0 • +25
Admission to accident and emergency does not require referral	Open for everyone	• Open for everyone • Referral from emergency doctor is required	• 0 • 1
Average waiting time for non-acute surgery (per month)	6 months	• 3 months • 6 months • 9 months	• −3 • 0 • +3
Frequency of treatment without complications	Less than average	• Less than average • Higher than average	• 0 • 1
Introduction of up-to-date treatment regime has priority	No	• No • Yes	• −1 • 0
The patient is primarily attended by one physician	Yes	• No • Yes	• −1 • 0
Number of beds per ward (per bed removed)	4	• 2 • 4 • 8	• −2 • 0 • +4
Out-of-pocket payment per hospitalisation (DKK)	0 DKK	• 0 DKK • 1,200 DKK • 2,500 DKK • 5,000 DKK • 10,000 DKK	• 0 • 1,200 • 2,500 • 5,000 • 10,000

Or

(continued)

TABLE 8.2. (continued)

Attributes/variables	Hospital A	Hospital B	B–A; encoding
Extra tax payment per year (DKK)	0 DKK	• 0 DKK • 1,200 DKK • 2,500 DKK • 5,000 DKK • 10,000 DKK	• 0 • 1,200 • 2,500 • 5,000 • 10,000
Out-of-pocket payment versus no out-of-pocket payment charge		If out-of-pocket payment > 0	1
		If out-of-pocket payment = 0	0
Or			
Tax increase versus no tax increase (TAX)		If increase in tax > 0	1
		If increase in tax = 0	0

The computer package SPEED 2.1 (Bradley, 1991) was used to obtain a fractional factorial design with 25 scenarios in which interactions among attributes were assumed to be insignificant. These 25 profiles were paired up into 13 choices, ensuring D-efficiency was maximised. To reduce the number of choices presented to each respondent, a block design was used. Each interviewee was asked to complete three choice questions. Data were analysed using a random effects probit model.

3.2. Method for Testing for Impact of Vehicle Payment

We sought to disclose the extent of opposition to the specific mode of payment as follows. First, we examined the quantitative effect of price on choice of hospital. This meant setting up two variables, one for each payment vehicle. If respondents faced increased income tax the out-of-pocket payment variable was coded zero and vice versa. Next, we examined the impact of payment vehicle *per se*. This was based on the assumption that the disutility associated with the payment consists of two dimensions: a principle attitude towards the concept of tax increase/introduction of user charges and the magnitude of the payment involved. This required two exogenous dummy variables to be created which represented the potential disutility associated with the notion of paying *per se*. These were constructed by setting the respective variables labelled as TAX and CHARGE, respectively in Table 8.2 equal to 1 when an option involved payments greater than zero (and equal to zero otherwise).

3.3. Method for Testing Lexicographic Preferences

When seeking to identify lexicographic preferences the most prevalent method applied in the health economics literature is to identify individuals who through their choices *appear* to have lexicographic preferences by observing dominant preference patterns (Scott, 2002; McIntosh and Ryan, 2002). In this approach, a respondent facing a large series of binary choices and consistently choosing the cheaper option would imply that compensatory decision making is not taking place. The analyst may choose to exclude such respondents from the analysis. The method requires a panel data set in which the individual respondent is faced with many discrete choice scenarios.

The problem with the approach is that identifying potential non-traders in this study is not sufficient evidence of non-compensatory decision making. Alternative explanations could include responses being an artefact of the experiment itself. Respondents may be unwilling to trade at given attribute levels but were the level range to expand may then demonstrate willingness to trade. It is not possible to test for all types of lexicographic preference structures simply through the observation of dominant preference patterns. Moreover, if respondents have lexicographic preferences with regard to payment, but each respondent has a different threshold for acceptable payment level, the analyst would not be able to detect this through the simple observation of individuals' choice patterns.

The present study took an alternative approach by testing the impact of the price attribute on the overall model. The idea was to suppose that individuals make choices in two steps; respondents are separated into those who cannot accept payment by any means and those who will. The latter then choose between hospital A and B on the basis of the remaining attributes. Clearly, such a two-part decision process violates the independence of irrelevant alternatives (IIA) criterion and renders the multinomial logit (MNL) model inappropriate (see Ryan and Skåtun, (2004) for a discussion of this issue).

The test comprised two stages (Jørgen Lauridsen, 2004, personal communication). First, the price variable is included in the regression analysis along with all other candidate explanatory variables (full model). This is followed by a reduced regression model in which price is the sole explanatory variable. The reduced model verifies whether the coefficient of the price variable remains unchanged relative to the full model. A pseudo *t*-test is performed to test for a statistically significant difference in the price coefficient as follows:

$$\text{Change 'price'} \, t = \frac{\beta_{\text{price, full model}} - \beta_{\text{price, reduced model}}}{\sqrt{(\text{SD}(\beta_{\text{price, full model}})^2 + \text{SD}(\beta_{\text{price, full model}})^2)}} \qquad (8.3)$$

where $\beta_{\text{price, full model}}$ is the coefficient from the full model, $\beta_{\text{price, reduced model}}$ is the coefficient from the reduced model and SD is standard deviation of the parameter.

The term "pseudo" is applied because the test is conservative due to overestimation of the standard deviation (the test does not take into account that the two coefficient estimates are based on the same sample). If some degree of trading is taking place between price and remaining attributes, then exclusion of all other candidate explanatory variables affect the estimated coefficient of the price variable. The relationship between the price variable and choice should in this case be more poorly explained, and the associated random error term must consequently increase. In discrete choice modelling each of the coefficients is scaled by $1/\sigma$, where the variance of the error term ε is σ^2. If a high proportion of the utility is unobserved the variance of the error term is high and the scale factor $1/\sigma$ diminishes. As the scale factor decreases the coefficients of the explanatory variables become smaller. Hence, we would expect the price coefficient to decrease due to this scaling effect. If, on the other hand, the initial choice between programmes A and B is solely based on the attitude towards payment and only subsequently on the other attributes, the exclusion of the other attributes as explanatory variables should not affect the model's ability to estimate the utility associated with payment and the coefficient should remain unaltered. If we are dealing with a stepwise decision-making procedure this means that the valuation of the other programme attributes are made independently of the price proxy, and hence exclusion of the price variable in the explanatory model should not affect the estimated parameters of the remaining variables.

Clearly, this test can only verify whether there is an extreme problem in the data set, i.e. whether all or a large majority of respondents are demonstrating lexicographic preferences. If only a fraction of respondents are refraining from performing compensatory decision making, other methods must be used in order to verify whether subgroups of respondents have a lexicographic preference structure. Inclusion of interactions variables such as socio-demographics may be a constructive method for identifying subgroups that have pure lexicographic preferences from those that do not (Bennett and Blamey, 2001). Application of the mixed logit model may also be useful in analysing heterogeneity in preferences amongst respondents.

3.4. Delta Method for Comparing Marginal Rates of Substitution

Our aim is also to test the hypothesis that the choice of payment vehicle will influence the observed relative weighting of the non-price variables. We can observe the results of regression models by payment vehicles but again must adjust for scale differences in the process. The relative scale of the estimates from the two data sets reflects the relative variance of the unobserved factors in the data sets. To the extent that the scale of the coefficients is in general higher in one data set than in another, this means that the unobserved portion of utility has less variance in this data set. Any difference in the magnitude of estimated coefficients across regression models based on different question formats may thus be a function of either varying degrees of random error across the two subgroups, or due to actual differences in expressed preferences. A larger degree of random error may occur when respondents are faced with tasks, which are more cognitively demanding. When making simple comparisons of regression models based on the two subsets of data we will observe how different the estimated indirect utility function may be when applying different payment vehicles in discrete choice. We cannot, however, isolate the impact of random error (scaling differences) from any difference in the underlying formed preference structures (Louviere et al., 2000). If random error is, for example, generally high amongst a subgroup of respondents estimated model coefficients will in general be lower, without there necessarily being a difference in the relative weighting of programme attributes. In order to test for any differences in elicited preference structures across the two subgroups in this study (those presented with out-of-pocket payment and those presented with increases in income tax) it is necessary to test for statistical differences in MRS between programme attributes across the two regression models (Ben-Akiva and Lerman, 1985). Note that MRS is applied because any scaling effect will be annulled when operating with fractions. There is a number of ways in which one may estimate variance around the mean for a fraction between two coefficients (see, e.g. Cameron and James, 1987; Kristrom, 1990). The method applied here is the Delta method (Greene, 2003; Hanemann and Kanninen, 1998).

If γ and λ represent coefficients for two programme attributes, then MRS is estimated as γ/λ. The variance for MRS is according to the Delta method calculated as follows:

$$VAR(\gamma/\lambda) = (\gamma/\lambda^2)^2 \times VAR(\lambda) + (1/\lambda^2) \times VAR(\gamma) - 2(\gamma/\lambda^3) \times COV(\lambda, \gamma) \quad (8.4)$$

Having estimated γ/λ (= MRS) and VAR (γ/λ) (=VAR(MRS)) we use the students t-test to test for whether the MRS for subgroup 1 differs from MRS for subgroup 2:

$$t = \frac{MRS_1 - MRS_2}{\sqrt{VAR(MRS_1) + VAR(MRS_2)}} \quad (8.5)$$

3.5. Results

3.5.1. Establishing impact of vehicle payment on preference

Table 8.3 shows the results of payment vehicle on preferences. It can be seen that the inclusion of the dummy variables had a significant impact on results. If the dummy variables were excluded (i.e. model 1) the price variables were associated with negative coefficients as expected and the signs of the coefficients associated with the remaining attributes were in line with expected hypotheses with one exception, frequency of treatment without complications. Inclusion of the dummy variables (model 2) rendered the price proxies insignificant, and changed model results such that all coefficients signs were in line with ex ante expectations. Inclusion of these dummy variables appeared to constitute a model that provided a better fit to the data. The results suggested that respondents reacted principally to the concept of non-zero payment and not to the magnitude of payments.

TABLE 8.3. *Model results (main effects and main effects and (dis)utility for payment vehicle). (From Slothuus Skjoldborg and Gyrd-Hansen, 2003.)*

Attribute	Model 1 Weight	Model 1 *p*-value	Model 2 Weight	Model 2 *p*-value
Travel time to hospital when driving by car (per minute)	−0.00899	0.0000	−0.00742	0.0000
Admission to accident and emergency does not require referral	−0.533	0.0000	−0.813	0.0000
Average waiting time for non-acute surgery (per month)	−0.0707	0.0000	−0.158	0.0000
Frequency of treatment without complications (higher than average versus lower than average)	−0.06314	0.1678	0.189	0.0000
Introduction of up-to-date treatment regime has priority	0.04223	0.4090	0.493	0.0000
The patient is primarily attended by one physician	0.546	0.0000	0.494	0.0000
Number of beds per ward (per bed removed)	−0.0833	0.0000	−0.203	0.0000
Extra tax payment per year (per DKK)	−0.000102	0.0000	Insignificant[a]	
Out-of-pocket payment per hospitalisation (per DKK)	−0.000185	0.0000	Insignificant[b]	
Tax increase versus no tax increase (TAX)	n.a.		−1.019	0.0000
Out-of-pocket payment versus no out-of-pocket payment (CHARGE)	n.a.		−1.437	0.0000
	n = 5,928 LogL = −2,614.3 McFadden = 0.00686		*n* = 5,928 LogL = −2,488.6 McFadden = 0.01969	

Model 1 represents standard model where price is included as continuous variable only. Model 2 included additional dummy variables for method of payment (= 1 if payment present; = 0 if payment absent).
[a]$p < 0.8955$
[b]$p < 0.1566$

This finding has a significant impact on subsequent interpretation of preferences. One cannot interpret MRS estimates between the price variable and the remaining attributes as measures of WTP in this case. However, if we had only applied the standard model (model 1) and not incorporated the dummy variables we would most likely have calculated WTP on the basis of MRS between the price coefficients and the remaining coefficients, and the data would have been misinterpreted. In another related study in which we elicited the public's preferences for health care systems (Gyrd-Hansen and Slothuus, 2002) we found that inclusion of similar dummy variables had a less-profound impact on the preference structure. The dummy variables were statistically significant, but the price proxy coefficients remained statistically significant. Hence, in this case the preferences were characterised by some degree of opposition towards payment, and also some degree of compensatory decision making.

3.5.2. Establishing preference structure

The question remains as to how one is to interpret the observed preference structure of model 2 in Table 8.3. In this specific context it appears that preferences are unaffected by the magnitude of payment and the highly statistically significant dummy coefficients reflect that disutility is associated with payment *per se*. Our results further indicate that the principle of out-of-pocket payment was associated with greater disutility than were increases in income tax. This is not surprising in a Danish context since almost all hospital beds are 100% publicly financed via income taxes. What we cannot directly determine from this analysis is whether this preference structure reflects homogeneity in preference structure (as is assumed in standard logit and probit regressions) or whether the result reflects an average preference structure over individuals with heterogeneous preferences and different principle attitudes towards the notion of additional payment. In other words, we may be identifying respondents who are principally opposed to paying for improvements in the quality of hospitals as long as this improvement is not large enough, but when the improvements are of an adequate magnitude the utility of these improvement by far override the disutility of the added payment, and henceforth the magnitude of payment has no impact on preferences. This would constitute some form of compensatory decision making, albeit with a rather unusual non-monotonic preference structure.

An alternative and perhaps more likely hypothesis is that we are dealing with a separate binary preference structure in which individuals are making choices in two steps. The first step involves the respondents' attitude to the concept of paying. In this initial step respondents are separated into those who cannot accept payment by any means and those who are, in principle, open minded towards additional payment (irrespective of the size of the payment). In the second step, those individuals who are willing to pay will choose between hospital A and hospital B solely on the basis of the remaining attributes. This is a demonstration of lexicographic preferences. In such a preference structure compensatory decision making is not being performed and hence results should not be interpreted as if trading is taking place.

In order to analyse the underlying nature of the preference structure observed in model 2 we performed the aforementioned pseudo *t*-test in order to disclose whether the dummy variable coefficients remained unchanged when only these are included as explanatory variables. We perform two sets of analysis, one for each method of payment. In Table 8.4, models 3a and b relate to user charges as the payment vehicle whilst models 3c and d relate to the tax payment method. In each case, the first of the pair presets the results of the full model and the second the reduced model.

Results show that both in the context of user charges and tax payments in the context of payment vehicle, the dummy coefficients remain unaffected ($p = 0.0000$). This signifies that we are dealing with pure lexicographic models where individuals are deciding for or against increased payment (irrespective of magnitude of payment) to hospitals and subsequently focusing on the remaining attributes (if a positive payment is deemed acceptable). If the appropriate model had been model 1 in Table 8.3 one could have performed the same type of analysis with the price proxy figuring as the only explanatory variable in the reduced regression model. Had we found that the coefficient of the price proxy variable remained unaltered when comparing the full and the reduced model this would have signified a scenario in which individuals initially focus on the magnitude of the payment when deciding for or against hospitals A and B, and if both prices were acceptable the choice between A and B would be based solely on the remaining attribute levels.

3.5.3. Marginal rates of substitution

MRS estimates were calculated for all 28 combinations of attributes in the hospital study. Since the aim is to analyse any changes in the relative weighting of attributes, MRS is also estimated for discrete variables in which case the fraction cannot be interpreted strictly as a MRS. It is nevertheless an indicator of the relative weighting of the attributes and an indicator of willingness to trade off between attributes.

Results in Table 8.5 show that out of the 28 different MRS estimates that can be derived on the basis of the list of explanatory variables included in the full models reported in Table 8.4, 11 were statistically significantly different across the two models. This result demonstrates that preference structures in the two settings are markedly different and that these differences are not induced by scaling effects alone. Statistically significant differences in MRS are observed. In six instances the MRS involves the price variable. This leaves five MRS estimates between non-monetary programme attributes that have been significantly affected by choice of payment vehicle. These differences in relative weightings of hospital attributes are largely explained by the lack of focus on travel time to hospital when payment vehicle is out of pocket. There may be several possible justifications for these variations in preferences. User charges may be associated with a private hospital setting in which case one does not expect to have a hospital close at hand. An alternative explanation to the marked difference in preference structure may also be that the insurance perspective induces other preference patterns because option value is incorporated. Finally, the observed preferences may be a result of different sets of heuristics being applied in the different settings. These hypotheses cannot be verified on the basis of the data we have available, and are merely presented in order to lay out possible explanations for the observed phenomenon.

TABLE 8.4. *Model results (full and reduced with respect to payment vehicle)*

Attribute	User charges		Tax payment	
	Model 3a (full) Coefficient (*p*-value)	Model 3b (reduced) Coefficient (*p*-value)	Model 3c (full) Coefficient (*p*-value)	Model 3d (reduced) Coefficient (*p*-value)
Travel time to hospital when driving by car (per minute)	−0.0008 (0.7417)	n.a.	−0.0093 (0.0000)	n.a.
Admission to accident and emergency does not require referral	−0.5698 (0.0000)	n.a.	−0.6081 (0.0000)	n.a.
Average waiting time for non-acute surgery (per month)	−0.0948 (0.0000)	n.a.	−0.1415 (0.0000)	n.a.
Frequency of treatment without complications (higher than average versus lower than average	0.0585 (0.3244)	n.a.	0.2738 (0.0000)	n.a.
Introduction of up-to-date treatment regime has priority	0.3157 (0.0003)	n.a.	0.3315 (0.0000)	n.a.
The patient is primarily attended by one physician	0.1879 (0.0044)	n.a.	0.4498 (0.0000)	n.a.
Number of beds per ward (per bed removed)	−0.1049 (0.0002)	n.a.	−0.1538 (0.0000)	n.a.
Tax increase versus no tax increase	n.a.		−0.8228 (0.0000)	−0.8310 (0.0000)
Out-of-pocket payment versus no out-of-pocket payment	−1.1516 (0.0000)	−1.1568 (0.0000)	n.a.	
	n = 2,888 LogL = −1,138.7 McFadden = 0.04639	*n* = 2,888 LogL = −1,217.8 McFadden = −0.01986	*n* = 3,040 LogL = −1,396.3 McFadden = 0.04825	*n* = 3,040 LogL = −1,667.7 McFadden = −0.13679

Separate analyses performed for choices involving different payment vehicles (models 3a and c). Reduced models presented in which dummy payment variables are only explanatory variables (models 3b and d).

TABLE 8.5. *Testing for differences in marginal rates of substitution (MRS) by payment vehicle*

MRS	*p*-value
Travel time, admission	0.0041
Travel time, average waiting time	0.0370
Travel time, frequency of treatment without complications	0.6086
Travel time, introduction of up-to-date treatment	0.0112
Travel time, primarily attended by one physician	0.1925
Travel time, number of beds per ward	0.0242
Travel time, payment	0.0004
Admission, average waiting time	0.2024
Admission, frequency of treatment without complications	0.4269
Admission, introduction of up-to-date treatment	0.9564
Admission, primarily attended by one physician	0.1160
Admission, number of beds per ward	0.2598
Admission, payment	0.0182
Average waiting time, frequency of treatment without complications	0.4781
Average waiting time, introduction of up-to-date treatment	0.3502
Average waiting time, primarily attended by one physician	0.3346
Average waiting time, number of beds per ward	0.9627
Average waiting time, payment	0.0000
Frequency of treatment without complications, introduction of up-to-date treatment	0.0276
Frequency of treatment without complications, primarily attended by one physician	0.3794
Frequency of treatment without complications, number of beds per ward	0.0920
Frequency of treatment without complications, payment	0.0004
Introduction of up-to-date treatment, primarily attended by one physician	0.0793
Introduction of up-to-date treatment, number of beds per ward	0.2381
Introduction of up-to-date treatment, payment	0.1990
Primarily attended by one physician, number of beds per ward	0.1370
Primarily attended by one physician, payment	0.0000
Number of beds per ward, payment	0.0073

Clearly, more research is warranted in order to conclude anything more general on this issue.

Looking at the relative magnitude of coefficients across models 3a and c suggests that the out-of-pocket payment scenario in general entails lower weights on all quality attributes relative to those observed when payment vehicle is increased taxes. Hence, not only is the opposition towards payment more pronounced in the context of out-of-pocket payment, but focus also appears to move away from the quality attributes – thus inducing higher levels of random error.

4. CONCLUSION

The issues that have been raised in the chapter whilst not an exhaustive represent a good push forward on the matter of using and interpreting a price proxy attribute in DCE. There is a range of issues that the analyst must be aware of. An important example is that of the cost-based responses to the price proxy in which case elicited responses may be an expression of the respondents' impression of the cost of the programme and the corresponding "reasonable" price rather than the respondents' WTP. Another pressing issue is whether the range of price values allows the analyst to estimate valid WTP values as addressed by Ratcliffe (2000). In the present chapter we have addressed the issue of non-trading with respect to the price proxy. For a health economist who applies DCE in order to estimate WTP for marginal programme changes or a programme as a whole it is of great importance to ensure that the underlying preferences are based on smooth continuous indifference curves. This chapter has illustrated that it is vital to analyse the preference structure in detail in order to avoid misinterpretation of data. This issue is especially important in relation to WTP estimates, but equally relevant in relation to estimation of MRS in general. The chapter has also focused on the possible impact that choice of payment vehicle may have on the general preference structure. Although future research is required in order to further understand the reasons for such preference changes, our empirical illustration does confirm that payment vehicle should be seen as an intrinsic characteristic of a programme and not just as at tool for eliciting WTP estimates. The analysis presented here demonstrates that the impact payment vehicle has on the valuation of a good does not necessarily take the form of a general increase or decrease in the overall valuation of the good, but may represent a more complex change in the relative importance of the good's characteristics. DCE may be seen as an instrument for further understanding changes in valuation of goods in the context of different payment vehicles.

In this chapter, we have discussed methods of data analysis with focus on detecting lexicographic preferences in relation to price proxy as well as the impact payment vehicle may have on preference structures. We envisage that these methods may be applied in order to improve data analysis and to gain insight into preference structures more generally. Whereas these tests are tools, which may produce insights into preferences at the group level, they cannot operate at the individual level. The field of experimental economics may be helpful in this regard.

Experimental questionnaire designs may involve more dynamic probing such that individuals' points of indifference may be disclosed and WTP thresholds elicited. Combining the knowledge gained through experimental economics with analysis of standard DCE questionnaires (within the same respondent group) may illustrate exactly how much we can infer about lexicographic preferences from data analyses of discrete choice data. More in-depth analysis of DCE data and more evidence from experimental economics is likely to improve our understanding of non-trading behaviour.

Finally, it should be noted that the extent to which payment vehicle affects results is bound to be both context and country specific.

ACKNOWLEDGEMENTS

We would like to thank Jørgen Lauridsen, Ph.D., Department of Economics and Business, University of Southern Denmark for discussions regarding tests for statistically significant difference in price coefficient.

ENDNOTES

[1] For further details about how to adjust the formula for alternative specifications of the utility function, see Louviere et al. (2000).

REFERENCES

Ben-Akiva, M. and Lerman, S. 1985. Discrete Choice Analysis: Theory and Application to Travel Demand. Cambridge, MA: MIT Press.

Bennett, J. and Blamey, R.K. 2001. The Choice Modelling Approach in Environmental Valuation. Cheltenham: Edward Elgar.

Bradley, M. 1991. User's manual for SPEED version 2.1 stated preference experiment editor and designer. The Hague: Hague Consulting Group.

Brookshire, D.S., Randall, A. and Stoll, J.R. 1980. Valuing increments and decrements in natural resource service flows. *American Journal of Agricultural Economics*, vol 62, 478–488.

Cairns, J., van der Pol., M. and Lloyd, A. 2002. Decision making heuristics in and the elicitation of preferences: being fast and frugal about the future. *Health Economics*, vol 11 (7), 655–658.

Cameron, T.A. and James, M. 1987. Efficient estimation methods for closed ended contingent valuation surveys. *Review of Economics and Statistics*, vol 69, 269–276.

Deaton, A. and Mullbauer, J. 1989. Economics and Consumer Behaviour. Cambridge, MA: Cambridge University Press.

Dolan, P., Olsen, J.A. and Menzel, P., et al. 2003. An inquiry into the different perspectives that can be used when eliciting preferences in health. *Health Economics*, vol 12 (7), 545–551.

Greene, W.H. 2003. Econometric Analysis. 5th edn. Upper Saddle River, NJ: Prentice Hall.

Greenley, D.A., Walsh, R.G. and Young, R.A. 1981. Option value: empirical evidence from a case study of recreation and water quality. *The Quarterly Journal of Economics*, vol 96 (4), 657–673.

Gyrd-Hansen, D. and Slothuus, U. 2002. The Citizen's preferences for financing public health care. A Danish survey. *International Journal of Health Care Finance and Economics*, vol 2 (1), 25–36.

Hanemann, W.M. 1984. Welfare evaluations in contingent valuation experiments with discrete responses. *American Journal of Agricultural Economics*, vol 66 (3), 332–341.

Hanemann, W.M. and Kanninen, B. 1998. The statistical analysis of discrete-response CV data, Working Paper 798, Department of Agricultural and Resource Economics and Policy, University of California, Berkeley.

Keeney, R.L. and Raiffa, H. 1976. Decisions with Multiple Objectives – Preferences and Value Tradeoffs. New York: Wiley.

Kristrom, B. 1990. A non-parametric approach to the estimation of welfare measures in discrete response valuation studies. *Land Economics*, vol 66, 135–139.

Lloyd, A.J. 2003. Threats to the estimation of benefit: are preference elicitation methods accurate? *Health Economics*, vol 12, 393–402.

Louviere, J., Hensher, D.A. and Swait, J. 2000. Stated Choice Methods, Analysis and Application, Cambridge: Cambridge University Press.

McIntosh, E. and Ryan, M. 2002. Using discrete choice experiments to derive welfare estimates for the provision of elective surgery: implications of discontinuous preferences. *Journal of Economic Psychology*, vol 23, 376–382.

Nakaruma, Y. 1997. Lexicographic additivity for multi-attribute preferences on finite sets. *Theory and Decision*, vol 42 (1), 1–19.

Neumann, P.J. and Johannesson, M. 1994. The willingness-to-pay for in vitro fertilisation: a pilot study using contingent valuation. *Medical Care*, vol 32 (7), 686–699.

Payne, J. et al. 1993. The Adaptive Decision Maker. Cambridge, MA: Cambridge University Press.

Posavac, S. 1998. Strategic overbidding in contingent valuation: stated economic value of public goods varies according to consumers' expectation of funding source. *Journal of Economic Psychology*, vol 19, 205–214.

Ratcliffe, J. 2000. The use of conjoint analysis to elicit willingness-to-pay values. *International Journal of Technology Assessment in Health Care*, vol 16, 270–275.

Ryan, M. and Gerard, K. 2003. Using discrete choice experiments to value health care programmes: current practice and future research reflections. *Applied Health Economics and Health Policy*, vol 2 (1), 55–64.

Ryan, M. and San Miguel, F. 2002. Revisiting the axiom of completeness in health care. *Health Economics*, vol 12, 295–307.

Ryan, M. and Skåtun, D. 2004. Modelling non-demanders in choice experiments. *Health Economics*, vol 13 (4), 397–402.

Scott, A. 2002. Identifying and analysing dominant preferences in discrete choice experiments: an application in health care. *Journal of Economic Psychology*, vol 23 (3), 383–398.

Slothuus Skjoldborg, U. and Gyrd-Hansen, D. 2003. Conjoint analysis: the cost variable: an Achilles' heel? *Health Economics*, vol 12 (6), 479–491

Slovic, P. 1995. The construction of preference. *Journal of American Psychology*, vol 50 (5), 364–371.

Train, K.E. 2003. Discrete Choice Methods with Simulation. Cambridge: Cambridge University Press.

CHAPTER 9

"IRRATIONAL" STATED PREFERENCES

A quantitative and qualitative investigation

FERNANDO SAN MIGUEL INZA

Institución Futuro, Navarra, Spain

MANDY RYAN AND MABEL AMAYA-AMAYA

Health Economics Research Unit, University of Aberdeen, UK

1. INTRODUCTION

When using discrete choice experiments (DCEs) it is crucial to ensure that subjects are answering in a "rational" (internally consistent) way. One approach to testing rationality is to test the axiom of non-satiation, i.e. more is preferred to less. Within DCEs satisfaction of this axiom has been explored by including choices where one of the options has no worse levels for any of the attributes and better levels for at least one (See Chapters 4, 5 and 7 in this book and Ryan et al., 2001). Johnson and Mathews (2001) carried out different tests of choice consistency, including dominance, monotonicity across different pairs and so-called stability (repetition of identical choices within the same questionnaire). Transitivity of preferences has also been explored (San Miguel, 2000).

Much of the work in health economics has concentrated on *just* the identification of "irrational" responses. Such responses have been generally dropped from further analysis. As discussed by Lancsar and Louviere (2006), there are a number of reasons why this practice should be avoided, including the possibility of biased results (see also Rouwendal and de Blaiej, 2004). However, it is still important to explain the inconsistencies found in individual choices (May, 1954; Earl, 1990; Sen, 1993). Consideration needs to be given to *why* individuals "fail" choice consistency tests. This chapter reports the results of a DCE set-up to test rational choice properties. Quantitative and qualitative methods are applied to better understand the reasons underlying "rationality" failures. Sections 2 and 3 describe the experiment including the various tests of rationality included (Section 2) and the quantitative and qualitative methods adopted to investigate "irrational" choices (Section 3).

195

M. Ryan, K. Gerard and M. Amaya-Amaya (eds.), Using Discrete Choice
Experiments to Value Health and Health Care, 195–215.

Results are then presented in Section 4. Section 5 discusses the results with consideration given to their implication for the design of DCEs.

2. THE EXPERIMENT

2.1. Setting and Sample

Rationality choice properties were investigated within a DCE embedded in the realistic context of a wider study concerned with assessing patient preferences for nurses in primary care (Caldow et al., 2000).[1] The conventional approach to investigating rationality within DCE is to include non-satiation (dominance) tests. However, it has been argued that such tests are easy to satisfy and that they may question the credibility of such experiments (Ryan et al., 2002; Ryan and Gerard, 2003). This study, in addition to traditional non-satiation tests, included two, arguably more stringent, rational choice tests based on Sen's choice consistency properties (Sen, 1993, p 500); the contraction property (CP) test and the expansion property (EP) test (see below for details).

Three versions of a DCE questionnaire were designed to allow a number of rationality tests to be conducted. Each version contained a different total number of choices (i.e. Q6, Q8, Q10 reflected the 6, 8 and 10 choices, respectively in each questionnaire) which were randomly allocated to respondents. These different lengths of version were included in the design of the experiment to pick up an important sequence effect that was thought to take place when respondents answered a series of choice questions (see Section 3.1 for more details) The tests carried out and their allocation across the questionnaires is summarised in Figure 9.1.

In each questionnaire, subjects were asked to imagine "you have been feeling slightly chesty with an irritating cough for 2 weeks. You are still able to do all the things you usually do, but notice that you are a little out of breath when exerting yourself. For the past three or four mornings you have coughed up a little phlegm and you decide to ask for an appointment at your practice". Respondents were told that their consultation could vary according to the attributes defined and offered a number of choices. For each choice respondents were asked to choose between two (A or B) or three (A, B or C) hypothetical consultations or a "neither" option. The "neither" option was included to give more realism to the exercise. Respondents were informed that choosing "neither" implied that they would not be seen in their practice about that illness. After completing the choices, respondents were asked to rate their difficulty on a scale from 1 (very easy) to 5 (very difficult).

The study population comprised a random sample of patients from 21 practices in Scotland. The practices were chosen from a list of general practitioner practices across Scotland about which information was available about the extended role of the nurse. Nine hundred and ninety-two postal questionnaires of Q6, 984 of Q8 and 975 of Q10 and two reminders were sent out.

2.2. Rationality Tests

Internally consistent choices require that if a choice set J is "*contracted*" or narrowed (to I) and the alternatives (or some of them) chosen from J are still in I, then no unchosen alternatives should be chosen now and no chosen alternatives should be

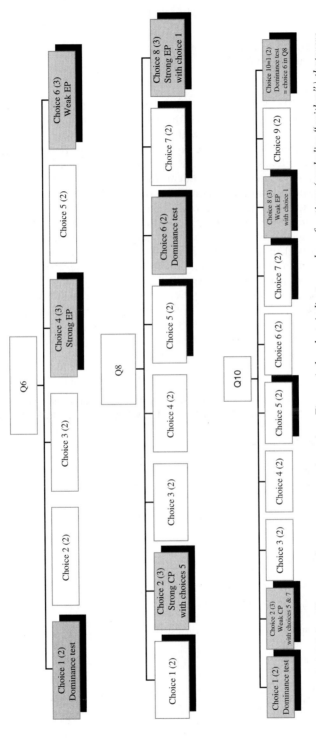

FIGURE 9.1. *Allocation of tests across questionnaires. Figures in brackets indicate number of options (excluding "neither") that were presented in each choice.*

unchosen now. Similarly, perceived preferences should be preserved under an expanded menu of choices.[2]

2.2.1. Contraction property tests

To test the CP choice property, respondents were first asked to choose a consultation out of a set of four alternatives (three consultations (A, B or C) and a "neither" option). This choice set was narrowed (in a non-consecutive choice) to a set of three alternatives (two consultations (A or B) plus a "neither" option) and respondents were asked again to choose one of the options (see, e.g. Table 9.1).[3]

The test was satisfied if a respondent who chose (say) option A in the first choice set did not choose option B or "neither" in the reduced choice set.[4]

Two variants of CP tests were used. If the tests included dominant options (i.e. an option that had no worse levels for any of the attributes and better for at least one of them), they are referred to as "weak CP" since it was considered that it would be easier to satisfy. The first test shown in Table 9.1 sets out an example of a weak CP test that was included in Q10 using the second, fifth and seventh choices. Otherwise, tests are "strong CP" tests. Strong CP tests were included in Q8 again using the second, fifth and seventh choices presented to respondents (see the second example in Table 9.1).

TABLE 9.1. *Choices used in the contraction property (CP) tests*

Test				
Attributes	Neither*	Consultation A	Consultation B	Consultation C
		Initial choice set		
Weak CP test (Q10)				
Who you see		Doctor	Doctor	Doctor
Waiting time (days)		2	2	4
Length of consultation (min)		10	10	10
Continuity of health professional		Yes	No	No
Likelihood of illness cured (%)		85	80	75
		1st contracted choice set		
Who you see		Doctor	Doctor	
Waiting time (days)		2	2	
Length of consultation (min)		10	10	
Continuity of health professional		Yes	No	
Likelihood of illness cured (%)		85	80	

(continued)

TABLE 9.1. (continued)

Test Attributes	Neither*	Consultation A	Consultation B	Consultation C
		2nd contracted choice set		
Who you see		Doctor		Doctor
Waiting time (days)		2		4
Length of consultation (min)		10		10
Continuity of health professional		Yes		No
Likelihood of illness cured (%)		85		75
		Initial choice set		
Strong CP test (Q8)				
Who you see		Practice nurse	Doctor	Practice nurse
Waiting time (days)		2	8	No waiting
Length of consultation (min)		30	5	20
Continuity of health professional		Yes	Yes	No
Likelihood of illness cured (%)		80	75	75
		1st contracted choice set		
Who you see		Practice nurse	Doctor	
Waiting time (days)		2	8	
Length of consultation (min)		30	5	
Continuity of health professional		Yes	Yes	
Likelihood of illness cured (%)		80	75	
		2nd contracted choice set		
Who you see			Doctor	Practice nurse
Waiting time (days)			8	No waiting
Length of consultation (min)			5	20
Continuity of health professional			Yes	No
Likelihood of illness cured (%)			75	75

*Attribute levels do not apply for the "neither" option as the respondent chooses not to visit the practice

2.2.2. Expansion property tests

To test the EP, respondents were first asked to choose a consultation out of a set of three alternatives (two consultations (A or B) and a "neither" option). This choice set was then widened to a set of four alternatives (three consultations (A, B or C) and a "neither" option), in a non-consecutive question where respondents had again to choose one of the options. For the property to be satisfied, a respondent that chose (say) option A in the first choice set, should not choose B or "neither" in the expanded one (Table 9.2 shows two examples).

TABLE 9.2. *Choices used in the expansion property (EP) tests*

Test	Description of choice sets			
	Expanded choice set (= initial choice + consultation C)			
	Initial choice			
Attributes	Neither*	Consultation A	Consultation B	**Consultation C**
Weak EP test (Q6)				
Who you see		Doctor	Doctor	**Doctor**
Waiting time (days)		2	4	**8**
Length of consul-tation (min)		20	20	**20**
Continuity of health professional		Yes	No	**No**
Likelihood of illness cured (%)		85	85	**80**
Weak EP (Q10)				
Who you see		Practice nurse	Practice nurse	**Practice nurse**
Waiting time (days)		No waiting	2	**4**
Length of consul-tation (min)		20	20	**20**
Continuity of health professional		Yes	No	**No**
Likelihood of illness cured (%)		80	75	**75**

(continued)

TABLE 9.2. (continued)

Test		Description of choice sets		
		Expanded choice set (= initial choice + consultation C)		
		Initial choice		
Attributes	Neither*	Consultation A	Consultation B	**Consultation C**
Strong EP (Q6)				
Who you see		Doctor	Practice nurse	**Practice nurse**
Waiting time (days)		2	No waiting	**2**
Length of consultation (min)		10	20	**30**
Continuity of health professional		No	Yes	**Yes**
Likelihood of illness cured (%)		75	75	**75**
Strong EP (8)				
Who you see		Doctor	Practice nurse	**Practice nurse**
Waiting time (days)		No waiting	8	**2**
Length of consultation (min)		5	20	**20**
Continuity of health professional		No	No	**Yes**
Likelihood of illness cured (%)		80	80	**80**

*Attribute levels do not apply for the "neither" option as the respondent chooses not to visit the practice

Again, two different versions of EP tests were used. When the choices included a dominant option, the test is referred to as "weak EP". Consistency using weak EP was tested in Q6 (using the first and sixth choices) and Q10 (using first and eighth choices). Strong EP was tested in both Q6 (using second and fourth choices) and Q8 (using first and eighth choices). Table 9.2 sets these out.

2.2.3. Non-satiation (dominance) tests

In addition to the EP and CP tests, traditional non-satiation tests (where one of the options has no worse levels for any of the attributes and better levels for at least one of them) were also included. Two tests were spread over the three questionnaires. These were as follows: one test each in Q6 (using first choice) and Q8 (using sixth choice) and two tests in Q10 (using first and tenth choices).

2.3. Qualitative Data

All respondents were asked to state the reason for their choice for the rationality tests. An open space was provided for such responses within the questionnaire. This was an opportunistic attempt to further investigate reasons for failing rationality tests.

3. EXPLORING "IRRATIONAL" RESPONSES

3.1. Quantitative Analysis

Initial quantitative analysis was conducted to investigate the frequency of failures across the different rationality tests. Samples were compared to ensure that if differences were found this was not the result of differences between respondent's characteristics. Respondents were compared according to gender, age, profession, education level and income level.

Regression techniques were used to explore reasons for failures. Given respondents completed more than one test, a random effect specification was used (Greene, 1997). The dependent variable was a dummy, taking the value of 1 if the respondent satisfied either version of the more stringent tests (i.e. weak and strong CP and EP) and 0 otherwise. Explanatory variables in the model took account of both the context of the experimental design and the characteristics of respondents (see the first two columns of Table 9.3). The role of each explanatory variable is discussed in turn below.

Respondents were expected to be less likely to fail the weak version CP and EP rationality tests, which both included a dominant option. Another important context variable is similarity between the alternatives (Tversky and Sattah, 1979; Shugan, 1980). This was captured by the dispersion of the standard deviation (SD) among attribute levels across alternatives (Deshazo and Fermo, 2002). The (absolute) difference between the values of this index for the choice sets compared in the rationality tests (*DdSD*) may be thought of as an indicator of the relative ease of the choice task in each case.[5] A priori it is hypothesised that as DsSD increases, choice sets become less similar, therefore making choices easier and in so doing increasing the probability of satisfying the rationality tests.

TABLE 9.3. *Quantitative investigation of "irrational" responses*

Variable	Coding and description	Regression results (random effects probit)	
		Coefficient	*p*-value
Dependent variable			
Rational	1 if respondent satisfies rationality test, 0 otherwise		
Independent variables			
Context factors			
Strong	1 if rationality test is strong; 0 if weak	−0.85	0.09*
DdSD	Difference between dispersion of standard deviation of choices included in the test	1.29	0.00**
Sequence	Position in the questionnaire of second choice in EP and CP tests	−4.06	0.06*
Sequence²	Position in the questionnaire of second choice in EP and CP tests (squared)	0.31	0.07*
DQ8	1 if rationality test is in Q8; 0 otherwise	1.24	0.02**
DQ10	1 if rationality test is in Q10; 0 otherwise	0.23	0.18
Difficulty dummies	("very easy" was the reference level)		
Dif2	1 if difficulty rating was 2; 0 otherwise	−0.28	0.03**
Dif3	1 if difficulty rating was 3; 0 otherwise	−0.21	0.10*
Dif4	1 if difficulty rating was 4; 0 otherwise	−0.21	0.35
Dif5	1 if difficulty rating was 5; 0 otherwise	−0.55	0.04**

(continued)

TABLE 9.3. (continued)

Variable	Coding and description	Regression results (random effects probit)	
		Coefficient	p-value
Dif3choices	Responses to the question "Did you find answering the questions with three choices more difficult?" "yes" = −1; "depended on the choices" = 0; "no" = 1	0.10	0.10*
Personal characteristics			
Age	Respondent's age	0.033	0.021**
Age²	Respondent's age (squared)	−0.0004	0.00**
Education dummies	School leaving certificate reference level		
Ed2	1 = O-level/GCSE; 0 otherwise	0.17	0.32
Ed3	1 = Highers/A-level; 0 otherwise	0.20	0.22
Ed4	1 = Further education college; 0 otherwise	−0.15	0.25
Ed5	1 = University degree; 0 otherwise	0.28	0.09*
Ed6	1 = Higher degree; 0 otherwise	0.71	0.03*
Constant		12.7	0.05**
	N = 2,625 (980 tests) pass: 88%		
	Log-likelihood function	−782.67	
	Restricted log function	−797.52	
	Chi-square (1 d.f.)	29.169	
	p-value	0	

*Significant at a 10% significance level
**Significant at a 5% significance level

It has also been argued that when answering DCE a dynamic process takes place: (i) respondents learn for some number of replications; (ii) they then apply the learned behaviour during another number of replications; and (iii) fatigue sets in (Swait and Adamowicz, 2001). If this dynamic process takes place, one would expect greater inconsistencies in earlier and later repetitions relative to the middle. To explore this, a variable indicating the position of the second choice set within the CP or EP tests, relative to the first, was included (*sequence*). The square of this variable (*sequence*^{2}) allowed testing the hypothesis of the inverted bell-shaped relationship between the position in the sequence of the test and the likelihood of an individual passing such test implied in the dynamic process.

The varying length (6, 8 or 10 choices) of the questionnaire allowed testing the hypothesis that as survey length increases individuals become fatigued or bored, lowering choice consistency (Elrod et al., 1992). Two dummy variables (*DQ8, DQ10*) were included to capture the effect of an increase in the survey length (relative to Q6). If fatigue or boredom set in longer questionnaires, we would expect these variables to have a negative effect on choice consistency.

The response to the question concerning whether respondents thought answering questions with three choices compared to two was more difficult was included (*dif3choices*). Here, it was hypothesised that those who answered "yes" would be less likely to pass the tests. In addition, it may be argued that the higher the perceived overall difficulty, the less likely subjects should be to answer the tests in a consistent manner. Four dummy variables were included (*Dif2, Dif3, Dif4, Dif5*) being "very easy" the reference level.

Personal characteristics, namely age (*Age*) and educational background, are also incorporated to the analysis of rationality failures. The squared value of age was also included to allow for potential non-linearities. A priori, it may be seen reasonable that younger and older respondents would be less likely to satisfy the tests. Regarding education, arguably it may be thought that those with higher education level would be more likely to provide "rational" answers to the tests. Five dummy variables were included (*Ed2, Ed3, Ed4, Ed5, Ed6*) being "*school leaving certificate*" the reference level.

3.2. Qualitative Analysis

A thematic approach was used to analyse the qualitative data (Aronson, 1994). Here, responses were read and reasons for answering in an "irrational" way were grouped into themes. Each time a new theme was defined, remaining transcripts were examined to see if they fit any of the themes. This process, carried out by one of the authors ([FSM]), was conducted until all reasons were analysed and categorised into different themes.

4. RESULTS

A total of 1,343 questionnaires were returned completed (45% response rate). Of these, 58% of the respondents were female and the mean age was 49 years, ranging from 16 to 90. Nineteen percent of respondents had a university degree or a higher one. On average, the difficulty of the questionnaire was given a value of 2.25 (in a scale from 1 = very easy to 5 = very difficult). Around 18% of respondents found choices with three alternatives more difficult to complete and around 22% said this depended on the choices.

4.1. Quantitative Results

No statistically significant differences were found between the samples completing the three questionnaires in terms of gender (χ^2 = 0.42, p = 0.8); age (anova = 1.015, p = 0.363); profession (χ^2 = 0.8; p = 0.567); education (LbL = 0.336, p = 0.562); or income level (LbL = 0.59, p = 0.442).

The results of the tests are presented in Table 9.4. Overall, satisfaction rates were high – between 80% and 99%. As expected, satisfaction was higher for the non-satiation tests than EP and CP tests. Also, weak versions of the tests were more likely to be satisfied than strong versions. No differences were found between the satisfaction of the non-satiation tests in the three questionnaires, despite their different position in each questionnaire (see Figure 9.1) and the differences in the dispersion of the SD of each choice. This was not the case in the EP and CP tests. Comparing the results of the strong EP properties in Q8 and Q6, the rate of failure was greater in the latter (16% compared to 5%), where the choices compared were more similar ($DdSD$ = 0 compared to 0.42).

Similar results are found comparing the weak EP in Q6 and Q10 – a higher rate of failure was found in the latter where the dispersion was smaller. Choices compared in this test were also more separated in the questionnaire, possibly indicating tiredness. However, these results were not found when comparing the CP tests in Q8 and Q10. Within each questionnaire, two CP tests were carried out comparing choices 2 and 5, and 2 and 7. Despite the existing differences in the dispersion of the SD of both tests, the rate of failure was nearly identical in both tests and questionnaires.

The results from the regression analysis are reported in the last two columns of Table 9.3. All variables show the expected signs and most are significant at the 10% level, except for the longest type of questionnaire ($DQ10$). As expected, strong tests are less likely to be satisfied, showing that choices between non-dominated options may be more difficult. The positive sign on $DdSD$ suggests that as choice sets become less similar (i.e. as $DsSD$ increases), choices become easier and respondents are more likely to answer the tests consistently. This is supported by the significance and negative sign of the dummy variables $Dif2$, $Dif3$ and $Dif5$ and the negative sign of $Dif3choices$, i.e. those who thought that the questionnaire was more difficult and those who thought that choices with three alternatives were more difficult were less likely to satisfy the tests.

The significant concave relationship between the relative positions of the second choice set in the rationality tests and the likelihood of passing the test supports the dynamic process hypothesis. Individuals are less likely to satisfy the test in the first choice of the questionnaire, they then learn, hence consistency improves for a number of questions, and finally fatigue sets in with satisfaction rates again decreasing for the final repetitions in the experiments. With respect to survey length, whilst there is no

TABLE 9.4. *Rationality test results*

Outcome		Questionnaire				
		Q10		Q8		Q6
Non-satiation tests						
1st test		DdSD = 1.83[a]		DdSD = 1.83[a]		DdSD = 0.29[a]
Number of respondents		$N = 388$		$N = 398$		$N = 384$
Dominated option[b]		4 — 1%		12 — 3%		8 — 2%
Dominant option[b]		252 — 65%		317 — 80%		368 — 96%
Neither[b]		132 — 34%		69 — 17%		8 — 2%
2nd test		DdSD = 1.83[a]				
Number of respondents		$N = 387$				
Dominated option[b]		6 — 2%				
Dominant option[b]		294 — 76%				
Neither[b]		87 — 22%				
Contraction property tests		*Weak*		*Strong*		
Number of respondents		$N = 388$		$N = 399$		
Choices 2 and 5		DdSD = 0.75		DdSD = 0.33		
Failure		22 — 6%		42 — 11%		
Pass		366 — 94%		357 — 89%		

(continued)

TABLE 9.4. Rationality test results (continued)

Outcome	Questionnaire					
	Q10		Q8		Q6	
Choices 2 and 7	DdSD = 0.99		DdSD = 1.13			
Failure	23	6%	40	10%		
Pass	365	94%	359	90%		
Expansion property test						
Number of respondents	*Weak* N = 388		*Strong* N = 399		*Weak* N = 384	
	DdSD = 0.25		DdSD = 0.42		DdSD = 1.37	
Failure	80	21%	22	6%	27	7%
Pass	308	79%	377	94%	357	93%
Strong EP in Q6					N = 384	%
					DdSD = 0.0	
Failure					63	16%
Pass					321	84%

a Tests involved only one choice hence dispersion of the standard deviation is reported
b Dominated, dominant and neither refer to the option chosen, i.e. how many chose the dominant option (passing the test), the dominated option (failing the test) and how many chose neither

significant difference between questionnaires with six and ten choices, individuals are more likely to pass tests in the questionnaire with eight choices.

As expected, a bell-shaped age effect is found. Younger and older people are less likely to pass the rationality tests. The significance and positive signs of dummy variables $Ed5$ and $Ed6$ indicate that respondents with higher level of education were more likely to pass the consistency tests. This supports the hypothesis that education would have a significant and positive effect on consistency. This result is in line with some previous studies looking at this issue (Johnson and Desvousges, 1997; Foster and Mourato, 2002; see also Saelensminde, 2002, who found the opposite).

Finally, the significant and relatively high value of the constant term indicates that there may be other factors influencing the likelihood of passing the rationality tests that we have not considered in this analysis.

4.2. Qualitative Results

Respondents' reasons for their responses could only be interpreted when provided for the two choices included in rationality tests. This resulted in 167 (51%) usable responses from those subjects that "failed" at least one test. Seven themes were established from the reasons provided. These are presented in Table 9.5.

4.2.1. Information from other choices (epistemic value of the menu)

Thirteen subjects (8%) acquired additional information from successive choices in the questionnaire or the expanded choice sets. This is what Sen (1993) referred to as "epistemic value of the menu". Consider strong EP test in Q6 in Table 9.2. Here, respondents were asked to choose between two options that implied seeing a doctor for 10 min (A), a nurse for 20 min (B) or "neither". This choice set was then expanded to include seeing a nurse for 30 min. One respondent chose option A in the first choice because he or she preferred to see a doctor. When the choice set was expanded he or she chose "neither", stating, "I want to see a doctor with a longer consultation". Hence, the new alternative added in the expanded choice set seems to have influenced the respondent's choice. Whilst this choice pattern violates the EP test, it seems consistent with respondent's preference to see a doctor and preferably for a longer time (which is not offered in any of the alternatives).

4.2.2. Additional information or assumptions made

Sixteen (9%) subjects introduced additional information or assumptions to that provided in the questionnaire, and chose according to such "new information". In the weak EP test in Q10 (Table 9.2), option A dominates B in the first choice and both B and C in the expanded choice set. In addition, all three options imply seeing a practice nurse. One respondent chose "neither" in the first choice stating that "It may be more serious than just a chest infection and the nurse may miss out this" implying that he or she preferred to see a doctor. In the expanded choice set he or she chose option A, but stated "If the doctor was not available, I would choose A as it seems the best option", hence whilst he or she stills prefers seeing a doctor, "given the lack of a doctor" he or she chose the best option available in the expanded choice set.

TABLE 9.5. *Themes defined as explanations of internally inconsistent choices*

Theme	Frequency (%)
"Epistemic value of the menu"	13 (8)
Additional information or assumptions	16 (9)
Own experience/protest answers	6 (4)
Consistent underlying preferences	20 (12)
Indifference between choices	17 (10)
Random error	21 (13)
Contradictory preferences	74 (44)

Note that this response satisfies dominance (in choice 1; Table 9.2) but not weak EP, because the same assumption about the seriousness of the illness was not made in both choices.

4.2.3. Own experience or protest answers

A small number of participants (6, 4%) either recalled their own experience of visiting their practice in completing the questionnaire, or *protested*, "demanding" a different scenario to that presented in the choices. For instance, in the strong CP test in Q8 (Table 9.1), one respondent chose option B (the only option that implies seeing a doctor) in the first choice arguing that "In our practice you can only see a doctor for a diagnoses or prescription. The practice nurse does not do this as far as I am aware". In the reduced choice set however he or she chose "neither" stating "In our practice you can insist on a 5 min emergency appointment if you phone early enough on the day of the consultation". This may be interpreted as this respondent "protesting" for having to wait 8 days to see a doctor. Hence, the respondent would seem not to have considered the hypothetical nature of the questions answering based on his or her experience.

4.2.4. Consistent underlying preferences

On 20 (12%) occasions, respondents' reasons for the "irrational" choices may indicate that, despite failing the tests, their underlying preferences were the same at all times. In the weak EP tests in Q10 explained above (Table 9.2) one respondent chose the "neither" option in the first choice stating "I would want diagnosed by GP and start treatment straight away". However, in the expanded choice set he or she chose option A arguing that "If doctors appointment not available I would seek advice from practice nurse, and hope she would be able to seek advice and prescription from GP". This respondent's arguments show his or her preference to see a doctor in both cases, and chose option A, based on the assumption that if necessary, he or she would see one (note this case could have been categorised as "additional assumption made").

4.2.5. Indifference

Seventeen (10%) respondents indicated indifference as an explanation for their seemingly "irrational" choices. In the strong EP test in Q6 (Table 9.2), one participant chose option A in the first choice but *changed* to option B in the expanded choice set. The respondent's reason for such response was that "Normally, I would rather go to a doctor as I feel that it is more confidential, but seeing as its not that bad a problem in this case, it would be easy to talk to a practice nurse also. I like the continuity of the health professional and I am very busy so no waiting time would be ideal". This respondent was willing to trade seeing a doctor for seeing a nurse given that such trade-off is compensated by improvements in the level of other attributes, indicating that the alternatives belong to the same indifference curve (or region), which is "rational". Similar arguments have been put forward to explain observed violations of the transitivity axiom (Tversky, 1969; Fishburn, 1970).

4.2.6. Random error

In a relatively high proportion of cases (20%), there was evidence of random error, i.e. the reasons provided indicated that respondents misread the value of the level of a specific attribute or did not choose the choice they intended to.

4.2.7. Contradictory preferences

The above reasons indicate that respondents often have "reasonable" arguments to explain their "irrational" responses (Simonson, 1989). However, up to 44% of the reasons suggest that respondents may lack a consistent and coherent choice criterion across choice sets (Drolet et al., 2000). In the strong EP test in Q6 (Table 9.2), one respondent chose option B (which implied seeing a nurse) in the first choice but chose option A (which implied seeing a doctor) in the expanded one stating that "I would always prefer a doctor in the first instance". This preference for seeing a doctor was expressed by eight other respondents who also reversed their preferences in the way indicated. A number of respondents also showed contradictory preferences in other attributes. For instance, one respondent stated that he or she chose option B in the expanded choice set (having chosen option A in the first choice) because of "No waiting time. Reasonable length of consultation. Continuity".

5. DISCUSSION

This study investigated alternative ways to test rationality of responses and the reasons why individuals may "fail" such tests. A key finding is that only a minority of subjects departed from rationality. The quantitative results indicate that satisfaction varied according to the questionnaire design and respondents characteristics. The more complex the DCE, the more likely the subject is to fail the rationality tests. Of particular interest is the significant direct relationship between the variable *DdSD* and choice consistency. This variable is related to the design of the experiment. DCEs are generally designed to satisfy certain statistical properties (Zwerina et al., 1996; Louviere et al., 2000). One such criteria may be utility balance, i.e. alternatives are similar in terms of utility, but these choices are likely to be the most difficult to make. The results in this paper suggest that such difficult choices affect respondents' consistency. A similar argument underlies Maddala et al. (2002) analysis with respect to the attribute levels "minimum overlap" criterion. In designing DCEs it is important to recognise that statistical efficiency must be considered alongside respondent efficiency (Severin et al., 2004).

The regression analysis supported the notion of a dynamic learning process. The first couple of choices may be used for "training" purposes, thus one may be tempted to conclude these should be excluded from policy analysis. Our findings also suggest that there may come a point at which individuals become bored or fatigued, and are less engaged with the task. Given individuals were given an opt-out alternative in all cases, this may results in individuals being more likely to choose this option as they proceed through the experiment. However, no evidence was found of this in our data.

Some evidence was found that that test failures are systematically related to observable respondent characteristics (e.g. age). Thus, the standard practice of dropping such responses from the analysis may induce selection bias (Mazzotta and Opaluch, 1995; Johnson and Desvousges, 1997; Johnson and Mathews, 2001; Foster and Mourato, 2002).

Qualitative analysis suggested that respondents often had reasonable arguments to explain their "'irrational'" choices. Despite describing in advance the scenario to be considered and the attributes and levels to be presented in the choices, some respondents did not consider (or remember) such information when completing the choice tasks. Experimental designs should ensure individuals acquire all relevant information before completing the choice task. Providing a summary sheet of all attributes and levels may help. Secondly, subjects who had experience of attending the practice and the condition described made additional assumptions. This suggests that when individuals are valuing familiar goods they may bring in "extra" information, which is not controlled for in the experiment. A similar argument was put forward by Ryan and San Miguel (2003) when testing for completeness of preferences in health care. Special emphasis should be put on making clear that respondents should answer according to the information provided and the scenarios described. Third, given that the rationality tests did not allow for indifference, some "irrational" responses were due to the lack of strict preferences. Further research should investigate the effect of allowing for indifference. However, it should be noted that subjects may choose such a response for other reasons than indifference, such as ease (Ryan and San Miguel, 2003). Further, given that some errors were random, respondents might be encouraged to go through their answers again, checking for errors.

An important finding from this study is that around 44% of respondents who failed the tests were defined as providing "contradictory preferences". One interpretation of this finding is that individuals have incomplete preferences, valuing each choice according to a different set of preferences (Slovic, 1995). However, given that the evidence is from a self-selected subsample, future work is need on completeness of preferences. Following on from this point, whilst asking respondent's reasons for their choices provided useful information at low cost, it is acknowledged that the information obtained was limited. Most notably, 49% of respondents who "failed" the test did not provide "usable" answers. Following useful information from this study regarding possible reasons (themes) for failures, preset responses to explain failures could be employed in future studies. Future work should also consider employing other survey methods (e.g. personal interviews) and qualitative techniques (e.g. verbal protocol analysis (Ericcson and Simon, 1993) to provide a better understanding of the reasons for rationality failures.

In conclusion, evidence was found that only a minority of subjects departed from rationality. Of those who did fail, a significant proportion appeared to have reformulated the experiment in some way in their mental processes. Whilst this may be inconsistent with economic theory, it is not surprising. As no reasonable person would suppose any definition of rationality to be universally and exactly satisfied, these findings do not appear to threaten economic theory. They do however have implications for the future development of DCEs, both at the design and analyses stages. Important issues arising with respect to design include: giving consideration to the trade-offs between statistical and respondent efficiency; encouraging respondents to read the questionnaire completely before completing the choices; providing a summary sheet of the attributes and all their possible levels; allowing for an indifference option; and inviting respondents to revisit their responses at the end of the choices. At the analysis stage consideration should be given to including warm-up questions and allowing for the systematic nature of the error term in modelling responses.

ENDNOTES

[1] Overcoming the limitations of experimental environments "stripped of context" (Loewenstein, 1999).

[2] The resemblance to a test of the weak axiom of revealed preference (WARP) is a necessary (but not sufficient) condition for utility-maximising behaviour (Lancsar and Louviere, 2006).

[3] These tests could be applied in a standard design DCE with constant set sizes, i.e. if individuals are provided with A, B and C in one option, and A, B and D in another option. One of the options provided could be a status quo or opt-out alternative.

[4] Since, generally, in a DCE participants are asked to choose only one option, the choice function in Sen's original formulation is restricted to be a singleton. Arguably, this assumption does not undermine the purposes on this study to the extent that indifference was not allowed for.

[5] Following Deshazo and Fermo (2002), the dispersion of SD for a choice set K including J alternatives is calculated as

$$\text{Dispersion } SD_K = \sqrt{\left[\left[\sum_{j=1}^{J}\left(SD_j - \text{Average } SD_K\right)^2\right]\middle/ J\right]}$$

where SD_j is the standard deviation among the x_{ij} normalised levels of the A attributes defining an alternative j defined

$$SD_j = \sqrt{\left[\left[\sum_{i=1}^{A}(x_{ij}-\bar{x}_j)^2\right]\Big/A\right]}$$

and average SD_k is the average SD for choice set K is calculated as follows:

$$\text{Average } SD_k = \left(\sum_{i=1}^{J} SD_j\right)\Big/J$$

REFERENCES

Aronson, J. 1994. A pragmatic view of thematic analysis. *The Qualitative Report*, vol 2 (1).

Caldow, J.L., Bond, C.M. and Ryan, M. et al. 2000. Treatment of minor illness in primary care: a national survey of patient attitudes to a wider nursing role'. Report to the Scottish Chief Scientist Office, K/OPR/2/2/D340.

DeShazo, J.R. and Fermo, G. 2002. Designing choice sets for stated preference methods: the effects of complexity on choice consistency. *Journal of Environmental Economics and Management*, vol 44, 123–143.

Drolet, A.L., Simonson, I. and Tversky, A. 2000. Indifference curves that travel with the choice set. *Marketing Letters*, vol 11, 199–209.

Earl, P.E. 1990. Economics and psychology: a survey. *The Economic Journal*, vol 100, 718–755.

Elrod, T., Louviere J.J. and Davey, K.S. 1992. An empirical comparison of rating-based and choice-based conjoint models. *Journal of Marketing Research*, vol 29, 368–377.

Ericcson, K.A. and Simon, H.A. 1993. Protocol Analysis. Cambridge, MA: MIT Press.

Fishburn, P.C. 1970. Intransitive indifference in preference theory: a survey. *Operations Research*, vol 18, 207–228.

Foster, V. and Mourato, S. 2002. Testing for consistency in contingent raking experiments. *Journal of Environmental Economics and Management*, vol 44, 302–328.

Greene, W.H. 1997. Econometric Analysis. Upper Saddle River, NJ: Prenctice Hall.

Johnson, F.R. and Desvousges, W.H. 1997. Estimating stated preferences with rated-pair data: environmental, health and employment effects of energy programs. *Journal of Environmental Economics and Management*, vol 34 (1), 79–99.

Johnson, F.R. and Mathews, K.E. 2001. Sources and effects of utility – theoretic inconsistency in stated preference surveys. *American Journal of Agricultural Economics*, vol 5, 1328–1333.

Lancsar, E. and Louviere, J.J. 2006. Deleting "irrational" responses from discrete choice experiments: a case of investigating or imposing preferences? *Health Economics*, vol 15 (8), 797–811.

Loewenstein, G. 1999. Experimental economics from the vantage-point of behavioural economics. *The Economics Journal*, vol 109, F25–F34.

Louviere, J.J., Hensher, D.A. and Swait, J.D. 2000. Stated Choice Methods. Analysis and Application. Cambridge: Cambridge University Press.

Maddala, T., Phillips, K.A. and Johnson, F.R. 2002. An experiment on simplifying conjoint analysis designs for measuring preferences. *Health Economics*, vol 37 (6), 1681–1705.

May, K.O. 1954. Intransitivity, utility, and the aggregation of preference patterns. *Econometrica*, vol 22, 1–13.

Mazzotta, M. and Opaluch, J. 1995. Decision making when choices are complex: a test of Heiner's hypothesis. *Land Economics*, vol 71 (4), 500–515.

Rouwendal, J. and de Blaiej, A.T. 2004. Inconsistent and lexicographic choice in stated preference analysis. Tinbergen Institute Discussion Paper. TI 2004-038/3. http://www.tinbergen.nl/discussionpapers/04038.pdf

Ryan, M. and Gerard, K. 2003. Using discrete choice experiments to value health care: current practice and future prospects. *Applied Health Economics and Policy Analysis*, vol 2 (1), 55–64.

Ryan, M. and San Miguel, F. 2003. Revisiting the axiom of completeness in health care. *Health Economics*, vol 12 (4), 293–308.

Ryan, M., Scott, D.A., Reeves, C., Bate, A., van Teijlingen, E., Russell, E., Napper, M. and Robb, C. 2001. Eliciting public preferences for health care: a systematic review of techniques. *Health Technology Assessment*, vol 5 (5), 1–186.

Ryan, M., Reeves, C. and Entwistle, V. 2002. Listening to respondents: a think aloud study of discrete choice experiment responses. Paper presented to the Health Economic Study Group Meeting, University of East Anglia, January.

Saelensminde, K. 2002. The impact of choice inconsistencies in stated choice studies. *Environmental and Resource Economics*, vol 23, 403–420.

San Miguel, F. 2000. Testing the assumptions of completeness, stability and rationality of preferences in health economics using discrete choice experiments. Ph.D. thesis. University of Aberdeen, Aberdeen.

Sen, A. 1993. Internal consistency of choice. *Econometrica*, vol 61, 495–521.

Severin, V.C., Burgess, L., Louviere, J. and Street, D.J. 2004. Comparing statistical efficiency and respondent efficiency in choice experiments. Research report, Department of Mathematical Sciences, University of Technology, Sydney, Australia.

Shugan, S.M. 1980. The cost of thinking. *Journal of Consumer Research*, vol 7 (2), 99–111.

Simonson, I. 1989. Choice based on reasons: the case of attraction and compromise effects. *Journal of Consumer Research*, vol 16, 158–174.

Slovic, P. 1995. The construction of preference. *American Psychologist*, vol 50, 364–371.

Swait, J. and Adamowicz, W. 2001. Choice environment, market complexity, and consumer behavior: a theoretical and empirical approach for incorporating decision complexity into models of consumer choice. *Organizational Behaviour and Human Decision Processes*, vol 86 (2), 141–167.

Tversky, A. 1969. Intransitivity of preferences. *Psychological Review*, vol 76, 31–48.

Tversky, A. and Sattah, S. 1979. Preference trees. *Psychological Review*, vol 86, 542–573.

Zwerina, K., Huber, J. and Kuhfeld, W. 1996. A General method for constructing efficient choice designs, SAS working paper. http://citeseer.nj.nec.com/rd/89088587,376089,1,0.25. Download/http:qSqqSqftp.sas.comqSqtechsupqSqdownloadqSqtechnoteqSqts629.pdf

CHAPTER 10

USING STATED PREFERENCE AND REVEALED PREFERENCE DATA FUSION MODELLING IN HEALTH CARE

TAMI MARK

Associate Director, Thomson, Medstat,
Washington, DC, US

JOFFRE SWAIT

Partner, Advanis, Inc., Adjunct Professor, University of Alberta, Alberta, Canada

1. INTRODUCTION

Economists have traditionally relied on retrospective analysis of actual consumer behaviour to understand the factors affecting the decisions of economic agents. This type of information is termed revealed preference (RP) data. Suppose we want to understand health plan choice. Typically, researchers will try to find a data set where consumers were offered and selected a number of different health plans. Then, they will examine the effect of the health plan attributes – price, services covered and quality ratings – on choice. The advantage of RP data is that it is based on actual decisions; thus, there is no need to assume that consumers will respond to simulated product markets as they do to actual market situations. This characteristic gives RP data high reliability and face validity. The disadvantage with this approach, in this case, is that the price of the insurance plan is highly correlated with the services covered and the actuarial value of the plan. What is needed is an estimate of the effect of prices for a wide range of benefit bundles.

As a second example, suppose one wants to estimate the demand for a new asthma medication that is available in once-daily dosing. There is no RP data available on the new medication because it has not yet come on the market. There is RP data available, however, on the choice of existing asthma medications, which vary in their side effects, efficacy rates and price. The variation of these attributes across existing medications may be sufficient to identify their relative impacts on prescription rates, but that is not guaranteed. Let us suppose that the existing medications are all multiple-daily dosing: this makes it impossible to identify the impact of dosing frequency from RP data. Hence, the RP data could not be used to extrapolate demand for the new medication,

M. Ryan, K. Gerard and M. Amaya-Amaya (eds.), Using Discrete Choice
Experiments to Value Health and Health Care, 217–234.
© 2008 *Springer.*

a major improvement of which is once-daily dosing. An alternative method would be to collect SP data, the range of which would cover medications similar to the new one in question due to the inclusion of a dosing attribute. By combining SP and RP data one can project the market impact of daily dosing on the prescription rate for the new medication.

Stated preference data has the advantage that it can allow the analyst to model the demand for new products with new attributes for which there is no RP history, such as in medications that are not yet on the market. In addition, SP data is collected under the "guidance" of a carefully designed experiment, with known statistical properties for parameter estimates. Key RP explanatory variables (e.g. medication prices) often exhibit little or no variability in the marketplace, and/or others may be highly collinear (e.g. side effects and compliance rates, prices and order of entry in market); SP data is able to introduce variability and eliminate/reduce collinearity, making possible more precise estimates of attribute contributions to product utility. Combining RP and SP data, also known as "data enrichment" and "data fusion", allows one to capitalise on the realism of the RP data and the favourable statistical properties of the SP data.

The data fusion literature, beginning with Morikawa (1989), recognised the need to reconcile the measurement characteristics of the different elicitation methods when combining data sources. Specifically, when combining multiple choice data sources, it was found theoretically necessary to control for error variance differences between them. Swait and Louviere (1993) combined two SP choice data sources using the multinomial logit (MNL) model, showing how to consistently estimate the relative error variance of one source with respect to the other. In their application, it was found that the two elicitation methods were measuring the same preferences up to a scale factor, which is the ratio of error variances. The combination of RP and SP data requires the same type of analytical and econometric framework.

In summary, data fusion can be gainfully employed for two major purposes. The first purpose is to improve the statistical properties of marginal utility estimates by augmenting RP data with SP data: we extend attribute ranges and introduce new attributes (from SP data) while we maintain the face validity of the joint model through the use of actual market behaviour (from the RP data). In general, in this context our interest will be in improved prediction of some form of market behaviour. Morikawa (1989) is typical of this form of data fusion. The second purpose for which data fusion is useful is when our substantive interest is in the explicit testing of whether two or more preference data sources exhibit the same marginal utilities. These data sources can be either RP or SP, in any mix. A pharmaceutical company may have conducted SP research in two countries concerning introduction of a new medication. The substantive question might be whether the markets in both countries exhibit the same marginal utilities, or attribute sensitivities. The result from this data fusion would indicate whether or not marketing activities to be pursued in the two countries should be the same (i.e. preference structures are similar) or differentiated (i.e. preference structures are dissimilar). This type of concern lay behind Swait and Louviere's (1993) work in data fusion.

2. BRIEF BACKGROUND ON ECONOMETRICS

Suppose that two preference data sources are available, one RP and one SP, both relevant to the same choice (e.g. physician choice). Each data source has a vector of attributes, and at least some of them are common to both data sets. Assume the attributes are represented by X^{RP} and X^{SP}, and let there also be unique attributes Z and W, respectively for each data set.

Assume the choice of products can be modelled using a random utility framework which can be represented by the following equations:

$$U_i^{RP} = \alpha_i^{RP} + \beta^{RP} X_i^{RP} + \omega Z_i + \varepsilon_i^{RP} \tag{10.1}$$

$$U_i^{SP} = \alpha_i^{SP} + \beta^{SP} X_i^{SP} + \Phi W_i + \varepsilon_i^{SP} \tag{10.2}$$

where i is an alternative in choice sets C^{RP} or C^{SP}, α_s are data source-specific alternative-specific constraints, β^{RP} and β^{SP} are utility parameters for the common attributes and ω and Φ are utility parameters for unique attributes in each data set. The whole point of data fusion exercise is to test whether $\beta^{RP} = \beta^{SP}$.

Typically, discrete choice experiment (DCE) models will be analysed using a conditional logit model, a name given to an MNL model when attributes or variables differ by alternative. MNL models assume that the random errors are IID Gumbel (type-I extreme value). Under the Gumbel distribution, the cumulative distribution function of the error term is

$$F(\varepsilon) = \exp[-\exp(-\mu\varepsilon)], \mu > 0 \text{ a scalar} \tag{10.3}$$

The scale factor μ is known to be inversely related to the variance of ε, i.e. $\sigma^2 = \pi^2/6\mu^2$, but it cannot be identified in any particular model because of confounding with the vector of utility parameters. In effect, in an MNL model estimated using either RP or SP data, the calculated parameters are actually the product of the scale factor and the desired parameter vector. Using Equation 10.1 as an example, an MNL model based on a single data source will yield estimates of $\mu(\alpha, \beta, \omega)$, *not* the desired vector $(\alpha, \beta, \omega)'$. This is very different from the situation in which the analysis involves a continuous, observable dependent variable, as in ordinary regression; there, an assumption of normality is made for the error terms in that analysis, and it is uniquely possible to separately estimate the mean and variance of the distribution, so no confound between them arises.

When working with a given choice data source, this confound is largely irrelevant since figures of merit (marginal rates of substitution, elasticities, choice probabilities, market shares, etc.) are not impacted. (It should be noted here that this basic taste parameter or variance confound is a characteristic of all discrete choice models, not just the MNL. Thus, nested MNL and multinomial probit models exhibit the exact same characteristic.) *However*, when working with two or more choice data sources, knowledge of this confound is crucial to interpretation and comparison: choice model parameters from two data sets are not directly comparable unless the relative scale differences (i.e. variance differences) are first isolated. Thus, it is not good practice to simply scan two comparable MNL parameter vectors (say, models from two cities, or two test groups) and reach conclusions of the type "The price parameter for City 1 is < larger| smaller > than that of City 2". (It is, however, perfectly proper to compare elasticities, choice probabilities, market shares and parameter ratios across different group models.)

In a data combination exercise, while it is not possible to actually estimate the error variances for the data sources separately, it is possible to normalise one and estimate the others, effectively implying that one can estimate the relative error variance of one data source with respect to another. Specialised estimation software can be written to estimate the joint model with relative scale factor, using maximum likelihood methods. Louviere et al. (2000) describe an equivalent full information maximum likelihood (FIML) method to estimate the constrained taste parameters ($\beta^{RP} = \beta^{SP} = \beta$) and relative scale factor simultaneously, using a nested logit (NL) model with two levels and as many clusters of alternatives as there are data sets. (This "trick", which involves interpreting the inverse of the inclusive value parameter as the relative scale parameter, will permit researchers with access to NL estimation software to execute data fusion exercises.).

Once combined, the hypothesis that $\beta^{RP} = \beta^{SP} = \beta$ can be tested using the likelihood ratio test statistic,

$$\lambda = -2[L_p - (L_r + L_s)] \tag{10.4}$$

where L_p is the pooled likelihood from the joint data, L_r is from an MNL model based on the RP data, and L_s is from an MNL model from the SP data. The test is asymptotically chi-squared distributed with ($|\beta| - 1$) degrees of freedom.

3. EMPIRICAL ANALYSIS

Mark and Swait (2004) used revealed and stated preference data to investigate physicians' prescribing decisions of alcoholism medications. At the time of the study two medications existed to treat alcoholism in the USA – disulfiram (brand name Antabuse) and naltrexone (brand name Revia). Neither medication was widely used. Combined revealed and stated preference data were used to indicate how widely new alcoholism medications with more favourable characteristics are likely to be prescribed.

3.1. Stated Choice Experiment Development

Attributes and levels are shown in Table 10.1. The seven attributes include two measures of the medication's efficacy, side effect rate, compliance rate, price, mode of administration and method of action.

There were seven attributes, two with two levels and five with four levels yielding $2^2 \times 4^5$ (4,096) possible product profiles. A sample was selected from the full factorial design satisfying the requirements that an explicit interaction between abstinence (A1) and side effects (A3) be estimable and that the percent having no heavy-drinking incidents (A2) be at least as large as the percent abstinent (A1) (see Table 10.1). The

TABLE 10.1. *Attributes and levels*

Attribute	Levels
A1: Percent of treated population who remained abstinent during a 3-month treatment period	20%, 40%, 60%, 80%
A2: Percent of patients who would have no incidence of heavy drinking during a 3-month treatment period[a]	20%, 40%, 60%, 80%
A3: Percent of patients that experience non-serious side effects such as nausea, headaches, dry mouth, dizziness, or nervousness during a 3-month treatment period[b]	10%, 15%, 25%, 35%
A4: Percent of patients who complied at a high rate (80% or more of doses) during a 3-month treatment period	20%, 40%, 60%, 80%
A5: Mode of action	Directly reduces drinking, causes an aversive reaction with alcohol
A6: Route of administration	Oral, long-acting injection
A7: Price per day	$0.25, $1.00, $3.00, $5.00

[a] Design constrained to make this attribute at least as large as A1
[b] Design included the interaction of A1*A3

inclusion of the interaction A1*A3 reflected researchers' expectations that physicians' responses to efficacy levels would vary depending on the level of side effects.

A heuristic optimisation routine was applied to the full factorial design to produce a random design with 128 runs that has near, but not exact, orthogonality between effects. The design was generated using a proprietary design technique that utilises exchange heuristics to achieve improvements to initial random designs. Improvements constitute decreases in intercolumn correlations, and are pursued until exchanges cannot find further improvements; this process may or may not produce orthogonal designs, but the degree of departure from that condition is known. Heuristic optimisation methods, of which exchange methods are an example, are computationally efficient methods of obtaining near-optimal solutions to complex problems. They do not, however, give the guarantee of optimal solutions. Nonetheless, such a flexible design process as described is most useful when orthogonal designs are unnecessary from the econometric perspective, too effortful to obtain without undue computational effort, or even undesirable (e.g. attributes are nested, or dependent, upon other attributes). SAS, in its Proc OPTEX, implements a number of optimal and heuristic search methods for design generation.

The adopted 128-run design was blocked into groups of four scenarios (for a total of 32 blocks); each respondent was randomly assigned to a block. Each choice scenario was comprised of three alternatives: two competing treatments, described in terms of the above attributes, as well as the option of rejecting both treatments. Specifically, physicians were asked whether they would prescribe medication 1, medication 2, or no medication.

The stated choice experiment asked physicians to select prescription of one of two medications, given their attributes, or to use no medication. The no medication alternative was provided since most treatment for alcoholism involves psychosocial interventions without medications. It was assumed that physicians would interpret the no-medication alternative as involving efficacy rates that they achieve in their standard practice for alcoholism patients.

3.2. Revealed Preference Data Elicitation

In this case, the RP data also came from the questionnaire. In other cases, RP data may come from a different data source. In this example, the RP and SP data sets were provided by the same individuals but this need not be the case (as long as the attributes are largely the same in the SP and RP data).

Physicians were asked "what percent of your patients with alcoholism were prescribed naltrexone in the past 3 months", and a similar question about disulfiram. Physicians were then asked to provide their perception of each medication's attributes: What percent of patients would relapse to any drinking and to heavy drinking over a 3-month period after taking disulfiram or naltrexone.? What percent of patients would have non-serious side effects when prescribed naltrexone or disulfiram? What percent of patients would comply at a high rate (take 80% more of their medications) over a 3-month period? (See Adamowicz et al. (1997) for a comparison of the use of self-reported and objective attribute measures in RP models.) Three of the attributes – price, mode of administration and method of action – did not need to be collected since they were fixed and known to the researchers. Specifically, there was only one price, one mode of administration and one method of action for each drug. In fact, this very lack of variability constitutes one of the main reasons that this RP data source would not permit estimation of the impact of these attributes on physician prescription of these medications, leading to our interest in complementary collecting SP data.

3.3. Data Collection

Data were collected from members of the two specialty medical societies for addiction medicine in the USA, the American Society of Addiction Medicine (ASAM) and the American Academy of Addiction Psychiatry (AAAP). Completed questionnaires were received from 1,388 respondents, for a response rate of 65%. Each of the 1,388 respondents provided a maximum of four choice responses, for a total of 5,552 possible choices. Of these, 5,053 were actually usable; the difference is accounted for by missing data.

3.4. Data Matrix and Specification

The resulting data matrix is shown in summary form below in Table 10.2. Each column represents a different variable and each row a different observation. The first column indicates whether the data is RP or SP. The next column indicates the respondent ID. In this example, only data from one respondent is shown. The next column indicates the alternatives. For the SP data, there were three alternatives, each of which is a different observation: choice of hypothetical alcoholism drug A, drug B, or no drug. The next column shows the observed choices, i.e. the dependent variable. For the SP data, respondent 1 selected drug B, therefore drug B is assigned a 1 and the other two choice variables receive a 0. The respondent also indicated that 20% of their patients were prescribed antabuse and 30% were prescribed naltrexone. The next three columns are intercepts, capturing the average utility of a treatment option after other sources of variation have been accounted for. There is an intercept for antabuse and another for naltrexone, both specific to the RP data source; the SP utility function also includes an intercept, which defines the average utility of hypothetical drugs A and B to be the same (since there is no branding occurring in this data source, which does occur in the RP data, there is no statistical reason to differentiate between the SP drug options in terms of average utility; the SP intercept simply captures the average utility of the drug treatments compared to the no-drug-treatment option). The next columns indicate the attributes of the product. In this example, one of the attributes was the efficiency level. In both the RP and SP cases, efficiency was measured as the percent of patients that are expected to remain abstinent for 3 months when taking the medication. Note that for the "no medication" alternative the attributes are set to 0. The next set of columns comprise the respondent attributes such as physician specialty, the intent of which is to capture heterogeneity among physicians due to identifiable characteristics. Since these physician characteristics do not vary by alternative, it is necessary to code them in such a way that one alternative serves as the base, hence the zeros in the no-drug options in both data sources for these variables. See Ben-Akiva and Lerman (1985) for a discussion of identification restrictions when including socio-demographic effects in choice models.

The general utility specifications are shown in Equations 10.5 and 10.6. The vector X represents the product attributes: efficacy (abstinence), efficacy (heavy drinking), side effects, compliance, price, mode of action and route of administration. Quadratic terms were tested for the efficacy and compliance attributes, reflecting the hypothesis that they would influence physician's choices at a marginally decreasing rate. In addition, efficacy was interacted with side effects, reflecting the hypothesis that physicians would be willing to have their patients tolerate higher side effects if they experienced better outcomes. Besides these attributes, the utility functions include certain physician characteristics that were a priori expected to explain differences in prescribing behaviour of the decision makers (sign indicates expected effect on utility): whether or not the physician is an addiction specialist (positive impact because specialists are likely to be more familiar with the latest information on alcoholism medications), percent of

TABLE 10.2. Sample RP and SP data matrix for one respondent

RP/SP	Respondent ID	Alternative	Choice	RP antabuse intercept	RP naltrexone intercept	SP intercept	Efficacy rate ETC	Specialist
SP	1	Drug A	0	0	0	1	0.5	3
SP	1	Drug B	1	0	0	1	0.5	3
SP	1	No treatment	0	0	0	0	0	0
RP	1	Antabuse	0.2	1	0	0	0.4	3
RP	1	Naltrexone	0.3	0	1	0	0.3	3
RP	1	No medication	0.5	0	0	0	0	0

patients with alcoholism (again, positive, because they are likely to be more familiar with the latest information on alcoholism medications), percent of time spent in administrative duties (negative impact because they have less time to research and develop a comfort level with new alcoholism medications), percent of patients with private insurance (negative or positive impact, depending on the coverage relative to other payers such as Medicaid). In essence, this specification allows for the average utilities (intercepts) to vary as a function of physician characteristics.

$$U_i^{RP} = \alpha_i^{RP} + \beta X_i^{RP} + \varepsilon_i^{RP}, \qquad (10.5)$$

$$U_i^{SP} = \alpha_i^{SP} + \beta X_i^{SP} + \Phi W_i + \varepsilon_i^{SP} \qquad (10.6)$$

These equations reflect the fact that the taste parameter β is restricted to be equal in the two data sources (per hypothesis) and that the RP data source has no unique variables (therefore, $\omega \equiv 0$).

Additional questions were asked to elicit attribute cut-offs (Swait, 2001), which are an especially interesting form of interacting decision-maker characteristics with product attributes. Consider situations where physicians have certain minimal or maximal requirements from a product for it to be acceptable (though not necessarily chosen). The question then arises as to what to do when a product that does not meet the requirement is offered for choice (whether RP or SP): the requirement can either be considered a "hard" constraint and the alternative removed from the model (reflecting the assumption that the physician completely ignores the drug in question), or it can be considered a "soft" constraint that generates disutility for the drug in question because it violates the constraint. The usual utility-theoretic framework completely ignores these types of behavioural constraints, opting to assume that they simply do not exist. Swait (2001) extended the basic utility maximising model underlying random utility models to incorporate such effects as "soft" constraints. The fact that the constraints are assumed "soft" leads to the existence of utility penalties, which are the utility function coefficients for cut-off variables. The theoretical justification for using cut-offs is the hypothesis that decisions may often be made in two stages in an effort to minimise cognitive effort: in the first stage, alternatives are screened by some attribute-based elimination rules, and in the second stage, remaining alternatives are evaluated in more detail and a final choice is made.

In the present context, physicians were asked what the minimal level of abstinence rate achieved with a medication would have to be so that they would use an alcoholism medication as a first-line therapy. This requirement varies, of course, from one physician to the next. The corresponding "cut-off" variable for this constraint captures the degree to which a particular medication violates the individual physician's requirement. For instance, say a physician requires that the 3-month abstinence rate achieved by a drug be at least 50% for it to be acceptable as a therapy he or she will prescribe. Suppose a drug presented for evaluation has an abstinence rate of 60%; for this physician, this drug is acceptable for further evaluation. Now suppose another drug, this one with an abstinence rate of only 20%. Clearly, this second drug falls short of the required minimum by 30% points. If we let A1 represent the drug's abstinence level, then the abstinence cut-off variable for this physician can be generally expressed as

$$\text{Abstinence cut-off} = \max (0, 50 - A1) \qquad (10.7)$$

For the first drug, the cut-off has a value of zero (it is acceptable); for the second drug, the cut-off has a value of 30 (= 50–20). The more positive the abstinence cut-off, the greater the amount by which the drug *underperforms* for this physician. Hence, the sign for the coefficient of this cut-off in the utility function should be negative. Note also that the estimation of the coefficients for cut-off variables, thus defined, does not need any special software: usual MNL estimation programmes are fully capable of implementing this type of utility function.

In general, cut-offs can be applied to minimum and maximum values of continuous attributes, as well as to discrete attributes. In the latter case, the cut-offs reflect requirements of the type "The drug must be administered orally". The reader is urged to consult Swait (2001) for further details about the theory of cut-offs, their use in the random utility framework, and their interpretation.

4. DATA ANALYSIS

The coefficients in the SP-only model were in the expected direction (Table 10.3) and statistically different from zero at the 95% confidence level; most of the coefficients from the RP model, however, were not statistically significant (also Table 10.3). Physicians' ratings of the efficacy of the medications in terms of promoting abstinence was one of the exceptions in the latter model, and was positively associated with the percent prescribed the medication. Thus, one interpretation of the RP data is that the attribute that matters most to physicians when making prescribing decisions is efficacy and the other attributes are relatively unimportant.

This general lack of attribute significance in the RP data may be due to correlation between the attribute variables. In the RP data matrix, efficacy in terms of abstinence and heavy drinking were both highly correlated with compliance (correlation coefficients of 0.67 and 0.81, respectively). Correlation coefficients were also high between abstinence efficacy and heavy-drinking efficacy and side effects (correlation coefficients of 0.44 and 0.52). Multicollinearity results in unstable coefficient values and deteriorated significance levels for the correlated predictors. A rule of thumb is that problems of multicollinearity are likely to occur if any of the correlations between any of the independent variables are greater than 0.7. Such levels of collinearity are not entirely uncommon in RP data, and have thus served as one of the main motivations for doing data fusion in the first place.

For three of the variables – mode of action, route of administration and price – there was no variation in the RP data. While this permits inclusion of RP prices in the data combination model (to be presented below), it does not permit identification of the price effect in the RP data alone since there is a one-to-one correspondence between prices and the medication intercepts.

Estimates from conditional logit analysis for RP data result from dependent variables, i.e. from percentage of patients with prescription of naltrexone, percentage with prescription of disulfiram and percentage prescription of no medication. For SP estimates, dependent variable is choice between two plans (A and B), plus no medication option. Note that the goodness-of-fit statistics of the RP model are uniformly better

TABLE 10.3. *Results of the conditional logistic regression analysis using the separate revealed preference and stated preference data*

	SP Model		RP Model	
	Coefficient	Asymp. *t*-statistic	Coefficient	Asymp. T-statistic
RP intercept 1			−2.94563	−4.00
RP intercept 2			−3.30918	−4.60
SP intercept	−3.2787	−10.70		
Efficacy (abstinence)/10	0.4647	3.10	0.21768	2.00
Efficacy^2 (abstinence)/1,000	−0.1594	−1.20	−0.15582	−1.60
Efficacy (heavy drinking)/10	0.1532	1.10	−0.14148	−0.80
Efficacy^2 (heavy drinking)/1,000	0.0843	0.80	0.15902	1.10
Side effects/10	0.1316	1.90	0.09462	1.10
Compliance/10	0.4351	6.90	−0.12174	−0.90
Compliance^2/1,000	−0.2101	−3.40	0.20875	1.90
Mode of action (+1 = aversive reaction, −1 = reduces drinking)	−0.4208	−15.40	NI	
Route of administration (+1 = long-acting injection, −1 = oral)	−0.0595	−2.40	NI	
Efficacy (abstinence) × side effects	−0.4998	−4.00	−0.17178	−1.30
Log (price) ($/day)	−0.2223	−9.90	NI	
Abstinence cut-off = max(0, minimum abstinence– abstinence)/10	−0.1889	−7.70	−0.04499	−0.80

(continued)

TABLE 10.3. (continued)

	SP Model		RP Model	
	Coefficient	Asymp. *t*-statistic	Coefficient	Asymp. T-statistic
Specialist in addiction	**0.4636**	**4.10**	**0.42786**	**2.00**
Percent of patients with alcoholism/10	**−0.0540**	**−2.80**	−0.02057	−0.60
Percent of time in administration/10	**−0.0445**	**−3.00**	0.03271	1.40
Percent of patients with private insurance/10	**−0.0363**	**−2.90**	**0.05183**	**2.60**
Goodness of fit				
Loglik @ convergence	−3,789.25		−918.948	
Number of parameters	17		15	
McFadden's Rho-squared	0.317		0.397	
Akaike Rho-squared	0.314		0.388	
% Right	56.7%		63.8%	

Bold indicates significant at < = 0.05 ($|t| \geq 1.96$), NI = not identified

than those of the SP model. While this may seem somewhat paradoxical, and even bring into question the motivation for pooling the two data sources, note that the main reason the RP model seems to fit better is due to the lack of variability in the independent variables. In fact, the better goodness of fit of the RP model is largely illusory, as confirmed by the large number of non-significant attributes. While the SP model may look like it is performing less well, in fact it is performing well on a much wider range of data.

4.1. Results of the Joint Model

A joint model that constrained taste coefficients across the two data sources to be equal was estimated; however, intercepts were not constrained. In Equations 10.1 and 10.2, only the α vectors were not constrained across RP and SP data sources. With respect to the intercepts, it is straightforward to justify their exclusion from the constrained parameters since they play different roles in each data source: in the RP data, the intercepts capture average medication-specific effects in the market, whereas in the SP data set the intercept is a contrast between designed medications and the no-medication option.

Table 10.4 shows the results of the parameter equality tests. The chi-squared statistic for the test that the parameter values from the separate models are equivalent to the pooled model equals approximately 29. Given 12 degrees of freedom and $\alpha = 0.01$, thus implying a critical chi-squared value of 26.2, this test statistic rejects the hypothesis of equal taste parameters. This means that the stated preference and RP data do not yield identical preference estimates, up to scale. Nonetheless, it should be noted

TABLE 10.4. *Testing of scaling and parameter equality*

Model	Log-likelihood	No. of parameters	Chi-squared value	Degrees of freedom	*p*-value
RP model	−918.948	15			
SP model	−3,789.25	17			
Total SP + RP (separate)	−4,708.20	32			
Joint model (RP + SP pooled)	−4,722.71	20	29.024	12 (= 32–20)	0.00391
Joint model (RP + SP pooled, physician variables by data source)	−4,713.99	24	11.583	8 (= 32–24)	0.17075
Joint model (RP + SP pooled, physician variables varied, efficacy quadratic effects removed)	−4,715.57	22	–	–	–

that the chi-squared statistic (29.0) is not much larger than the critical values for usual levels of α; thus, despite the formal hypothesis rejection, we find this comparison is empirically indicative of how strongly the proposed mechanism of taste parameter equality up to scale differences is actually able to describe both sets of preferences.

An examination of the separate model parameters using graphical methods described in Swait and Louviere (1993) and Louviere et al. (2000) suggested that a possible reason for the rejection of the hypothesis is that the impact of the socio-demographic variables (e.g. addiction specialist status) is significantly different in the two data sources. Accordingly, a second pooled model was estimated in which the four physician characteristic variables were not constrained to be equivalent in the SP and RP joint model; however, all attribute coefficients remained constrained. The chi-squared statistic from this second joint model equals 11.58 (Table 10.3), indicating that the models are not significantly different ($p = 0.17$).

Thus, in this application, it seems that the scalability hypothesis holds across strict taste parameters (i.e. those that apply to product attributes), but does not apply when physician characteristics are included as intercept shifts. The impact of these charac-teristics seems to differ significantly between data sources. This final result is most encouraging since it indicates that the marginal utility estimates for the attributes are equal across the two elicitation methods, once error variance differences and individ-ual physician differences have been accounted for. This would support the interpreta-tion that the SP experiment fulfilled its main objectives: it provided carefully controlled preference information that permitted more accurate measurement of physician trade-off than was possible with only RP data, and it did it in a manner that led respondents to behave consistently with their market behaviour despite the elici-tation being a paper-and-pencil task.

The final joint model is presented in Table 10.5. This model is actually a simplifi-cation of the models just discussed: in the model for which scalability cannot be rejected, it was found that the quadratic effects of both efficacy measures were not sig-nificantly different from zero, hence have been eliminated from the final joint model. (The chi-squared statistic is 3.16 with two degrees of freedom for the restriction of these two quadratic effects, hence cannot be rejected at the 95% confidence level. The restricted final model does not nest the full joint model, hence cannot be compared using a chi-squared test.) The final joint model has an estimated relative SP scale parameter of about $\exp(1.37) \approx 3.93$. This scale factor can be compared to the nor-malised RP scale of unity, indicating that the error variance of the SP data is smaller than the error variance of the RP data.

5. DISCUSSION

This chapter begins by describing how combining RP and SP data can com-pensate for the weaknesses in each of the data sets. We then present a brief overview of the technical approach to combining RP and SP data. For a fuller explanation, readers are referred to Louviere et al. (2000, Chapter 8). The present chapter contin-ues on to present an example of how SP data, based on hypothetical prescription choices given medication attributions, and RP data, based on perceived medication attributes and reported medication usage, might be employed to understand the factors influencing physician prescribing decisions.

TABLE 10.5. *Final results of the conditional logistic regression analysis using the joint revealed preference and stated preference data*

Parameters	SP and RP joint model	
	Coefficients	Asymp. *t*-statistics
RP – intercept	**−3.6434**	**−11.15**
RP – intercept	**−4.2476**	**−11.62**
SP – intercept	**−0.7981**	**−4.73**
Efficacy (% abstinence)/10	**0.0777**	**4.14**
Efficacy^2 (abstinence)/1,000	0	–
Efficacy (% no heavy drinking)/10	**0.0637**	**3.56**
Efficacy^2 (heavy drinking)/1,000	0	–
Side effects/10	**0.0364**	**1.95**
Compliance/10	**0.104**	**4.11**
Compliance^2/1,000	**−0.0467**	**−2.68**
Mode of action (+1 = aversive reaction, −1 = reduces drinking)	**−0.1067**	**−4.83**
Route of administration (+1 = long-acting injection, −1 = oral)	**−0.0149**	**−2.13**
Efficacy (abstinence) × side effects/1,000	**−0.1312**	**−3.35**
Log (price) ($/day)	**−0.0561**	**−4.53**
Abstinence cut-off = max (0, minimum abstinence–abstinence)/10	**−0.0497**	**−4.29**
RP – specialist in addiction	**0.4912**	**2.27**
RP – percent of patients with alcoholism/10	−0.0258	−0.75
RP – percent of time in administration/10	0.0339	1.44
RP – percent of patients with private insurance/10	**0.0503**	**2.54**
SP – specialist in addiction	**0.1178**	**3.18**
SP – percent of patients with alcoholism/10	**−0.0137**	**−2.45**

(continued)

TABLE 10.5. (continued)

Parameters	SP and RP joint model	
	Coefficients	Asymp. *t*-statistics
SP – percent of time in administration/10	**–0.0113**	**–2.58**
SP – percent of patients with private insurance/10	**–0.0091**	**–2.48**
ln(RP scale)	0.0	–
ln(SP scale)	**1.3677**	**6.85**
Goodness of fit		
Loglik @ convergence	–4715.57	
Number of parameters	22	
McFadden's Rho-squared	0.334	
Akaike Rho-squared	0.331	
% Right	58.2%	

Bold indicates significant at ≤0.05 ($|t| \geq 1.96$)

As explained in our introductory remarks, obtaining better models for predicting a certain behaviour is one motivation for data fusion. Another is to explicitly test whether two preference data sets (e.g. two RP data sets from different populations, an RP and an SP data set on the same or different populations) exhibit the same marginal utilities. If this type of comparison is of substantive interest, hypothesis testing can lead to two possible outcomes: either the preferences of common attributes are identical up to scale, or they are not. If one concludes that they are identical, one should make use of the pooled model coefficients for policy setting.

If one concludes they are not identical, then one must rely on the individual models for policy setting. This may well involve a difficult decision about which model to use to answer-specific policy questions. Let us say that one wants to understand the effect of health status on choice of Medicare drug plan. One could use Medicare part D data as RP claims data along with Medicare part D drug data to answer this question. However, access to such data might be limited and expensive. Further, the variation in drug plans is relatively small. This may lead one to also collect SP data on choices through a survey. If the two data diverge, one might conclude that consumers cannot adequately describe their choices in the SP data and that the investment in RP data must be made in order to answer this question. Alternatively, it could also be due to the fact that there are data limitations inherent to the RP source such as limited price variation. The selection of a particular data source mainly depends on the question of interest.

Data enrichment techniques have not been widely applied to health economics, but clearly there are many opportunities to benefit from this approach. The public health system in the USA has been increasingly looking towards a competitive model in which consumers choose among health plans and providers. One example is the Medicare Prescription Drug benefit which went into effect in 2006. RP and SP fusion can be used to determine how consumers value various aspects of different Medicare drug plans: relative consumer preference for higher copayments versus unrestricted access can be evaluated by merging RP data on actual plan choice and plan attributes with SP data on hypothetical choices associated with plans described with common and proposed attributes. The addition of the RP data to the estimation "mix" allows one to model the market at the current equilibrium, thus providing a better and more realistic sense of how plans market shares might shift if they offered enhanced benefits. As a second example, similar studies can be conducted to understand patients' decisions to select among treatments or providers, thus providing estimates of the value of attributes of treatment or providers.

Data enrichment allows one to capitalise on the realism of actual health care choices with the favourable statistical characteristics of hypothetical choices. In modelling drug plan choice under Medicare, plans may tend to offer similar packages at similar prices, therefore allowing little variation with which to estimate the value of different attributes. Moreover, certain characteristics may always be offered together. A plan offering an open formulary may always charge high copayments. By adding SP data collected through experimental design to RP data one may overcome the problems of low variation and confounding. On the other hand, utilities collected from only SP data can be subject to the criticism that respondents' choices of plans in hypothetical situations differ from their actual choices. Moreover, RP allows one to pinpoint market equilibrium and thus determine the initial equilibrium from whence changes will be evaluated. This can lead to better estimates of the effect of changing particular attributes as well as their marginal utility.

In short, by combining information on what people say they will do with information on what they did do, one can have a richer (and likely more robust) understanding of their preference structures and their implications for future decisions.

ACKNOWLEDGEMENTS

The preparation of this manuscript was supported by a National Institute of Alcohol Abuse and Alcoholism (NIAAA) grant R01-AA12146-01A1. The second author acknowledges the support of Advanis Inc. in the preparation of this article.

REFERENCES

Adamowicz, W., Swait, J., Boxall, P., Louviere, J. and Williams, M. 1997. Perceptions versus objective measures of environmental quality in combined revealed and stated preference models of environmental valuation. *Environmental Economics and Management*, vol 32, 65–84.

Ben-Akiva, M. and Lerman, S. 1985. Discrete choice analysis: theory and application to predict travel demand. Cambridge, MA: MIT Press.

Louviere, J.J., Hensher, D.A. and Swait, J.D. 2000. Stated choice methods: analysis and applications. Cambridge: Cambridge University Press.

Mark, T.L. and Swait, J. 2004. Using stated preference and revealed preference modeling to evaluate prescribing decisions. *Health Economics*, vol 13 (6), 563–573.

Morikawa, T. 1989. Incorporating stated preference data in travel demand analysis, Ph.D. dissertation. Department of Civil Engineering, Massachusetts Institute of Technology, Cambridge, MA.

Swait, J. 2001. Non-Compensatory choice model incorporating attribute cutoffs. *Transportation Research Part B*, vol 35, 903–928.

Swait, J. and Louviere, J. 1993. The role of the scale parameter in the estimation and comparison of multinomial logit models. *Journal of Marketing Research*, vol 30, 305–314.

PART 4

CONCLUSIONS

CHAPTER 11

CONCLUDING THOUGHTS

MANDY RYAN AND MABEL AMAYA-AMAYA

Health Economics Research Unit, University of Aberdeen, UK

KAREN GERARD

Faculty of Medicine, Health and Life Sciences, University of Southampton, UK

1. SUMMARY OF THE BOOK

Over the last 15 years, discrete choice experiments (DCEs) have proved a very useful technique both within the framework of an economic evaluation, and for modelling behaviour and preferences in a variety of contexts within health economics. This book has presented important issues in the design and analysis of DCEs (Part 1), demonstrated their application in a number of different settings in the health and health care arena (Part 2) and looked at some emerging methodological issues (Part 3).

We have come a long way since DCEs were first applied in health economics by Carol Propper, to look at the value of reducing waiting time (Propper, 1990). Consider the experimental design component of a DCE. Initially, we used catalogues or computer software to generate an orthogonal main effects plan. Choices were created by randomly pairing the profiles into choice sets (e.g. 16 profiles would become eight choices) or by choosing a constant comparator. Health economists were simply not familiar with the budding literature on experimental design of DCEs. Recent advances have seen awareness of important design properties such as orthogonality, minimum overlap and level balance, and more recently, a movement striving for the maximisation of statistical efficiency when designing DCEs (Chapters 2 and 3).

Similarly, developments have taken place in the methods of analysis of DCEs, partly reflecting the increasing efficiency of computers. Early applications of DCEs mainly involved binary forced choices (e.g. A or B) and so the most common models used for analysis were the binary probit and logit, often including a random effects specification to account for the multiple observations obtained from each respondent (see Chapters 5–7 in Part 2). However, recognition of the importance of including opt-out options (such as neither or the status quo) led to increased use of the multinomial logit (MNL) model, and developments of this relaxing some of its restricted

M. Ryan, K. Gerard and M. Amaya-Amaya (eds.), Using Discrete Choice Experiments to Value Health and Health Care, 237–248.

assumptions, such as the nested logit (see Chapter 4), and more recently mixed logit models (e.g. Hall et al., 2006).

At the applied level, whilst DCEs were introduced into health economics to go beyond health outcomes and to value "non-health" outcomes (e.g. patient choice, satisfaction and information) and process attributes (e.g. reassurance), the technique is now applied to a broader range of policy-relevant questions. The collection of studies presented in Part 2 demonstrates this. Indeed, recently the technique has been applied to inform cost-utility analysis (CUA). Ryan et al. (2006) used DCEs to estimate quality weights in the development of a programme-specific quality-adjusted life year (QALY). Work is also underway using DCEs to estimate willingness to pay (WTP) for a QALY (Baker et al., 2003; Viney et al., 2005). So long as the policy question can be broken down into attributes the DCE approach is potentially useful. The applied chapters demonstrated the different policy outputs that can be generated from a DCE. Whilst DCEs to date have been most commonly used to estimate the monetary values of individual attributes, and overall welfare from defined policy changes, the tool is now starting to be used to predict the take-up of new services (see, e.g. Chapter 5; Hall et al., 2002, 2006).

2. DIRECTIONS FOR FUTURE RESEARCH

Perhaps more interesting in this chapter is the question: where should we go from here? To answer this question it is useful to present the key findings and expert commentary reported in five peer review papers (Viney et al., 2002; Ryan and Gerard, 2003; Ryan et al., 2003; Hanley et al., 2003; Bryan and Dolan, 2004) and a key working paper (Fiebig et al., 2005) which have looked at the role of DCEs in health economics. Table 11.1 summarises the practice and development of DCEs in health economics from about 1990 to 2004, which amounts to some 60 applications published in the literature. This provides a reasonably accurate and informative summary of the point reached to date. The table also provides a synthesis of possible directions for future research. Below we discuss some key areas where more work is needed within the field. This list is far from exhaustive, but reflects crucial issues we think will attract research efforts in the future (for other topics at the leading edge, see special issues in Marketing letters (2005, 16 (3)) and Environmental and Resource Economics (2006, 34 (1))).

2.1. Experimental Design

The importance of the experimental design component of a DCE is being increasingly recognised. As demonstrated in Part 1, experimental design methods in health economics have progressed in recent years. However, this is not an area that is standing still. In this book, we have demonstrated one approach to designing DCEs, based on maximising D-efficiency as defined in Chapter 2. This method, originating from the work of Street et al. (2001), starts with orthogonal plans and uses matrix algebra to create choices. Given this, overlap in choice sets is minimised, thus ensuring information obtained from making choices is maximised. As outlined in Chapter 1, a number of alternative approaches are being developed in the literature. Following on from

TABLE 11.1. Key issues in the practice and development of DCE in health economics at a glance

References	Objective	Key findings
Viney et al. (2002)	To offer expert opinion on use of DCE and future research directions	*Current*: literature shows potential of DCE and that consumers value more than just health outcomes *Future*: use DCE to inform resource allocation and policy decisions (e.g. indirect WTP estimates in CBA), demonstrate greater potential than existing multi-attribute utility methods to explore the nature of the utility function and inform CUA, demonstrate greater use as a tool for predicting demand in rapidly changing circumstances; take opportunity to complement existing data sets to allow more complex analyses of a number of health questions
Ryan and Gerard (2003)	To systematically identify and describe the conduct of DCE studies, 1990–2000, and offer expert opinion on future research directions	*Current*: increasingly used in health economics for variety of reasons – e.g. benefit valuation, valuation of generic health status domains; labour supply characteristics, predicting/planning health insurance uptake, but concerns over quality of conduct of studies appraised ($n = 34$) *Future*: need paced development, particularly regarding: complexity issues, relationship with direct WTP, presentation of attributes, construction of efficient experimental designs, appropriate estimation procedures, validity, reliability and generalisability
Ryan et al. (2003)	To offer expert opinion on methodological issues in monetary valuation of benefits (using CV and DCE) and future research directions	*Current*: acceptable to respondents, few inconsistent responses, little evidence on reliability, high levels of internal consistency, inconclusive and limited evidence on convergent validity and external validity *Future*: systematically explore: more rigorous tests of external validity and data enrichment through combining RP and SP data; context and complexity effects; social interdependence and benefit transfers

(continued)

TABLE 11.1. (continued)

References	Objective	Key findings
Hanley et al. (2003)	To offer expert opinion on key DCE issues and debates in environmental economics, consider how health economists have addressed them and future research directions	*Current*: health economists are addressing some of the key issue that have been debated in environmental economics: e.g. experimental design, data analysis and validity although the potential for benefit transfer analysis is largely unproven *Future*: more effort to be focused on external validity of DCE, exploration of a possible "social distance-decay" function with respect to valuation and applications of benefit transfer
Bryan and Dolan (2004)	To offer expert opinion to encourage reflection on potential uncertainties and weaknesses of DCE	*Current*: too rosy a picture painted about DCE in the literature; need to encourage more reflection on important uncertainties and weaknesses of the approach with respect to normative, psychological, technical and generalisability issues *Future*: better understanding of: results to inform policy decisions, processes of elicitation on the construction of preferences, cognitive burden placed on respondents, validity of linear additive models, generalisability of results for broad health policy
Fiebig et al. (2005)	To systematically identify and describe the conduct of DCE studies, 1990–2004 and critique current practice in experimental design and generation of choice data and data analysis	*Current*: between 1990 and 2000, and 2001 and 2004, rapid increase in DCE studies often conducted in a stylised way, e.g. simple and small designs based on random assignment of scenarios to pairwise choice sets using an orthogonal main effects plan and simple econometric models (e.g. random effects probit) which do not embrace richer formulations of heterogeniety ($n = 59$) *Future*: greater use of larger experimental designs and richer econometric models, key unresolved issues lie in the areas of optimal design and variance-scale confounds

the work of Huber and Zwerina (1996), who considered minimum overlap, level balance, orthogonality and utility balance, Sandor and Wedel (2001) relax all criteria other than level balance in minimising D-error (an *inefficiency* measure based on the determinant of expected asymptotic variance–covariance matrix). In their more recent work, they also relax level balance (Sandor and Wedel, 2002, 2005). Such approaches normally require prior assumptions regarding parameters. A third approach, developed by Kanninen (2002), is concerned with designing experiments that result in choice probabilities for each situation such that the elements of the variance–covariance matrix are minimal and so the overall design optimal. This approach also requires using prior beliefs on parameter values to estimate the choice probabilities. Like Sandor and Wedel, Kanninen's work also minimises the D-error of the design. However, this is done through choice probabilities. Rose and Bliemer (forthcoming) provide more details on these three approaches. They discuss their advantages and disadvantages, and compare their relative performance. The primary message to take away is that the statistical experimental design of a DCE has developed to become quite a complex component when carrying out a DCE. It is, however, important that practitioners of the DCE familiarise themselves with such methods and, whenever possible, have expert help available from a specialist. The challenges for the future are: (1) for design experts to be able to convey information on good designs to practitioners using DCEs, and (2) for practitioners to keep on top of an ever-developing field of expertise.

2.2. Econometric Modelling

Chapter 1 indicated the developments which have taken place in econometric modelling of DCE data over the last decade. To date, these developments have seen limited application in health economics. Fiebig et al. (2005) emphasise the importance of using richer econometric models in the analysis of DCE data. In particular, they identify a need for looking at what is being singled out as "the most salient feature of consumer demand on the micro level", that of heterogeneity (Wansbeek et al., 2001). Random effects specifications provide some insight but they account for heterogeneity in a rather simplistic way. The health economics literature has yet to embrace the movement to richer formulations of heterogeneity (e.g. mixed logit) that is happening in other fields. The same is true when it comes to analysing other sources of unobserved variability in responses (Louviere et al., 2002) that might lead to model misspecification and endogeneity biases (Louviere et al., 2005). With increasing computational power and increasingly rich data sets, models such as those outlined in Chapter 1 can be practically applied and offer great potential to better understand behaviour and test behavioural hypotheses. We believe that, now that the feasibility of the DCEs technique in health economics has been established, this movement will happen naturally, as research efforts get directed to important methodological issues for which more advanced econometric analysis is required. Some examples are presented below (see, e.g. Section 2.7). It is also important to reinforce the idea in Chapter 1 that caution is needed when choosing a more advanced model for analysis, given the data requirements of these more flexible econometric specifications (Louviere, 2006).

2.3. Validity of Responses

Given DCEs, like other health economic valuation techniques, rely on responses to hypothetical data, investigating external validity of responses has been identified as an important area for future research (Ryan and Gerard, 2003; Ryan et al., 2003). External validity refers to testing whether individuals behave in reality as they state in the hypothetical survey. Given that many of the applications of DCEs have taken place in countries with a publicly provided health care system, availability of data on actual choices to compare real and stated behaviour may be limited. As a result, a number of alternative validity tests have been applied. Current practice indicates that much emphasis is placed on theoretical validity (Ryan and Gerard, 2003). This involves checking that model coefficients have the signs expected given theory or previous evidence, with results generally being positive.

Validity has also been assessed by looking at the "*rationality*" of responses (often referred to as internal consistency). This has been mainly tested by including dominance tests (choice sets where one alternative is clearly superior), though tests of transitivity and Sens' expansion and contraction properties have also been employed (see applied chapters for an application of the dominance tests and Chapter 9 for an application of Sen's properties as well as the dominance tests). Whilst results are again favourable, there is a lack of research investigating reasons for "*irrational*" responses and future work should explore "irrational" responses in more detail. Qualitative research techniques will prove useful here – Chapter 9 presents an example of this.

The "true" test of validity is whether stated preference (SP) behaviour is the same as real behaviour. Imaginative methods are required to test the external validity of DCEs in health economics. Consideration should be given to setting up tests in areas where patients have to pay for health care, such as in the UK NHS prescription drugs, dental care, assisted reproduction and some prenatal screening programmes. Laboratory tests may also prove useful in testing external validity. Furthermore, following the identification of invalid responses, consideration should be given to factors influencing this response strategy in order that they may be fed back into the design process to help reduce hypothetical bias in future experiments. Qualitative work will prove useful here.

2.4. Data Enrichment

Viney et al. (2002) suggest an important area for research is "data enrichment", i.e. combining different sources of preference data to allow more complex analyses of a number of health questions. Most often SP data from DCEs are combined and jointly estimated with revealed preference (RP) data to exploit the contrasting strengths of the various approaches while minimising their weaknesses. This approach emerged in the marketing and transportation literatures and from there extended to other disciplines (see Whitehead et al. (2005) and references therein). Chapter 10 by Mark and Swait provided an example of this "data enrichment" approach in a health care context. Their study is an example where RP data is limited. There is no RP data available for the new therapies. The effects of attributes cannot be estimated, as there is no variation in them (as was the case for price, mode of administration and method of action). They show how SP data collected alongside the RP data can complement estimation of behaviour beyond the range of historical experience. The challenge ahead for health economists lies in identifying suitable contexts where this RP–SP data combination can be fruitfully exploited. RP data may exist already. RP data from the Labour Force Survey could be used alongside a DCE to investigate job choices. Or, as with Chapter 10, the researcher could collect information on previous choices (RP) as part of a SP survey. It is also important to note that data fusion does not only involve combining RP and SP. It may also involve the bringing together of SP data sets obtained by different elicitation methods, e.g. the contingent valuation method (CVM) and DCEs. The overall objective is to improve welfare estimates or policy recommendations by drawing on the strength of the different valuation approaches (as opposed to seeing alternative techniques as competing with each other). "Data enrichment" within health economics is likely to be a challenging but exciting area in the near future.

2.5. Complexity Effects

The ability of respondents to fully comprehend valuation tasks has always been the subject of some scepticism. DCEs require respondents to understand in general terms the attributes of options, the way the attributes vary across a number of levels and the way various combinations of attributes at varying levels may result from alternative resource use options under consideration. They also often require respondents to make a sequence of choices between multiple alternatives. In general, the complexity of a given choice task depends on the number of alternatives in each choice task, the number of attributes used to describe the alternatives, the correlation structure among attributes and the number of replications within a survey. Design strategies seeking to maximise *statistical efficiency* (see Chapters 2 and 3 and Section 2.1) may lower *respondent efficiency* (Severin, 2001).

An important question is how do individuals cope with the "complex" setting of a DCE? Will their cognitive challenge lead to non-compensatory decision making as advanced by cognitive psychologists and behavioural researchers (see more below) or more subtle effects such as status quo bias or choice deferral (Samuelson and Zeckhauser, 1988; Dhar, 1997)? If so, parameter estimates and/or variance components may be affected. Research on the impact of task complexity is growing (Amaya-Amaya and Ryan, forthcoming, for a review). Some of this work is in health economics (Cairns et al., 2002; Maddala et al., 2003; Cairns and van der Pol, 2004; Amaya-Amaya and Ryan, forthcoming), but more research is clearly needed.

Further, as noted by Kahn et al. (1997), in the medical context, the complexity of the task might be increased because decisions often require "impossible" trade-offs such as survival versus quality of life or life expectancy versus monetary considerations, which can be highly stressful and emotional. Whereas, emotions are typically considered outside of economic analysis, recent research has begun to explore the role of emotions in judgements and decisions (Ryan et al., 2003). Future research exploring the role of emotions in responding to DCEs in a health care context is warranted.

2.6. Non-Compensatory Behaviour

The issue of non-compensatory behaviour deserves further attention. It may not be surprising that DCE respondents use non-compensatory strategies: the costs of assimilating the information provided, and making choices, are current and real, whereas the benefits are likely to be perceived as uncertain and distant. As a result, as a DCE progresses, respondents may move from fully compensatory rules towards simplified non-compensatory strategies (Swait and Adamowicz, 2001). Such behaviour might compromise the consistency with which choices are made, impacting parameters estimates and welfare analysis. Whilst this poses theoretical and methodological challenges, researchers may still enjoy the advantages that DCEs offer if they intervene at two junctures: the *design* of the experiment and the *analysis* of responses.

At the *design* stage, choice sets should be designed with an awareness of how much and what type of information will be considered. Whilst evidence is emerging here (Hensher et al., 2005; Hensher, 2006), more research is needed. Possible areas for future research include modifying the design strategy according to information obtained from focus groups (Sandor and Wedel, 2001) and the use of pictorial representations (Vriens et al., 1998) along with warm-up and training exercises (Louviere, 1987; Bateman et al., 2004) to help individuals engage in the experiment. Research is also needed on design strategies that are efficient both from the statistical and respondent viewpoints.

At the *analysis* stage, the goal is to incorporate psychological insights related to non-compensatory behaviour into the models. Exploration of the impact of context on the nature of both the systematic and random components of the utility function is needed (Swait et al., 2002). Researchers should enrich the basic discrete choice model by identifying, parameterising and controlling for context-dependent choice behaviour. Possible methodologies include flexible error structures (Ben-Akiva et al., 2002a); explicitly representing latent constructs such as experience, perceptions or beliefs (Ben-Akiva et al., 2002b); or latent classes that exhibit different taste parameters, choice sets and decision protocols (Ben-Akiva and Boccara, 1995). The difficulty of estimating such models suggests the need for a modest initial research agenda. However, the sophisticated econometrician might attempt integrating all these extensions in a generalised framework (Walker, 2001).

Another issue is whether non-compensatory strategies result into observed choices that provide information about underlying preferences. If individuals structure their preferences lexicographically, focusing on a single attribute (see Chapter 8), non-compensatory behaviour is consistent with utility theory. Alternatively, individuals may use rules of thumb or choice heuristics (Simon, 1955). Here, there is debate around whether such heuristics maximise welfare (Kahneman and Tversky, 1982); lead to increased mistakes or errors (De Palma et al., 1994) or are powerful tools for making nearly optimal decisions (Gigerenzer et al., 1999). Clearly more work is needed.

2.7. Benefits Transfer

Conducting a DCE is often time consuming and expensive. Thus, strategies need to be put in place for dealing with transferability of valuation results. There has been an interest in health economics in generating generic benefit measures which can be applied in a number of contexts. EQ-5D has been developed to value alternative health outcomes across a wide range of interventions (Drummond et al., 2005). To date DCEs have mainly been used to value specific interventions, thus raising concerns about generalisability of results (Bryan and Dolan, 2004). Within the environmental literature generalisability has been discussed within the context of "benefit transfer" (Morrison and Bennett, 2000; Hanley et al., 2003). Hanley et al. (2003) note that evidence here is limited and mixed, and it is unclear as to whether benefit transfers works. The key question for researchers is whether a primary study in a new site would be more efficient than applying existing work to the study site.

In the health economics literature benefit transfer research is further behind, but as DCE becomes increasingly popular and the stock of data and methodological knowledge increases it is essential to develop this aspect of research. Yet applying benefit transfer to health economics DCEs raises a number of further issues. One concerns the quantity, scope and quality of potential primary DCEs as reference studies. Exercises in benefit transfer are "data hungry". The larger the pool of (good quality) studies the better the chances that the type of benefit of interest has been valued elsewhere, that it has been valued in appropriate units for transfer and a number of explanatory variables are reported that could be used to adjust transfers. In all, there is a greater potential for increased accuracy of transfers. It, therefore, follows there is a strong argument for taking stock of the way in which DCE studies build up in the literature so that research is compatible with longer-term research needs such as ensuring good quality studies. Perhaps, it is timely to explore the need for a clearing house to keep track of DCE studies. Lessons could be learnt from the Environmental Valuation Reference Inventory (Environment Canada, 2006).

3. CLOSING

In closing the book, the words of Professor Jordan Louviere (Louviere, 2006) seem appropriate:

> DCEs and associated choice models have come a long way in a short academic time, but this research is in its infancy, with many unresolved issues and problems. . . . . Indeed, only 15 years ago there were few applied economists and only a small number of marketers and others interested in these problems.

We have clearly come a long way in the development and applications of DCEs in health economics, and the technique clearly has potential to answer a broad range of questions. However, DCEs are constantly evolving to accommodate the requirements of specific applications. For more progress to be made, there are still a number of methodological questions to be addressed. This is an exciting field of research, where a deep understanding of the underlying theoretical assumptions is necessary both to apply and further develop the applications of DCEs within health economics, for improved understanding of individuals' preferences for health care and better informed resource allocation decisions.

REFERENCES

Amaya-Amaya, M. and Ryan, M. (forthcoming). Between contribution and confusion: between contribution and confusion: an investigation of the impact of complexity in stated preferences choice experiments. *Journal of Health Economics*, under review.

Baker, R., Chilton, S., Donaldson, C., Jones-Lee, M., Metcalf, H., Shackley, P. and Ryan, M. 2003. Determining the societal value of a QALY by surveying the public in England and Wales: a research protocol. Birmingham, UK: NCCRM Publications.

Bateman, I.J., Day, B.H., Dupont, D., Georgiou, S., Louviere, J.J., Morimoto, S. and Wang, P. 2004. Preference formation in choice experiments (CE): task awareness and learning in the cognitive process. Paper presented at the 13th annual conference of the European Association of Environmental and Resource Economics (EAERE). Budapest, 25–28 June 2004. http://eaere2004.bkae.hu/download/paper/bateman2paper.doc

Ben-Akiva, M. and Boccara, B. 1995. Discrete choice models with latent choice sets. *International Journal of Research in Marketing*, vol 12, 9–24.

Ben-Akiva, M., McFadden, D., Train, K., et al. 2002a. Hybrid choice models: progress and challenges. *Marketing Letters*, vol 13 (3), 163–175.

Ben-Akiva, M., Walker, J., Bernardino, A.T., et al. 2002b. Integration of choice and latent variable models. In: Perpetual Motion: Travel Behaviour Research Opportunities and Application Challenges. Mahmassani (ed.). Amsterdam: Elsevier, pp 431–470.

Bryan, S. and Dolan, P. 2004. Discrete choice experiments in health economics. *Applied Health Economics and Health Policy*, vol 5, 199–202.

Cairns, J. and van der Pol, M. 2004. Repeated follow-up as a method for reducing non-trading behaviour in discrete choice experiments. *Social Science and Medicine*, vol 58, 2211–2218.

Cairns, J., van der Pol, M. and Lloyd, A.J. 2002. Decision making heuristics and the elicitation of preferences: being fast and frugal about the future. *Health Economics*, vol 11, 655–658.

De Palma, A., Myers, G.M. and Papageorgiou, Y.Y. 1994. Rational choice under an imperfect ability to choose. *American Economic Review*, vol 84, 419–440.

Dhar, R. 1997. Consumer preferences for a no-choice option. *Journal of Consumer Research*, vol 24, 215–231.

Drummond, M., Sculpher, M., Torrance, G., O'brien, B., Stoddart, G. 2005. Methods for the Economic Evaluation of Health Care Programme, 3rd edn. Oxford: Oxford University Press.

Environment Canada. Environmental Valuation Reference Inventory. 2006. www.evri.ca/ (acc 2/2/06)

Environmental and Resource Economics. 2006. Special issue: Frontiers in Stated Preference Methods. Adamowicz, W. and Deshazo, J.R. (eds). 34(1).

Fiebig, D., Louviere, J. and Waldman, D. 2005. Contemporary issues in modelling discrete choice experimental data in health economics. Working paper, University of New South Wales, http://wwwdocs.fce.unsw.edu.au/economics/staff/DFIEBIG/ContemporaryissuesHEv120Apr05 .pdf. Last accessed 13 July 2006.

Gigerenzer, G., Todd, P. and the ABC Research Group. 1999. Simple Heuristics that Make Us Smart. Oxford: Oxford University Press.

Hall, J., Kenny, P., King, M., Louviere, J.J., Viney, R. and Yeoh, A. 2002. Using stated preference discrete choice modelling to evaluate the introduction of varicella vaccination. *Health Economics*, vol 11, 457–465.

Hall, J., Fiebig, D., King, M., Hossain, I. and Louviere, J.J. 2006. What influences participation in genetic carrier testing? Results from a discrete choice experiment. *Journal of Health Economics*, vol 25, 520–537.

Hanley, N., Ryan, M. and Wright, R.E. 2003. Estimating the monetary value of health care: lessons from environmental economics. *Health Economics*, vol 12, 3–16.

Hensher, D.A. 2006. Revealing differences in willingness to pay due to the dimensionality of stated choice designs: an initial assessment. *Environmental and Resource Economics*, vol 34 (1), 7–44.

Hensher, D.A., Rose, J. and Greene, W.H. 2005. The implications on willingness to pay of respondents ignoring specific attributes. *Transportation*, vol 32 (3), 203–222.

Huber, J. and Zwerina, K. 1996. The importance of utility balance in efficient choice designs. *Journal of Marketing Research*, vol 33, 307–317.

Kahn, B.E., Greenleaf, E., Irwin, J.R., et al. 1997. Examining medical decision making from a marketing perspective. *Marketing letters*, vol 8, 361–375.

Kahneman, D. and Tversky, A. 1982. Judgement under uncertainty: heuristics and biases. Cambridge: Cambridge University Press.

Kanninen, B. 2002. Optimal designs for multinomial choice experiments. *Journal of Marketing Research*, vol 39, 214–227.

Louviere, J. 2006. What you don't know might hurt you: some unresolved issues in the design and analysis of discrete choice experiments. *Environmental and Resource Economics*, vol 34, 173–188.

Louviere, J., Train, K., Ben-Akiva, M., Bhat, C., Brownstone, D., Cameron, T.A., Carson, R., DeShazo, J.R., Fiebig, D., Greene, W., Hensher, D. and Waldman, D. 2005. Recent progress on endogeneity in choice modelling. *Marketing Letters*, vol 16, 3–4.

Louviere, J.J. 1987. Analysing Decision Making: Metric Conjoint Analysis. Newbury Park, CA: Sage Publications.

Louviere, J.J., Street, D., Carson, R., et al. 2002. Dissecting the random component of utility. *Marketing Letters*, vol 13, 177–193.

Maddala, T., Phillips, K.A. and Johnson, F.R. 2003. An experiment on simplifying conjoint analysis designs for measuring preferences. *Health Economics*, vol 12 (12), 1035–1047.

Marketing letters. 2005. Special Issue: Sixth Invitational Choice Symposium, vol 16 (3–4), 173–454.

Morrison, M. and Bennett, J. 2000. Choice modelling, non-use values and benefit transfer. *Economic Analysis and Policy*, vol 30 (1), 13–32.

Propper, C. 1990. Contingent valuation of time spent on NHS waiting list. *The Economic Journal*, vol 100, 193–199.

Rose, J. and Bliemer, M. (forthcoming). Stated preference experimental design strategies. In: Handbook in Transport Modelling. Hensher, D.A. and Button, K. (Series and volume eds). Oxford: Pergamon Press.

Ryan, M. and Gerard, K. 2003. Using discrete choice experiments to value health care programmes: current practice and future research reflections. *Applied Health Economics and Health Policy*, vol 2, 55–64.

Ryan, M., Watson, V. and Amaya-Amaya, M. 2003. Methodological issues in the monetary valuation of benefits in healthcare. *Expert Review of Pharmacoeconomics Outcomes Research*, vol 3, 89–99.

Ryan, M., Netten, A., Skåtun, D. and Smith, P. 2006. Using discrete choice experiments to estimate a preference-based measure of outcome – an application to social care for older people. *Journal of Health Economics*, vol 25, 927–944.

Samuelson, W. and Zeckhauser, R. 1988. Status quo bias in decision making. *Journal of Risk and Uncertainty*, vol 1, 7–59.

Sandor, Z. and Wedel, M. 2001. Designing conjoint choice experiment using mangers' prior beliefs. *Journal of Marketing Research*, vol 38, 430–443.

Sandor, Z. and Wedel, M. 2002. Profile construction in experimental choice designs for mixed logit models. *Marketing Science*, vol 21, 455–475.

Sandor, Z. and Wedel, M. 2005. Heterogeneous conjoint choice designs. *Journal of Marketing Research*, vol XLII, 210–218.

Severin, V. 2001. Comparing statistical and respondent efficiency in choice experiments. Unpublished Ph.D. dissertation. Department of Marketing, University of Sydney.

Simon, H.A. 1955. A behavioural model of rational choice. *Quarterly Journal of Economics*, vol 69, 99–118.

Street, D.J., Bunch, D.S. and Moore, B.J. 2001. Optimal designs for 2^k paired comparison experiments. *Communications in Statistics, Theory, and Methods*, vol 30, 2149–2171.

Swait, J. and Adamowicz, W. 2001. The influence of task complexity on consumer choice: a latent class model of decision strategy switching. *Journal of Consumer Research*, vol 28, 135–148.

Swait, J., Adamovicz, W., Hanemann, M., et al. 2002. Context dependence and aggregation in disaggregate choice analysis. *Marketing Letters*, vol 13, 195–205.

Viney, R., Lanscar, E. and Louviere, J. 2002. Discrete choice experiments to measure consumer preferences for health and healthcare. *Expert Review of Pharmacoeconomics Outcomes Research*, vol 2, 319–326.

Viney, R., Savage, E. and Louviere, J.J. 2005. Empirical investigation of experimental design properties of discrete choice experiments in health care. *Health Economics*, vol 14, 349–362.

Vriens, M., Loosschilder, G.H., Rosbergen, E. and Wittink, D.R. 1998. Verbal versus realistic pictorial representations in conjoint analysis with design attributes. *Journal of Product Innovation Management*, vol 15, 455–467.

Walker, J. 2001. Extended discrete choice models: integrated framework, flexible error structures, and latent variables. Ph.D. dissertation. Massachusetts Institute of Technology, Cambridge, MA.

Wansbeek, T., Meijer, E. and Wedel, M. 2001. Comment on microeconometrics. *Journal of Econometrics*, vol 100/101, 89–91.

Whitehead, J.C., Pattanayak, S.K., Van Houtven, G.L. and Gelso, B.R. 2005. Combining revealed and stated preference data to estimate the nonmarket value of ecological services: an assessment of the state of the science. Working paper. http://econ.appstate.edu/RePEc/pdf/wp0519.pdf. Last accessed November 2006.

INDEX

The Economics of Non-Market Goods and Resources